SHAKESPEARE'S DELIBERATE ART

William Bache

William B. Bache
and
Vernon P. Loggins

University Press of America, Inc.
Lanham • New York • London

Copyright © 1996 by
University Press of America,® Inc.
4720 Boston Way
Lanham, Maryland 20706

3 Henrietta Street
London, WC2E 8LU England

Library of Congress Cataloging-in-Publication Data

Bache, William B.
Shakespeare's deliberate art / William B. Bache and Vernon P.
Loggins.
p.   cm.
Includes index.
1. Shakespeare, William, 1564-1616--Criticism and interpretation.   I.
Loggins, Vernon P.   II. Title.
PR2976.B224   1996   822.3'3--dc20   96-10396 CIP

ISBN 0-7618-0300-9 (cloth: alk. ppr.)
ISBN 0-7618-0301-7 (pbk: alk. ppr.)

⊖™ The paper used in this publication meets the minimum
requirements of American National Standard for information
Sciences—Permanence of Paper for Printed Library Materials,
ANSI Z39.48—1984

For Maryann and Nancy; Becky and Josh

Preface

Except for the Introduction and two chapters (the chapter on *The Tempest*, a chapter on *Troilus and Cressida*), *Shakespeare's Deliberate Art* is the combined effort of two Shakespeare teachers. Although much has been written on them, Shakespeare's plays have not been sufficiently recognized as works of art. Because most critical and scholarly discourse has ignored, neglected, or misunderstood the nature of Shakespeare's art, we have tried to identify the main components of that art, those elaborate procedures (patterns, strategies, systems) that are in evidence throughout the canon. We have tried to make clear in specific plays how Shakespeare variously employed and necessarily modified those often interrelated procedures. Shakespeare employed all of his literary skill in order to render the evolving plight of each of his memorable characters in plays of enduring human value.

As a rule, we have dealt with the most famous plays, but we have also considered a neglected history (*King John*), a neglected comedy (*All's Well That Ends Well*), and a neglected tragedy (*Coriolanus*). Part One of the study concentrates on the comedies and the histories; it concludes with a consideration of a structural pattern (recapitulative lists) and with a consideration of a thematic strategy (roles and offices). Part Two concentrates on the world-famous tragedies; it concludes with a close consideration of *King Lear*, generally recognized as Shakespeare's greatest play, and of *Troilus and Cressida*, generally recognized as Shakespeare's most difficulty play. The study itself concludes with a recapitulative examination of an elaborate play-ending pattern of closure.

Permission has been granted to reprint the following: "Affirmation in *Troilus and Cressida*," *Discourse* 10 (1967): 446-55 and "Shakespeare and Received Opinion," *The Sewanee Review* 101.4 (1993): 549-55. The Purdue Research Foundation has been helpful in supplying a grant.

West Lafayette, Indiana
December, 1995

Contents

PART TWO

A Note on the Text

All quotations from Shakespeare are taken from *The Riverside Shakespeare*, ed. G. Blakemore Evans, (Boston: Houghton Mifflin, 1974).

Introduction

Shakespeare and Received Opinion

I'm going to consider William Shakespeare, but not the person, not the man. There is no Shakespeare: all of the assertions, all of the beliefs, all of the emotions and passions are fictive. Although his expressive language is alive and well, there is no distinctive *I*, no persona. Shakespeare never says anything, not even in the sonnets, in his own voice. Shakespeare's personality is sublimated in and to his art. All we have, as well as all we need to have, is what Shakespeare has bequeathed to us. He has become what he has achieved: he has transformed himself into his studied art. Thus if we want to understand Shakespeare, we must attend to his work; everything else is of secondary importance. We receive but what we give.

Strange as it may seem, the main impediment to an understanding of Shakespeare is the familiarity everyone has with the material. *Hamlet* is the world's most familiar literary work; *King Lear* may well be the world's most celebrated literary work. For generations *Hamlet* and *King Lear* have headed our list of literary obsessions. Everyone has read and seen them; everyone has an opinion about them; everyone apparently understands them. But, in considering any literary work, we must try to distinguish what the work says from what the work signifies. We respond to what we've come to expect: we receive but what we give, our expectations. *Hamlet* and *King Lear* signify too much. They have entered our consciousness and our imagination and taken over: their significance appropriates their meaning. We are hostage to the literary icons that Hamlet and *King Lear* have become. That is what happens to a famous literary work of art: it becomes something accepted and known. We receive but what we give, and we fail to give enough.

Often what we take to be meaning is a product of received opinion: our attitude toward *Hamlet* and *King Lear* is conditioned by what we have heard and read and are supposed to feel. We accept received opinions, together with their implications, as having the validity of scripture and the comfort of sugar candy. But received opinion is only opinion packaged: it narrows the concern, disables thought, corrupts meaning. Like a rock it is there, defying inspection. There is it, as Falstaff says.

In attempting to distinguish meaning from significance, E. D. Hirsch, Jr., remarks that "'significance' is textual meaning as related to some context, indeed any context, beyond itself." Significance forgets the text. As Whitehead reminds us, teachers teach by contact, and we must remain in contact with the meaning of a Shakespeare text. We have been led to misunderstand Shakespeare by the opinions received from friends, teachers, scholars, critics, authorities on Shakespeare. Consider a few of these staples of received opinion: the tragic hero, the tragic flaw, comic relief. Taken together, these particular terms unhappily contribute to an oversimplification of Shakespeare's tragedies and, on a deeper level, to a diminution of Shakespeare's human achievement. Let me give a simple illustration.

Although Othello is commonly referred to as a jealous murderer, he is never called that in the play. Othello himself remarks that, though perplexed, he is not easily jealous. The crucial point is that the only characters in the play who slander Othello as being jealous are Iago and his wife, Emilia, both of whom, for very different reasons, want to see Othello come to grief. In the play Othello is *never* jealous or *never merely* jealous. In fact he enters the long last scene of the play, the one in which Desdemona is killed, like a priest and a bridegroom: he has almost completely recovered from the trauma of destructive emotion. The point is that to label Othello as a jealous murderer or to see jealousy as Othello's tragic flaw is a dangerous abstraction and a gross distortion of the character of Othello and of the meaning of the play.

A different kind of received opinion is that of considering Shakespeare mainly as a Renaissance artist. Spenser, Jonson, Donne—Shakespeare's remarkable contemporaries—were, in one way or another, hostage to their extraordinary time: they can be considered true disciples of the Renaissance. They were Shakespeare's contemporaries, but Shakespeare is our contemporary. He is modern. For, as Emerson asserts, to be perpetually modern is the mark of merit in any work of art. To consider a Shakespeare play as being primarily a Renaissance text is dangerously close to thinking of *King Lear* as an antiquated plaything, as a disguised history lesson, as an outmoded social document.

It is often remarked that a Shakespeare play was not meant to be read, that Shakespeare never intended one of his plays to be scrutinized. "Don't you know that Shakespeare wrote for the stage?" Imagine a received opinion that seems deliberately meant to slander an acknowledged master like Shakespeare as being just another playwright. Anyone who has ever written a poem or a story or even a play must expect his or her work to be able to withstand scrutiny. Any decent writer should want his or her work to be studied. To assert that a play was meant for the stage doesn't mean that it is mindless, though most plays are frivolous—not worth watching, let alone reading. Every real playwright writes for himself or herself. No first-rate playwright is sloppy; no first-rate play, slovenly.

The deconstructionists have urged upon us a received opinion about the instability of words, the sloppiness of language. Dealing with something so recalcitrant as language is what any real writer learns early and never forgets. Indeed the real writer must master the medium if he or she is going to create something that, as Milton hoped, the world will not willingly let die. As G. B. Shaw remarks, words are all we have. Most of these modern theorists fail in not making valid distinctions among texts and among the writers of these texts. Although most writers are at the disposal of language, Shakespeare isn't one of them. He has language at his disposal. If Swift can assert that prose is proper words in proper places, surely we can agree that the poetic Shakespeare uses the only appropriate words in the only appropriate places.

When Eliot said that the poet must destroy language in order to create language anew, he must have been thinking of Shakespeare. Shakespeare's verbal strategies are dazzling. His puns and other wordplay are startling and elaborate. His use of malapropisms is apparent (a Shakespeare fool will say *salvation* when he means *damnation*: Shakespeare means both *salvation* and *damnation*). Shakespeare even employs letters as words (in *Twelfth Night* C, U, T, P become C's [seas/sees/seize], U's [use], T's [tease], P's [peace/peas/piece]); in *Twelfth Night* he also uses letters as graphic symbols (M, O, A, I). In order to secure needed complexity, Shakespeare, as William Empson notices, often relies on the floating pronoun. Witness Shakespeare's use of misplaced periods in order to present alternative readings of a passage: for example, Peter Quince's prologue in *A Midsummer Night's Dream*.

Apparently a great many people read Shakespeare the way E. M. Forster is purported to have read Jane Austen: with the mouth open and the mind closed. The truth is that Shakespeare should be read and reread with the mind open and the mouth closed. Harold Goddard, one of the most astute Shakespeare critics, goes even so far as to state that no one who knows Shakespeare can ever be entirely pleased with any stage production of Shakespeare. You are bound to be disappointed with some aspect of a production. Too often on stage Shakespeare is not Shakespeare, but Shakespeare transformed, even mangled. If for purposes of novelty or other unenlightened reasons a director takes liberties with the text, no one can have a serious objection. Shakespeare will survive. We should object, however, to directorial arrogance and to the pretense that what is being presented is Shakespeare. The producer, the director, the actors, even the set designer determine to a considerable extent what and how we see and hear and understand. And so, even in a good production, we get Peter Hall's *Tempest*, not Shakespeare's. To make the main point differently: a Shakespeare play is, to use the current jargon, *writerly*. It is too much like a poem to ever be translated properly into a satisfactory public enterprise like a play.

When we read a Shakespeare play, we can turn the pages back to a past scene or ahead to a future scene. We can interrupt our reading to ponder, to reconsider. We can't do that in the theater. As Goddard might say, we can never get a satisfactory public expression of what is essentially a private experience. Shakespeare is not Mozart. What generally happens is that a Shakespeare production often simplifies the play into something like a cartoon, or a production distorts the play into something like a happening, or a production perverts a play into something like a catfight.

Alfred Harbage, a good Shakespeare critic, says that all he asks from a Shakespeare production is that the actors read the lines loudly and clearly. That's not much of a solution. I don't want to be misunderstood: Shakespeare's plays were meant to be performed; his art is presentational. The plays must be staged. But at least those people most involved in the delicate task of Shakespeare production should scrutinize a play before deciding to move forward with a plan. Difficult decisions have to be made, and these decisions ought to be informed by Shakespeare's intention and meaning, as they can be discerned. Still the actual production may not satisfy everyone, but the result can be instructive, stunning, brilliant: Peter Hall's decision at the Old Vic in 1974 to emphasize Stephano and Trinculo at the expense of Caliban in *The Tempest*; Maggie Smith's rendition of Desdemona's plight in the bedroom scene in Olivier's movie version of *Othello*; Helen Mirren's performance as Rosalind in PBS's *As You Like It*; Brian Bedford's almost comic interpretation of Richard II in Stratford, Ontario.

A Shakespeare play presents a simple dramatic situation: a young man is ordered by a ghost to revenge a murder; an old king disinherits his beloved youngest daughter. Shakespeare takes such an apparently simple situation, develops it, and explores its implications: he shows us what the *Hamlet* story means and implies. Every part of the play is implicated in every other part. *Hamlet* as an artistic creation becomes a seamless web. For something like recapitulation is the essence of Shakespeare's art. To put the matter bluntly: you cannot understand a complete play unless and until you understand every part of the play; you cannot understand any part of a play unless and until you understand the complete play. It is as simple and as difficult as that.

The main reason that Shakespeare is so intellectually restless and so incredibly resourceful is that he wants to be understood.

Because he is as clear as an artist can be and because he demands our cooperation and, indeed, our complicity, Shakespeare is not only the world's greatest artist but also the world's best teacher. All we need do is to recognize the patterns and strategies and systems that inform his art and then to employ them to the best of our ability.

For example, act 3 of *Hamlet* is composed of four recapitulative point-of-view scenes: Hamlet coming upon Ophelia at prayer and delivering his "To be or not to be"(3.1.55) soliloquy; Hamlet presenting the Mousetrap to the onstage audience, a scene in which the murder of his father is reenacted; Hamlet coming upon King Claudius at prayer; Hamlet, after murdering Polonius, berating his mother, Gertrude, in her bedroom.

We readily perceive similarities between the scenes: Hamlet berates Ophelia in scene 1 and Gertrude in scene 4. The King and Polonius are eavesdropping behind an arras in the Ophelia scene; Polonius, an agent of the King, is eavesdropping behind an arras in the Gertrude scene. Ophelia only seems to be praying in her scene; Claudius only seems to be praying in his scene. An old man, the "player-king," is "murdered" in Hamlet's scene (3.2); an old man, Polonius, "a player-king," is murdered in Gertrude's scene (3.4).

Although unnoticed by the voluminous *Hamlet* criticism, the primary strategy is simple and conclusive: the first scene of act 3 is from Ophelia's perspective; the second from Hamlet's; the third from Claudius's; the fourth from Gertrude's. Thus act 3 presents the developing plot in terms of the four main characters, the two essential couples (the future queen and king; the present king and queen): Ophelia and Hamlet; Claudius and Gertrude. In effect four distinct but related Hamlets are paraded before us: Ophelia's Hamlet; Hamlet's Hamlet; Claudius's Hamlet; Gertrude's Hamlet.

All of this is true, but it isn't the only truth. For instance, Hamlet's haphazard murder of Polonius in 3.4 transforms the action: now Hamlet is the murderer, and Laertes will be the avenger. In addition *Hamlet* follows a pattern deployed famously in *Richard II* and followed, for example, in *Macbeth*, *King Lear*, *Measure for Measure*, *The Winter's Tale*. In each of these plays the last scene of act 3 is essentially choric: it is designed to further our larger understanding of the action. The appearance of the ghost in 3.4 is a version of his appearance in the first scene of *Hamlet*: a murder prompts the ghost's first appearance; a murder prompts his second and final appearance.

The end of act 3 of a Shakespeare play is almost always the end of an action: the murder of Polonius and the last appearance of the ghost make the point. In *Hamlet* Polonius is killed at the end of act 3; Ophelia's death is reported at the end of act 4; Laertes is killed at the end of act 5. Hamlet kills the characters of the subplot: he is directly responsible for all of these deaths (Polonius, Ophelia, Laertes) as well as for such other deaths as those of Rosencrantz and Guildenstern. So much then for Hamlet as tragic hero.

An assertion: the closely inwoven texture of *Hamlet* mandates poetic tension, ambiguity, irony, paradox—in other words, literary complexity.

A comment: imagine Joyce and Eliot believing that a masterpiece like *Hamlet* is a failure. Even a word-besotted old teacher like Kittredge knew better than that: he says that one should begin with the assumption that there are no mistakes in *Hamlet*.

A confession: although I have been teaching *Hamlet* since 1949 and although I have read the play more than six hundred times, I cannot read it, even today, without my head in a whirl.

A question: what is the poor old teacher to do?

Answer: take the next step; widen the perspective.

In considering the art of fiction, Henry James espoused the value of a survey of the whole field: a full fictive landscape is important. I suppose we can partially blame James then for all of those big, clumsy, ugly novels that populate the best-seller lists. But James was right: a survey of the whole field supplies the needed moral energy. In art nothing should come in partial: art cannot be allowed to remain partial, incomplete. Everything has to be accommodated. As Aristotle observes, a small masterpiece can be only neat: to be beautiful a work of art must have magnitude. Truly great art is full and complete and moral.

But, unless you are Eugene O'Neill, you can't put a loose and baggy monster on the stage with any success. As I have been trying to make clear, Shakespeare manages to survey the whole field by keeping the plot relatively simple, by condensing the action, by being poetic. *Hamlet* gets its moral energy because it surveys the whole field as a poetic drama.

The stage cannot adequately present such novels as *Anna Karenina* or *Ulysses*, even if they were turned into poetic drama. Shakespeare must have been sharply aware of the limitations of drama as a genre. That, I think, is part of the reason that Shakespeare wrote two historical tetralogies, eight plays that chronicle almost a century of English history. The necessity of going beyond a single play into a cycle of plays in order to achieve a fuller historical survey—this kind of necessity also prompted Shakespeare to write a social tetralogy, made up of four comedies: *Much Ado About Nothing*, *As You Like It*, *Twelfth Night*, *Measure for Measure*. When considered together, these four comedies are enriched and deepened. *Measure for Measure*, the play that concludes the cycle, has as its theme the subsuming one of justice and mercy.

In the same way *Hamlet*, magnificent as it unquestionably is, must be seen as part of a cycle that includes *Macbeth* and *King Lear*. These three together make up an historio-tragic trilogy, a sublime human, rather than just an historical or social, vision. The strategies in *Macbeth* and *King Lear* depend upon and reflect those in *Hamlet*. One cannot understand these individual masterpieces unless and until one considers them in the context of a gigantic enterprise. Let me make the easy, salient point. Hamlet is a son and a prince; Macbeth is a husband and usurper; Lear is a father and a king. Each protagonist is restricted to his particular position, a private role and a public office. Having written *Hamlet*, Shakespeare recognized the necessity of completing what he started. *Macbeth* and *King Lear* thus fulfill the implications of *Hamlet*. Shakespeare never left anything unfinished: that is what makes him such a consummate artist.

Let us end by turning to John Keats, another consummate artist. In reading Shakespeare, we must practice what Keats calls negative capability: don't be upset by what you don't readily understand. In addition, instead of merely reading *King Lear*, you must "burn through" it. Imagine that. Ultimately we receive from Shakespeare but what we give to Shakespeare.

Part One

1

Shakespeare's Deliberate Art: *The Tempest*

> I do not think . . . that Milton's mind was (so to
> speak) greater than the *Paradise Lost*; it was just big
> enough to fill that mighty mould; the shrine contained
> the Godhead. Shakespeare's genius was, I should say,
> greater than anything he has done, because it still
> soared free and unconfined beyond whatever he
> undertook—ran over; and could not be 'constrained by
> mastery' of his subject.
>
> —William Hazlitt, "On the Qualifications
> Necessary to Success in Life."

Although I do not subscribe to his judgment on Milton, I do think
that Hazlitt, with his odd combination of romantic feeling and
English common sense, refers to a truth about Shakespeare that I
have spent a lifetime trying to convey: Shakespeare controlled his
creations; he composed them; he mastered them. I would not,
however, conclude with Hazlitt that Shakespeare was greater than
his creations. Hazlitt's comment is only a romantic quibble:
Shakespeare was just distinct from his creations. My
uncomplicated argument would be that, though a Shakespeare play
is not free and unconfined, our responses to that play certainly are:
meaning is both transmuted by and overcome with significance.
Shakespeare was a realist; we are the romantics.

The chief reason that our responses to a Shakespeare play are so mixed, so varied, so unconstrained is that Shakespeare's presentation of the material mandates, as it must, ambiguity, irony, paradox, and tension. For a Shakespeare play is vitally concerned (as all great Western literature is) with the human response to ethical problems and moral dilemmas, with those epistemological difficulties that were Shakespeare's ultimate concern and that must then be our epistemological concern as we are engaged by and in a Shakespeare play. Our responses must be mixed and varied, unconstrained. Shakespeare presents the world, not as a philosopher might, but as a superb literary artist must.

As an artifact a Shakespeare play is architectonic: it coolly displays or unfolds a particular society in all of its human foibles and self-centered errors. This epic-like or god-like spectacle is proffered to us with lively humor and trenchant wit, with rare subtlety and true sophistication, with great understanding but no patronization. We are not burdened by, as Eliot would put it, Shakespeare's personality: Shakespeare dramatically surveys the whole field in a manner quite unlike the baggy survey conducted by a Henry James. In considering a Shakespeare play, we should be conditioned and directed by its closely controlled structure.

A Shakespeare play is a deliberate construct; a Shakespeare play is of intense human value. Both of these propositions, taken either separately or together, may cause either anxiety or consternation to students and teachers and critics. Therefore in order not to be thought to contradict myself or not to be thought patronizing or reductive or rude, I should like to demonstrate these propositions with the ideal example, *The Tempest*, which is, as everyone knows, the first play in the Folio and which is the last play completely the product of Shakespeare. It is not muddied by the textual problems that beset *Hamlet* or *King Lear*. All of its cruxes are relatively insignificant. But before I begin this demonstration, I should like to declare that Shakespeare will always do whatever he can to teach his audience both the necessity of and the intransigence of being human. I also want to endorse emphatically Frank Kermode's declaration: "*The Tempest* is unquestionably the most sophisticated comedy of a poet whose work in comedy is misunderstood to a quite astonishing degree."[1] For, though I am not so bold as to hope to explicate satisfactorily or to demystify

The Tempest, I am brave enough to use it in an attempt to clarify the procedures that bear upon my two propositions.

The action of *The Tempest* proceeds along three distinct lines (the Ferdinand-Miranda line; the Alonso-Antonio-Sebastian line; the Caliban-Stephano-Trinculo line) until these lines come together at Prospero's cell. Prospero is on stage throughout acts 4 and 5; he delivers the epilogue. After leaving the stage at the end of act 4 and at the end of act 5, he returns in each instance at once. Prospero is thus the center of attention in the second half of *The Tempest*; the perspective, we may say, is his. The audience seems intended to observe and to judge him as he responds to and is affected by the action that is the product of his decision to call up the tempest of the first scene. Anyone can and may quarrel with the following broad assertion (I make it almost exclusively for descriptive purposes): in the second half of *The Tempest* Prospero in turn confronts and is confronted by Ferdinand and Miranda; Alonso, Antonio and Sebastian; the Boatswain and the Master; Caliban, Stephano and Trinculo; the audience.

In the second half of the play Prospero also has two other strange, deliberate confrontations with Ariel, his chief servant and only disciple. At the beginning of act 4, after Prospero orders Ariel to fetch the rabble (Caliban, Stephano, Trinculo), Ariel responds:

> Before you can say "come" and "go,"
> And breathe twice, and cry "so, so,"
> Each one, tripping on his toe,
> Will be here with mop and mow.
> Do you love me, master? no?
> *Pros.* Dearly, my delicate Ariel. Do not approach
> Till thou dost hear me call.
> (4.1.44-50)

At the beginning of act 5 Ariel sings and helps to attire Prospero:

> Where the bee sucks, there suck I:
> In a cowslip's bell I lie;
> There I couch when owls do cry.
> On the bat's back I do fly
> After summer merrily.

Merrily, merrily shall I live now,
Under the blossom that hangs on the bough.
Pros. Why that's my dainty Ariel! I shall miss thee,
But yet thou shalt have freedom. So, so, so.

                                        (5.1.88-96)

The similarities between the two occasions are so striking (the way "my dainty Ariel" echoes "my delicate Ariel"; the five rhyming short lines in each Ariel passage; the five uses of *so*; the subsequent immediate departure of Ariel from the stage) that it is indeed odd that no critic, so far as I can determine, has ever even noticed the similarities between the two. I should like to make, but not press, the importance of the five *O* rhymes and the five *I* rhymes and the five uses of *so*. In addition to other significations in Shakespeare (*O* is a homonym for *eau* or *owe;*[2] *I* for *aye* or *eye*; *so* for *sew* or *sow*), *O* generally refers to the community or society; *I* to the individual; *so* to causality or consequence. In act 5 Prospero actually draws a circle or a large O on the stage platform.

I do not wish to pursue the equation that may be readily drawn between the rabble on the one hand and the Master and the Boatswain on the other. Nor do I want to consider the easily recognized equations between Ariel and Caliban and between Ariel and Miranda. Nor do I want to do more than mention the importance of the play-wide tension between the *I* (the individual) and the *O* (the community). Let it suffice for me to make two points: first, the two occasions demonstrate one major feature of the play, that of closely related incidents or episodes; second, these "similarities" cannot be the product of chance. I shall return to Ariel and his importance to our understanding of Prospero and the play, but I should like to say a little more about dramatic relationships.

In the third scene of the play, 2.1, Gonzalo, Alonso's chief counselor, presents an ideal commonwealth to his king in order to "bring the plaster"(2.1.140) to Alonso's dismay and sorrow. Alonso is grief stricken because he has just married off his only daughter (against the advice of his court and her feelings for the king of Tunis) and because he thinks he has just lost his only son and heir. Gonzalo's impossible world of fabricated lies is at the service of his desire to comfort and aid his king: like a good fool he will say and do whatever is humanly required in order to be helpful. The churlish Antonio and Sebastian, who are stage audience to all this, make clear to us how unrealistic and foolish they think Gonzalo and his ideal commonwealth are. By the end of the scene, these two men, who relish power and despise conscience, are about to murder Alonso and the good Gonzalo; acting on Prospero's behalf, Ariel intervenes to prevent murder.

In intention, in structure, in theme, act 4 is like 2.1. Whereas in 2.1 Gonzalo proffers an ideal world fashioned of words to and for his king, in act 4 Prospero presents through the "vanity of [his] art"(4.1.41) a vision, fashioned by spirits as actors, of an ideal world, where spring follows harvest (thus obviating winter) to and for the future king.[3] If we perceive it, as we should, the equation of Prospero with Gonzalo serves to demonstrate Prospero's kind humanity; it also serves to demonstrate Prospero's folly and vulnerability. On a related but deeper structural and thematic plane, Alonso seems meant to be seen as Prospero's double: Alonso helps us "measure" Prospero. Antonio's comment, "what's past is prologue"(2.1.248), shortly followed by Sebastian's retort, "Thy case, dear friend,/Shall be my precedent"(2.1.285-86), establishes Alonso's position on the island as being much like Prospero's position twelve years before in Milan.[4] Act 4 ends with Caliban, Stephano, and Trinculo (instead of Antonio and Sebastian as in 2.1) ready to murder the king of the island, Prospero, and being prevented from doing so.

In intention, in structure, in theme, act 5 is like both 2.1 and act 4. Now, however, the vision is, not the easy one of words as in 2.1 or the seductive one of dramatic action as in act 4, but the effective, realistic one of two human beings (of the future king and queen, of the lost son and daughter, of a boy and a girl, of two actors, of two real-life boys) playing chess. Ferdinand and Miranda then leave Prospero's cell to join the onstage audience. Although this "vision" of the two young people at play is not discounted or rejected or broken off as the earlier versions are, the young couple may still be only an impossible ideal. The rules of chess are factitious. Playing chess is not necessarily a preparation for ruling a kingdom. Chess is adversarial. Miranda may be cheating so that Ferdinand can win.

* * * * *

As we discover at the beginning of the play's second scene, the first scene (which presented the great danger faced by men on a ship in a violent tempest) was only a vision: the tempest, we are now told, was not real. Let me now peremptorily comment that, although I have seen as many as twenty productions of *The Tempest*, including Peter Hall's remarkable one with Gielgud at the Old Vic in 1974, I have never witnessed the first scene of *The Tempest* satisfactorily done: it ought to serve to clarify intention, structure, theme. It is true (and should prompt our applause) that most productions allow the audience to hear Gonzalo above the noise, as they should, for one of the primary functions of Gonzalo is to help us to measure and thus to understand Prospero, as I have tried to demonstrate. As we watch and listen to the first scene, we, as usual audience, pay almost no attention to the words spoken, except for Gonzalo's choric speech, while the Boatswain is briefly off stage, and except for Gonzalo's final, epilogue-like comment.

The practice of words being spoken to little or no effect on stage becomes an important feature of *The Tempest* and has a crucial bearing upon the general subject of audience and audience response. Words spoken on stage are often not heard or heard not as words or heard differently or misheard by one or more of the other characters on stage. The truth is that an understanding of this complicated strategy is essential to an understanding of *The Tempest*. Although I will not try to do justice to the strategy and to its function, I should like to emphasize that by exercising an enlarged awareness we, as audience, make and must try to make those connections that none of the characters on stage is in the position of making or is able to make or does make.

In 1.2 Ferdinand, who was present but silent in 1.1, is led on stage by a song sung by Ariel. Ferdinand hears, not the words, but the music: "Come unto these yellow sands,/And then take hands"(1.2.377-78).[5] He does not hear the first burden of the watchdogs barking, nor the second burden of the "strain of strutting chanticleer"(1.2.386). Ferdinand does hear more music and, this time, the words of the new song: "Full fadom five thy father lies"(1.2.397), and he responds as, in his self-concerned state, he would: "The ditty does remember my drown'd father"(1.2.406). Prospero's political intention or the general nature of his plan for vengeance seems by now quite clear to even an uninstructed audience. Prospero has split Ferdinand from his father and the court; he wants Ferdinand to believe that his father is dead; he wants Ferdinand and Miranda to discover each other and to fall in love. To put his moral and political purpose in brutal terms, Prospero intends to use his daughter in order to destroy his enemies; he wants his daughter to become a queen. He is using his daughter as Alonso, so we will soon be told, used his daughter, Claribel, not for her and the court's good, but for his own. The early Prospero is almost totally self-concerned.

After the tempest Prospero finds it necessary to tell Miranda something of their past: he tells her only what he wants her to know; he, for instance, doesn't mention Ferdinand. Ferdinand will be revealed to Miranda at the proper time: she will discover him, like a vision, "A thing divine"(1.2.419). The central point is that Prospero, like a Pandarus, is staging this meeting for a particular effect and a specific result. Miranda lies on stage asleep until he wakes her. If she were to hear the second song, she would take "thy father" in the first line to refer to Prospero, her father. The other significant point is that Prospero is being false, that he is lying: "Full fadom five thy father lies"(1.2.397). In Shakespeare, as the beginning of 3.4 of *Othello* and the beginning of 2.3 of *Macbeth* emphatically prove, *lying* is a meaningful pun. We should not be bemused by the belief that Prospero is a benign magus.

Again, I should like to make the general comment that every aspect or part of *The Tempest* is inextricably implicated in every other part or aspect of the play. The first act helps to make this essential point clearly and simply: the first scene is a symbolic representation of the present;[6] Prospero's interviews with Miranda, Ariel, and Caliban are essentially an exposition of the past; the songs with their three burdens concern the future. Like its polar opposite (the tempest of 1.1) the episode of songs and burdens in 1.2 expresses in condensed, recapitulative terms the thematic concerns of the play. Both the actual tempest (where the emphasis is on action and the present) and the songs and burdens (where the emphasis is on words and the future) must be brought to bear on the rest of the play rather than be allowed to remain distinct and apart from it.[7] For example, the specific function of the first burden (the barking of watchdogs) seems certain, since the watchdogs will appear at the end of act 4 as the means of controlling the tempestuous Caliban group. Although the function of the second burden, which concerns the love plot, is not readily apparent, it is quite clear that Shakespeare wants us to consider Ferdinand as the strutting chanticleer; my guess would be that we, the audience, are being urged to listen for and to hear his future crowing. Thus the third burden (the bell) must have to do with the court group; we are apparently being asked to listen to and for an ominous knell.

The metaphoric tempest on stage at the end of 2.1 is the intended murder of Alonso and Gonzalo (two of Prospero's many doubles) by Antonio and Sebastian. The murder is prevented by Ariel's singing a song in Gonzalo's ear. Alonso hears nothing; Sebastian hears the bellowing of bulls or lions; Antonio hears the roar of a whole herd of lions; Gonzalo hears a humming. These are the words of the song as we hear them:

> While you here do snoring lie,
> Open-ey'd conspiracy
>   His time doth take.
> If of life you keep a care,
> Shake off slumber, and beware.
> Awake, Awake!
>   (2.1.300-05)

Gonzalo's waking words are these: "Now, good angels/Preserve the King!"(2.1.306-07)

As an informed audience we should have no trouble seeing a connection between this situation and the one in the scene before it (Miranda on stage asleep and then awaking) and between this situation and the one in the scene after it (Caliban and Trinculo on stage under the gaberdine and then "awaking" to Stephano). But, again, the substantive point is that the song is also, on a deeper level, addressed to us, the audience. We are asleep; we are unaware. The play seems to assert that, if we care about life, we must shake off slumber and beware. Directed by the song, our awareness must be larger than and thus accommodate the various awarenesses of the characters on stage.

In 1.2 Prospero thrusts Ferdinand and Miranda together for his own purposes; now, in 3.1, the fifth scene of the play, Prospero, a stage audience of one, watches unseen the ensuing private meeting between the young couple. Although his first comment is the critical "Poor worm, thou art infected!/This visitation shows it"(3.1.31-32), Prospero doesn't seem to recognize or to mind that his daughter is willing to subvert her father's wishes ("My father/Is hard at study; pray now rest yourself,/He's safe for these three hours"[3.1.19-21]); that she can tell a kind of lie (". . . nor have I seen/More that I may call men than you, good friend,/And my dear father"[3.1.50-52]); that she can wantonly throw herself at Ferdinand ("I am your wife, if you will marry me;/If not, I'll die your maid. To be your fellow/You may deny me, but I'll be your servant/Whether you will or no"[3.1.83-86]). Nor does Prospero seem suspicious that this vainglorious boy ("A prince, Miranda; I do think, a king"[3.1.60]), the product, as Prospero too well knows, of a vicious court, would seize the opportunity to use Miranda in order to strike back at the tyrannical magician who has turned him into a Caliban. In the parodic next scene Caliban will seize the opportunity presented by Stephano to want to destroy the tyrannical Prospero.[8] The bemused Prospero hears what the young people say, but he does not truly listen, for this is his gullible, epilogue-like comment:

> So glad of this as they I cannot be,
> Who art surpris'd [withal]; but my rejoicing
> At nothing can be more. I'll to my book,
> For yet ere supper-time must I perform
> Much business appertaining.
>
> (3.1.92-96)

It is true that later Prospero is aware of the danger of leaving Ferdinand and Miranda alone together. At the beginning of act 4, he warns Ferdinand of the evil consequences of breaking her virgin-knot before marriage. Because Ferdinand has "strangely stood the test"(4.1.7), Prospero will present the "vanity of [his] art"(4.1.41). Toward the end of the dance between the Reapers and the Nymphs, forgetful Prospero suddenly remembers the rabble's foul conspiracy against his life, and he breaks off the dance. Now Prospero has forgotten Caliban, but Ariel, as we soon discover, has not, and we, the audience, should not. From the perspective of 2.1, we ought to expect the dramatic pageant to be in vain, precisely because it excludes Caliban and what he represents: ingratitude, winter, death. Like a bad audience, the all-too-human Prospero has been so caught up in the staged performance that he has forgotten what he ought to remember.

Prospero's most famous speech, "Our revels now are ended"(4.1.148), which has so influenced our perception of *The Tempest* and our understanding or, rather, misunderstanding of Shakespeare, must be seen for what it is: a dodge, a fabrication, a lie.[9] Prospero gives the famous speech, not to make a philosophic point, but as an excuse to get Ferdinand, his limited audience, and Miranda off stage, so that Prospero and Ariel can deal with the Caliban threat. I do not mean just to discountenance or to disavow the substance of Prospero's speech. But primarily the speech ought to be considered in its dramatic context. The significance, a product of our indoctrinated familiarity with "Our revels now are ended"(4.1.148), has obscured its dramatic meaning and purpose.

Prospero's famous "lie" is made not just because of Caliban and the others but because of Ariel: Miranda must be removed before Ariel can enter, for Prospero is always intent upon keeping Miranda ignorant of Ariel. She isn't told that Ariel was instrumental in the tempest in 1.1. She is put asleep while Prospero has his interview with Ariel in 1.2, and when Ariel and Miranda are twice on stage together, later in the scene, she is unaware of Ariel, to whom Prospero speaks only in asides. Ariel is not on stage in 3.1; and in act 4, as I have said, Prospero has Miranda leave before Ariel comes on stage to control Caliban. When Miranda is discovered playing chess, Ariel is off stage, and when he returns, Ariel is spoken to only by Prospero and only in asides. Miranda never knows that Ariel was either Ceres or Iris in the pageant. To Ariel Prospero is primarily magus; to Miranda Prospero is primarily father. Prospero attempts to keep the role of father separate from the role of magus. Moreover, the two roles of magus and father seem meant to be viewed by us as being incompatible. The regained office of Duke of Milan will cost Prospero not only the role of magus but also that of father: Miranda will become Ferdinand's wife.

In act 5 Prospero may be said to be instructed in turn by the three other denizens of the island, the ones instructed by him in 1.2: Miranda, Ariel, Caliban. First, the non-human spirit gives his master an instructive lesson in humanity: Ariel feels for the distracted, sorrowful men of the court, and this expressed feeling provokes Prospero's famous reply:

> Hast thou, which art but air, a touch, a feeling
> Of their afflictions, and shall not myself,
> One of their kind, that relish all as sharply
> Passion as they, be kindlier mov'd than thou art?
>
> (5.1.21-24)

In helping to attire Prospero, Ariel enables his master to give up vengeance: "The rarer action is/In virtue than in vengeance" (5.1.27-28). In regaining the office he has lost, Prospero becomes the virtuous Duke of Milan again, a prospective victim.

When alone with the members of the court, the Duke of Milan embraces Alonso and receives back his dukedom. "But," asks Alonso, "how should Prospero/Be living, and be here?"(5.1.119-20) Prospero, so newly the reinstated duke, is now faced with a moral dilemma: his initial plight has been transformed into his present plight. Should he say that he, as magus, caused the tempest and wanted revenge but has changed his mind? Should he lie to his king and fabricate a past? He doesn't answer Alonso's question. Instead he compromises himself and eventually everyone else: he refers to all the members of the court as his friends, and (as if to prove the assertion) tells Antonio and Sebastian, his deadly enemies, that he knows of their sinful behavior toward Alonso but will tell no tales.

Prospero's curious reference to "some subtleties o' th' isle"(5.1.124) enables us to understand Prospero's strange actions. If Prospero were to answer Alonso's question and to reveal how he came to be on the island, he would have to divulge the behavior of the noble Neapolitan Gonzalo:

> Out of his charity, who being then appointed
> Master of this design, did give us, with
> Rich garments, linens, stuffs, and necessaries,
> Which since have steaded much; so of his gentleness,

Knowing I lov'd my books, he furnish'd me
From mine own library with volumes that
I prize above my dukedom.

(1.2.162-68)

Rather than to incriminate Gonzalo, who, by disobeying his king, made it possible for Prospero to reach the island and to become a powerful magus, Prospero is willing to put himself and the court at the mercy of Antonio and Sebastian: from their evil perspective it is now imperative that the Duke of Milan be destroyed. There is little evidence that these evil, desperate men have been converted to goodness.

The relationship of the Boatswain to the Master is a gloss on the other servant-master relationships that are so central to the structure and thought of the play.[10] In 1.1 the Boatswain is called a blasphemous dog: he cares about only himself. But this self-centered man, who cares not at all for others, directs his men to do what must be done in a tempest if the ship is not to sink with all aboard. Shakespeare's trenchant paradox is that a ruthless, self-centered man can serve a useful purpose because he cares about only himself. The Boatswain has no intention of drowning, and to that end he will do whatever he can do to keep the ship afloat. His pursuit of a clear-eyed, single-minded end may preserve the lives of others. Unintentionally and unwittingly he can do good, though, as we soon discover, the ship was in no danger. The Boatswain's parable (if I can call it that) forms part of the complex theme of the play. The king's ship is the ship of state, society, the court. We are reminded of the parable when the Boatswain and the Master next appear on stage, in act 5, by Gonzalo, who repeats what he said in 1.1: "I prophesied, if a gallows were on land,/This fellow could not drown"(5.1.217-18). Presumably, now that the Boatswain is on land, he may be hanged. The thought is ominous, in part because the Boatswain is a double for Prospero.

As Ariel's last song (made while transforming Prospero into the Duke of Milan on stage) indicates, Ariel will now be free to serve only himself; he will have no master, no one to control and direct him: he will "fly/After summer merrily"(5.1.91-92), thus excluding the other three seasons.[11] As the Duke of Milan, Prospero will be bereft of his servant, Ariel, and of Ariel's service. Before being freed, Ariel's last two tasks are almost perfunctory: he leads the amazed Boatswain and the Master on stage; he drives in Caliban, Stephano, and Trinculo. As Shakespeare's way of reinforcing the significance of the onstage Boatswain and his parable, Stephano, upon his entrance, makes the following remark:

> Every man shift for all the rest, and let no man
> take care for himself; for all is but fortune.
>
> (5.1.256-57)

That man must shift for others and not take care for himself is precisely the lesson that the new Duke of Milan has decided to take for his own: he doesn't tell Alonso about Gonzalo's "betrayal"; he tells Antonio and Sebastian that he will tell no tales; he acknowledges Caliban (ingratitude, winter, death) as his own. It is no wonder that the epilogue is a prayer.[12]

Stephano is a reduced version of Prospero: his wine is a version of Prospero's art. The butt is out; Prospero has drowned his book. Prospero's reasons for his actions in act 5 are more responsible and more complex than Stephano's; he cannot believe that life is just a matter of fortune. But his conclusion is the same. The Boatswain was capable of doing good because he loved only himself; the Duke of Milan is capable of encouraging evil because he cares about others and doesn't take care for himself: he willingly acknowledges those things that Caliban represents.[13] And the significant point is that the original tempest has been transformed into a human tempest; only an instructed audience can and will recognize its features. Again, to be concerned for only one's self can be useful; to be concerned for only others is to be in immediate danger; it is an impossible vision, a fabrication, a lie.

Thematically, *The Tempest* seems to proceed from endorsing the Boatswain's parable at the beginning (the importance of an individual in a tempest) to endorsing Stephano's parable at the end (the importance of the community in a tempest). The play begins with a choric demonstration of Prospero's plight in terms of the Boatswain; the play ends with a choric demonstration of Prospero's transformed plight in terms of Stephano. A human society in a tempestuous world must value both the individual and the community: both must be accommodated. The epilogue dramatizes Prospero's plight as a supplicant.

In the first scene of the play a sailing ship is dismantled on stage: the topsail is taken down and then the topmast.[14] The Boatswain gives orders to put up the foresail and the mainsail, but to no good end.[15] All is lost; all pray; a confused noise is heard; the men are split from their wives and children at home and from one another on the ship. Similarly, in act 5 Prospero dismantles himself as magus on stage: he puts aside his mantle, breaks his staff, drowns his book, and, at the end of the play, releases Ariel, thus finally divesting himself of all of the accouterments of magic and its power. During the first four acts Prospero has moved between the roles of magus and father. Now, having surrendered the roles of magician and father, he takes up the composite human role-office of old man-brother-Duke. Having done their job, art, love, and necessity are surrendered by Prospero and, on a deeper level, by Shakespeare to the risky world.

The play has ended; we, the audience, are asked to draw near. And so in the epilogue Prospero turns to us in a prayer-like speech of short-line rhymes, like the two sets of short-line rhymes given by Ariel to Prospero with which I began this chapter. But who is this man? He can be variously identified as the erstwhile tyrant, the old magician, the new duke, a lonely dragon (like Coriolanus), a surrogate for Ariel, a double for Stephano, an actor, a spokesman for the acting company, a provost for Shakespeare, whatever. His diverse roles function in the epilogue as an index to what should be our complex awareness of the emerging, changed plight of Prospero, of the dynamic tension between the individual and the community or between goodness and evil that *The Tempest* has explored. And we, the audience, are now asked to become a human Ariel and clap our hands and produce a wind capable of sending this person home. But if he has been dismantled, what good can home do? What good can he do?

The decisive point is that the epilogue delivers the completed play with all of its intransigence to us.[16] *The Tempest* has been an emotionally charged and extended vision, and we must try to implement that vision in our own lives for our own good. Finally, like the rest of Shakespeare's major plays, *The Tempest* should leave us, as I implied at the outset, with the realization that it is a

remarkable human document because it is a deliberate construct.
Shakespeare's deliberate art is at the service of teaching us the
value of what it means to be human; it demands that we
imaginatively respond to it.

NOTES

1. Frank Kermode, "Introduction" to the Arden *The Tempest*
(Cambridge, MA: Harvard UP, 1958), lxxxvii-lxxxviii. I am indebted to
Kermode's discussion of *The Tempest* criticism of Coleridge, G. W.
Knight, D. G. James, E. M. W. Tillyard, and Theodore Spencer.

2. According to the Concordance *O* as a vocative is used 2,434 times.
In the Prologue to *Henry V* the theater is referred to as "this wooden
O"(Pro. 14). See the footnote in The Riverside *Tempest*: "So, so, so.
Probably an expression of approval as Ariel finishes attiring him"(1633).

3. "The betrothal masque Prospero stages for the couple is a figuration
of Gonzalo's utopia and enacts on a mythological level the human action
of the play" (Howard Felperin, *Shakespearean Romance* [Princeton, NJ:
Princeton UP, 1972], 266).

4. Harry Berger says that Caliban is like Gonzalo in his attitude toward
the island and that Gonzalo and Prospero are alike ("Miraculous Harp:
A Reading of Shakespeare's *The Tempest*," *Shakespeare Studies* 5 [1969],
260-65). Joan Hartwig comments: "Sebastian and Antonio reenact the
preplay crisis of Prospero's betrayal and exile when they plot to kill
Alonso" (*Shakespeare's Tragicomic Vision* [Baton Rouge, LA: Louisiana
State UP, 1972], 164). Kenneth J. Semon observes that "The wonder
which Ferdinand and Miranda experienced in I,2 is parodied by the
meeting of Trinculo, Stephano, and Caliban in II,1" ("Shakespeare's
Tempest: Beyond a Common Joy," *ELH* 40 [1973], 30). Clifford Siskin
remarks, "The Caliban-Stephano-Trinculo and Antonio-Sebastian
conspiracies undoubtedly reenact the events in Milan twelve years earlier,
providing Prospero with the opportunity to demonstrate convincingly his
new political acumen" ("Freedom and Loss in '*The Tempest*,'"
Shakespeare Survey 30 [1972], 147).

5. By taking hands a human circle is effected.

6. In his introduction to The Riverside *Tempest* Hallett Smith
comments, "The word *now* occurs seventy-nine times in the course of the
play" (1609). For further emphasis on the present see Stephen Kitay
Orgel, "New Uses of Adversity: Tragic Experience in *The Tempest*." *In*

Defense of Reading, Ed. Reuben A. Brower and Richard Poirer (New York: Dutton, 1962), 110-32.

7. "The one fairly constant musical metaphor in *The Tempest* is the symbolic opposition of confused noise, especially storm sounds, and harmonious music" (Reuben A. Brower, *The Fields of Light* [New York: Oxford UP, 1951], 109).

8. Act 3.1 has the same design as the previous scene, 2.2. In 2.2 Caliban comes on stage carrying wood; he delivers a soliloquy; he is then joined by, first, Trinculo and, then, Stephano. In 3.1 Ferdinand comes on stage carrying wood; he delivers a soliloquy; he is then joined by Miranda. Prospero is also on stage but is unseen by Ferdinand and Miranda.

9. Commenting on Prospero's "Our revels now are ended" speech, Reuben A. Brower declares, "We can now realize that metamorphosis is truly the key metaphor to the drama . . ." (*Fields*, 120).

10. In a footnote Joan Hartwig makes the following observation: "The fact that Prospero is actually the 'master' who controls the tempest makes the Boatswain's questions more dramatically ironic at the same time it complicates the already intricate question" (142).

11. As Herbert Coursen, Jr., remarks, ". . . *The Tempest* explores the nature of freedom and concludes that freedom and responsibility are linked, that freedom without responsibility is license and, ultimately, bondage" ("Prospero and the Drama of the Soul," *Shakespeare Studies* 4 [1968], 317).

12. Joan Hartwig asserts, "The paradox is a familiar one: man must lose his world in order to gain it" (139). Speaking about the epilogue Herbert Coursen, Jr., comments, "This is as close a paraphrase of Christ's injunction on prayer in The Sermon on the Mount or of the words on forgiveness in His prayer as could be found" (329).

13. Robert Egan makes the interesting observation that "we need only remind ourselves that Prospero is the Italian for Faustus" (*Drama within Drama* [New York: Columbia UP, 1975], 97). Frank Davidson remarks that Prospero's failure as duke was a type of error keenly recognized by the Renaissance: "As Frye shrewdly observed, Prosper 'appears to have been a remarkably incompetent ruler of Milan!'" ("*The Tempest*: An Interpretation," *JEGP* 62 [1963], 504).

14. See Guy Back, "Dramatic Convention in the First Scene of *The Tempest*," *Essays in Criticism* 21 (1971), 74-85; and Juliet McLauchlin, "Dramatic Convention in the First Scene of *The Tempest*," *Essays in Criticism* 21 (1971), 424-26.

15. In a famous article written a long time ago Nevill Coghill made the stunning observation that *The Tempest* is "at the start and at the end a ship-play." He goes on to remark:

> Be that as it may the dialogue makes it quite clear that the audience is looking at a stage representing a ship that is going away from them. At the end of the play, when Prospero comes forth from his cell to speak the Epilogue, the sails are hoisted again; up goes the rigging with the mariners in attendance, and the curtains of the inner stage part to show the whole and happy company as a background to Prospero's speech:
> > Gentle breath of yours my sailes
> > Must fill, or else my project failes,
> > Which was to please. (11-13)
> If, with whatever scenic additions, the stage at the start and finish of the play represents a ship going away from the audience, we only now have to ask 'Where was it going?' And the answer must be, at the end of the play, 'Home. It's a play about going home. ("The Basis of Shakespearian Comedy," *Essays and Studies* 3 [1950], 24).

16. "Only in a world of art, an enchanted island, or the play itself, does order arrest mutability and control disorder; but art must be abandoned, and then nothing is left mankind but to sue for grace" (Rose Abdelnour Zimbardo, "Form and Disorder in *The Tempest*," *Shakespeare Quarterly* 14 [1963], 56).

2

King John: The Plight of the Bastard

In *King John*, after rejecting his heritage as a Faulconbridge, Philip is knighted as Richard Plantagenet, the bastard son of Richard the Lionhearted. Promising to follow Elinor, his new grandmother-patroness, till death, the Bastard goes with the English army to France in order to secure the throne for King John. The world at the beginning and at the end of the play, as the Bastard expressly recognizes, is deceitful (". . . though I will not practice to deceive,/Yet to avoid deceit, I mean to learn"[1.1.214-15]), self-interested ("Commodity, the bias of the world"[2.1.574]), and dangerous ("I am amaz'd, methinks, and lose my way/Among the thorns and dangers of this world"[4.3.140-41]). At the beginning, having nothing to lose, the Bastard discloses to himself that "[deceit] shall strew the footsteps of my rising"(1.1.216) and that "Gain, be my lord, for I will worship thee"(2.1.598).

Unquestionably, the Bastard is much more admirable than, for instance, Richard III or the bastard Don John (*Much Ado*) or the bastard Edmund (*King Lear*). If we delay for a moment a consideration of the Bastard's plight, we may assert that the only other characters in the play who elicit our respect and sympathy (largely because of a relative absence of deceit and self-interest) are those that, like the Bastard, are outsiders and victims: Arthur, Blanch, and Hubert. Yet even they are self-interested. Arthur can shamelessly beg and flatter Hubert in order to save his own life; Lady Blanch can acknowledge that, now betrothed to the Dauphin, a victory for either England or France would still be a defeat for her; having agreed to kill Arthur, Hubert does not obey, and then he leads John into believing that Arthur is dead. It is the opportunistic Bastard who best articulates the extent of Hubert's guilt: "If thou didst but consent/To this most cruel act [of killing Arthur], do but despair . . ."(4.3.125-26). The Bastard is usually seen as setting the standard by which the other characters are judged. Indeed, his behavior is unlike that of his brother (Robert), King John, Elinor, King Philip, Constance, Pandulph, Austria, Blanch, Lewis (the Dauphin), Hubert, Salisbury, or Prince Henry. He never indulges in immoderate grief ("I am no woman, I'll not swound at [ill news]"[5.6.22]), like Constance; he is never openly political for his own ends, like France or Pandulph or Lewis; he is never treacherous, like Bigot or Pembroke or Salisbury; he is never vacillating or weak, like King John. Although he recognizes John's bias (commodity) and although he can refer on stage to the dead Arthur, rather than to the living John, as being England, and although he can later chide John for inaction, this blunt, brave soldier is loyal to his liege, King John, who anointed him as knight. But that is not to say that the Bastard is without self-interest, the bias of the world.

Upon learning that Arthur, the legitimate claimant to the English throne, has been abandoned, Constance, Arthur's mother, is understandably furious at her erstwhile friends, France and Austria. When Austria, who wears the lion skin of the slain King Richard, tries to silence Constance ("Lady Constance, peace"[3.1.112]), the Bastard reiterates Constance's rebuke to Austria ("And hang a calve's-skin on those recreant limbs"[3.1.129,131,133]). So, even at the risk of offending his patron, King John ("We like not this, thou dost forget thyself"[3.1.134]), the Bastard affronts the man who killed his father and who, so he would say, insolently wears a stolen lion's skin. We safely assume that the Bastard is self-interestedly seeking an opportunity to avenge his father's death.

The next scene, 3.2, is one of those short, strange scenes in Shakespeare that demand close attention:

> *Alarums, excursions. Enter* BASTARD *with Austria's
> head.*
>   *Bast.* Now by my life, this day grows wondrous
>   hot;
> Some aery devil hovers in the sky
> And pours down mischief. Austria's head lie there,
> While Philip breathes.
>   *Enter* [KING] JOHN, ARTHUR, HUBERT.
>   *K. John.* Hubert, keep this boy. Philip, make up.
> My mother is assailed in our tent,
> And ta'en, I fear.
>   *Bast.*   My lord, I rescued her;
> Her Highness is in safety, fear you not.
> But on, my liege, for very little pains
> Will bring this labor to an happy end.   *Exeunt.*
>   (3.2.1-10)

We are surprised to witness Austria's head, which the Bastard carries on stage and then puts down and which John, Arthur, and Hubert apparently fail to notice: neither Austria nor his head will be mentioned thereafter in the play. Although we are surprised at the Bastard's reference to himself as Philip (as if he still thinks of himself as a Faulconbridge), we are not surprised at John's addressing the Bastard as Philip rather than as Richard or cousin. For the King means to rebuke his protege, as he did in the previous scene. The Bastard's acceptance of the rebuke ("Philip, make up"[3.2.5]) is acknowledged by his "My lord" and "my liege." Hubert, who is so casually introduced into the play in this scene, is told to "keep this boy"(3.2.5); in the next scene John will get Hubert to agree to kill "this boy," Arthur.

Since at the end of 3.1, John equates heat and burning with his inflamed wrath at France, an anger that can be allayed only with "The blood and the dearest-valued blood of France"(3.1.343), we can take the reference in 3.2 to the day as being "wondrous hot"(3.2.1) and to some aery devil pouring down mischief as being Shakespeare's symbolic reference to John's anger. Near the end of 3.1 John orders the Bastard to gather together the English army: "Cousin, do draw our puissance together"(3.1.339). Off stage in addition to, or instead of, gathering the army, the Bastard pursued, killed, and decapitated Austria. Either before or after that event, he rescued Queen Elinor and took her to safety. We readily surmise that by saving Elinor he intended to mitigate his illegitimacy: doing a noble deed for a king and a queen would seem to be a sure way to erase a blot and to rise to power in this kind of world. The scene ends with the Bastard's attempt to ingratiate himself with King John:

> But on, my liege, for very little pains
> Will bring this labor to an happy end.
>
> (3.2.9-10)

We get a sense of the difference between a great and a merely good Shakespeare play by noting, for instance, that commodity and honor, the prevailing thematic concerns of *King John*, are pungently objectified in *1 Henry IV* in the persons of Falstaff (commodity) and Hotspur (honor). Yet, though no one can safely assert that *King John* is a masterpiece like *Richard II* or *1 Henry IV*, one may quietly observe that *King John* is both a misunderstood and an unappreciated Shakespeare history play.[1] So far as we can determine, no one has dealt with the meaning of *King John* seriously or successfully. The surest way to redeem the play from readerly neglect and critical ignominy is to demonstrate that in design and structure it is a work of Shakespeare's accustomed artistry, employing recognizable patterns, strategies, systems. Shakespeare's deliberate art is at the service of daring, incisive meaning. *King John* is not a relic but a work of Shakespeare's literary imagination.

The typical Shakespeare play has two main parts: the first three acts; the final two acts. A Shakespeare play begins with a piece of decisive, startling action: the ghost roams the battlements; a king decides to divide his kingdom; Roderigo demands his jewels and money from a spendthrift Iago. The ramifications of this initial action are translated into the dramatic action of the first three acts. Then, after reaching a climax or a culmination, the action of the second part of the play moves at a faster pace and in a changed direction. Often the second half of a Shakespeare play is a reversal of the first half: Hamlet and Claudius exchange roles, as do Othello and Iago; Richard, king in the first half of *Richard II*, is replaced by Henry in the second half; the tavern, the chief setting of the first half of *1 Henry IV*, is replaced by the battlefield in the second half. In the first half of *King John* England invades France; in the second half France invades England. The motivating force in a Shakespeare play is often an unhappy, dissident young man: Romeo and Orlando are easy examples. Shakespeare's accustomed practice is to establish in an early soliloquy the essential nature of this displeased young man: Prince Harry, Hamlet, or Edmund has at least one soliloquy in the second scene of the play in question. Iago's first soliloquy comes at the end of the first act. In *King John* the Bastard has two related soliloquies, in 1.1 and in 2.1. In Shakespeare most of the soliloquies and asides are a function of first-half action, which culminates in the next-to-last scene of act 3. For example, in the penultimate third-act scene Hamlet comes upon Claudius at prayer; Lear puts his imagined daughters on trial; Othello surrenders his power and will to Iago. Descending to the base court, Richard II surrenders to Bullingbrook. Prince Harry promises his father, Henry IV, to kill Hotspur. In *King John* the culminating first-half action consists of two orders given by the King: to assault the church and to assassinate the boy who has a legitimate claim to the crown. The Bastard is told to seize the wealth of the church; Hubert is told to kill young Arthur.

Generally in Shakespeare the last scene of act 3 is choric and symbolic. One feature of such a scene is the presence on stage of a woman or women: *Hamlet* (Gertrude), *King Lear* (Goneril and Regan), *Othello* (Desdemona, Emilia, Bianca), *Richard II* (the Queen and two ladies), *1 Henry IV* (the Hostess), *King John* (Constance). The second feature is that of male violence: the killing of Polonius; the putting out of Gloucester's eyes; Othello's brutal treatment of Desdemona. In *Richard II* the Gardener is cruelly frank about the dispossessed king; in *1 Henry IV* Falstaff is heartless toward the Hostess. In *King John* no one is affected by Constance's heartfelt grief. In the second half of this choric scene, Pandulph uses the death of Arthur to encourage Lewis to claim the English throne. The general point is that in the last, choric scene of act 3 in Shakespeare the heart (a woman) is brutalized by, or sacrificed to, the will of the head (a man). In *King John* we witness the immediately ironic effect of the King's decisions to rob the church and to kill Arthur.

In 3.2 the Bastard comes on stage with Austria's head. Absent from the stage from 3.3, the Bastard reports to the King in 4.2 with, in effect, the large sums of money he has collected from the clergymen and with, in fact, a prophet named Peter:

> And here's a prophet that I brought with me
> From forth the streets of Pomfret, whom I found
> With many hundreds treading on his heels;
> To whom he sung, in rude harsh-sounding rhymes,
> That, ere the next Ascension-day at noon,
> Your Highness should deliver up your crown.
>
> (4.2.147-52)

The Bastard wants the King to know that the common people are aroused. He may well believe that Arthur is dead; he should be aware that Elinor is no more; he would not be surprised to learn that the nobles are hostile. And so, in this much-troubled world, the Bastard wants his king to realize that he has a redoubtable friend in his cousin Richard. And if indeed King John is going to have to abdicate the throne, he may wish to consider the excellent son of Richard I as a likely successor.

But, fearing an angry rebuke (as he received in 3.1 and 3.2) for the news he bears, the Bastard has shrewdly brought along the seer as a buffer against authority. And the kingly rebuke when it comes is directed, not at the Bastard, but at the prophet: Hubert is ordered to imprison Peter and to have him hanged on this Ascension day. In this manner the Bastard has escaped a rebuke and indeed has even been commanded to fetch the renegades (Bigot, Pembroke, and Salisbury): the king has "a way to win their loves again."(4.2.168) After the Bastard joins the rebels, Arthur's dead body is discovered on stage. And, perhaps for political reasons, Salisbury addresses the Bastard as Sir Richard. Since Bigot will shortly rebuke Hubert as a commoner (". . . dar'st thou brave a nobleman?"[4.3.87]), the Bastard is encouraged to think of himself as being a legitimate agent of the King and as being, unlike Hubert, a nobleman. Alone with Hubert at the end of the scene, the Bastard voices his awareness of the "thorns and dangers of this world"(4.3.141): ". . . powers from home and discontents at home/Meet in one line"(4.3.151-52). But he will continue to serve his king as faithfully as his unexpressed self-interest allows:

A thousand businesses are brief in hand,
And heaven itself doth frown upon the land.
(4.3.158-59)

When the Bastard tells John in 5.1 that "Your nobles will not hear you, but are gone/To offer service to your enemy"(5.1.33-34), he is making the rebels serve his private interest. He distinguishes himself from them and proffers himself as a loyal subject. It is therefore in his self-interest to encourage the King to fight: "But wherefore do you droop? Why look you sad?/Be great in act, as you have been in thought"(5.1.44-45). If the Bastard, as the leader of the English force, can defeat the invading French, he will achieve the status of a true Richard Plantagenet. Upon discovering that his king has made "a happy peace with [the legate of the Pope]"[5.1.63], the Bastard is more determined than ever to fight: "Let us, my liege, to arms"(5.1.73). For, having witnessed the abuse and disgrace that Peter, an innocent prophet, and Hubert, a political instrument, have endured, the Bastard surely knows that a wily Pandulph and a subservient John would not hesitate to cast aside the person directly responsible for ransacking the treasuries of the church: the Bastard will be discarded for having obediently carried out the orders of his king.

In the next scene, when Pandulph tells the Dauphin that John and the church have been reconciled, Lewis responds, "What is that peace to me?/I, by the honor of my marriage-bed/After young Arthur, claim this land for mine"(5.2.92-94). By continuing the war the Dauphin thinks he can win England. Upon entering to his enemies, the Bastard, claiming to speak with King John's voice, abuses not just the French but the English rebels, who are present: "And you degenerate, you ingrate revolts,/You bloody Neroes, ripping up the womb/Of your dear mother England"(5.2.151-53). If the Bastard can provoke the Dauphin and the rebels, as he had earlier provoked Austria, he may be able to defeat them in combat and thus convince John that the King's league with the church can be safely abandoned. As the English victor, he will deserve the highest reward that a no-longer-weak but downcast king can give. The bemused Dauphin, who would welcome the chance to kill John, dismisses the Bastard as a brabbler.

The setting of the next-to-last scene of a Shakespeare play is often explicitly symbolic: the churchyard in *Much Ado*; the prison in *Richard II*; the graveyard in *Hamlet*. Often the action takes place in the night: the death watch in *Much Ado*; the street scene in *Othello*. In *King John* the Bastard and Hubert, the two instruments of the King, discover each other in the night. Hubert has been seeking the Bastard in order to deliver news that will "better arm you to the sudden time"(5.6.26): King John has been poisoned by a monk. And Hubert has other bad news:

> . . . the lords are all come back,
> And brought Prince Henry in their company,
> At whose request the King hath pardon'd them,
> And they are all about his Majesty.
>
> (5.6.33-36)

When the rebels were informed by Melun, a French lord, that after the battle the Dauphin was going to have them killed, they returned to the English camp, but not before enlisting Prince Henry to intercede for them. Henry is the presumptive heir. As in *Hamlet* (Fortinbras), in *King Lear* (Albany), and in *Othello* (Cassio), in *King John* Henry is rewarded for what someone else has done.

The Bastard's response to all this bad news is heartfelt and sincere:

> Withhold thine indignation, mighty heaven,
> And tempt us not to bear above our power!
>
> (5.6.37-38)

And then he reveals to the sympathetic Hubert his own bad news: his forces have been devoured by the "Lincoln Washes"; all of his soldiers have been drowned, and he is powerless. Now his best hope is to reach the dying King. If he can just persuade John to continue to fight against the French, he may still be able to salvage something from the wreckage of his enterprise. But when the King dies, the Bastard can only declare, "I do but stay behind/To do the office for thee of revenge"(5.7.70-71). All is perhaps not lost if he can still confront the Dauphin in battle. And then he learns to his deep chagrin and shattered dream that Pandulph is inside Swinstead

Abbey and that the Dauphin, who, like the Bastard, has lost all his soldiers in a flood, has accepted the English offer of peace. Having no other recourse, the Bastard turns to Prince Henry:

> And happily may your sweet self put on
> The lineal state and glory of the land!
> To whom with all submission, on my knee,
> I do bequeath my faithful services
> And true subjection everlastingly.
>
> (5.7.101-05)

When the rebels kneel beside him and echo his declaration, the Bastard rises and makes the speech with which the play ends:

> O, let us pay the time but needful woe,
> Since it hath been beforehand with our griefs.
> This England never did, nor ever shall,
> Lie at the proud foot of a conqueror,
> But when it first did help to wound itself.
> Now these her princes are come home again,
> Come the three corners of the world in arms
> And we shall shock them. Nought shall make us rue,
> If England to itself do rest but true.
>
> (5.7.110-18)

Here the Bastard makes a distinction between "us" (Henry, the rebels, himself) and England. If they will submerge their self-interest to mother England, all will be well. But he is surely aware that these rebels are now his unremarkable enemies. As we can see, this victory of hope over experience is the logical end to which the battered Bastard has been brought in clearly marked steps in the second half of the play. Gain, his proclaimed lord in act 2, has had to be sacrificed to his need for survival as the faithful servant of the dead King John. And we are meant to realize that the Bastard is like a lost lamb bleating in the wilderness for its mother. He will be both a victim and a scapegoat. And he knows it.

NOTE

1. See E. M. W. Tillyard, *Shakespeare's History Plays* (New York: The Macmillan Company, 1946); Adrien Bonjour, "The Road to Swinsted Abby: A Study of the Sense and Structure of *King John*," *ELH* 18 (1951): 253-74; James L. Calderwood, "Commodity and Honor in *King John*," *University of Toronto Quarterly* 24 (1960): 341-56; Julia C. Van der Water, "The Bastard in *King John*," *Shakespeare Quarterly* 11 (1960): 137-46; Alexander Leggatt, "Dramatic Perspectives in *King John*," *English Studies in Canada* 3 (1977): 1-17; Jay L. Halio, "Alternative Action: The Tragedy of Missed Opportunities in *King John*," *Hebrew University Studies in Literature and the Arts* 11 (1983): 254-69; Virginia Mason Vaughan, "Between Tetralogies: *King John* as Transition," *Shakespeare Quarterly* 35 (1984): 407-20; A. R. Braunmuller, Introduction to the Oxford *The Life and Death of King John* (Oxford: Clarendon P, 1989), 1-93.

3

Richard II: The Garden Scene
as a Clarification of the End of the Play

Although the garden scene, 3.4, of *Richard II* has been much
discussed, no one has demonstrated that an important function of
the scene is to clarify the end of the play. The garden scene takes
place right after Richard, in 3.3, descends to the base court and
acknowledges to Bullingbrook that he knows he must go to London
and give up the crown; the last scene of the play, 5.6, takes place
right after the murder of Richard by Exton. At the beginning of
the garden scene, the Queen, disconsolate over her husband's
misfortune, enters with two of her ladies: "What sport shall we
devise here in this garden/To drive away the heavy thought of
care?"(3.4.1-2) Playing bowls and dancing are mentioned but
rejected by the Queen. Telling either joyful or sorrowful tales will
bring the Queen only more sorrow. One of the ladies says that she
will sing, and, if that will not help, she will weep. The Queen
responds, "And I could sing, would weeping do me good,/And
never borrow any tear of thee"(3.4.22-23). When the Gardener
enters with two of his men, the Queen and her ladies retire.

The growing concern of the list of activities mentioned by the
women (bowling, dancing, telling tales, singing, and weeping) is,
not toward driving out the Queen's heavy thought of care, but
toward her accepting the intransigence of sorrow and weeping. The
play concludes, as the garden scene does, with men. And in the

final scene the conflicting emotions of joy and sorrow are also of growing concern: these men may be said to be joyful that civil unrest has ended; these men may be said to be sorrowful that the double cost of that peace is the murder of Richard and the heartfelt grief of Henry, the new king. In the fifty-two lines of heavily rhymed verse that make up the scene, a procession of five characters, in addition to the coffin containing Richard's body, comes on stage to King Henry, his uncle York, and other lords. Fourteen different men are mentioned by name in the scene. As in 3.4, lists in 5.6 serve to convey intention and meaning.

The surrender of Richard to Bullingbrook in 3.3 prompts the Gardener's cold assessment (". . . Bullingbrook/Hath seiz'd the wasteful King"[3.4.54-55]) of Richard's fall in 3.4 and culminates in the chilling announcements made directly to King Henry in 5.6. The King tells York that he doesn't know whether the rebels who destroyed Ciceter have been taken or slain. Northumberland enters with the news that he has sent the heads of Salisbury, Spencer, Blunt, and Kent to London. Fitzwater comes on stage with the announcement that he has sent the heads of Brocas and Sir Bennet Seely from Oxford to London. Harry Percy arrives with the information that the Abbot of Westminster has "yielded up his body to the grave"(5.6.21). Exton presents the dead body of Richard to Henry.

The Gardener and his men are responsible only for the upkeep of the garden; to the Queen their political remarks, which she has overheard, are impertinent and rude. As the public official who is responsible for the upkeep of England as well as for putting down civil unrest, Henry accepts, as he must, the series of entering men and their reports. He himself begins with a statement about the uncertain end of some rebels. He is then informed about the death of Salisbury and three others; then he hears about the death of (as Fitzwater puts it) two "dangerous consorted traitors"(5.6.15); then he hears from Harry Percy about the death of the Abbot, "The grand conspirator"(5.6.19); Exton asserts that dead Richard is "The mightiest of [Henry's] greatest enemies"(5.6.32). The movement of this list is from an unspecified number of rebels to four men, to two men, to one man, to the body of the dead king. It is also from those least reprehensible to King Henry (rebels rather than traitors or a conspirator) to his mightiest enemy, Richard.

The deposition of Richard (an inevitable consequence of Richard's submission to Bullingbrook in 3.3) has resulted, as might be expected, both in the growing rebellion of men loyal to Richard and in the needed reprisals against these increasingly threatening figures: to Henry the most dangerous of them is still the rightful king of England, the dead Richard. But the Abbot didn't have his head chopped off; Richard's body was not sent to London but delivered to Henry. For understandable reasons, King Henry desired the murder of Richard.

The gardeners enter 3.4 with the instruments of their trade and indulge in political gossip. Northumberland enters 5.6 alone, with a piece of paper. Fitzwater comes on stage with news. But Harry Percy is accompanied by the Bishop of Carlisle; and Exton enters with Richard's coffin. As the men gather, Henry mentions six of them by name. He addresses "Kind uncle York"(5.6.1); he calls Northumberland "gentle Percy"(5.6.11); he thanks Fitzwater by name; he does not mention Harry Percy's name, but he does Carlisle's; he does not mention Richard's name, but he does Exton's: "With Cain go wander thorough shades of night"(5.6.43). Henry's list of names proceeds from the one most in his favor to the one that is least: uncle York, Percy, Fitzwater, Carlisle, Exton, Cain.

The first three men that he names were partisans of Richard who became followers of Henry; the last named of the three is Fitzwater, who, when introduced into the play in the deposition scene, significantly remarks: "As I intend to thrive in this new world"(4.1.78). These named men are the source of Henry's joy. The men named in the second group, all of whom are or were both guilty and banished, are the source of grief and sorrow. The memory of Carlisle's prophecy in the deposition scene must be painful to Henry now:

> My Lord of Herford here, whom you call king,
> Is a foul traitor to proud Herford's king,
> And if you crown him, let me prophesy,
> The blood of English shall manure the ground,
> And future ages groan for this foul act.
> Peace shall go sleep with Turks and infidels,

And in this seat of peace tumultuous wars
Shall kin with kin and kind with kind confound.
(4.1.134-41)

By the end of 5.6 Henry has come to feel both love and hate, both joy and sorrow; he could both sing and weep: "I hate the murtherer, love him murthered"(5.6.40).

When Exton comes on stage in 5.6 he refers to Richard in three different ways: Richard is Henry's "buried fear"(5.6.31); Richard is "The mightiest of thy greatest enemies"(5.6.32); Richard, for the first and only time in the play, is called by his rightful name, "Richard of Burdeaux"(5.6.33). This short list or three-fold identification of the dead king serves to explain Henry's joy and sorrow as well as his anger and need for penance.[1] Strangely, Henry first refers to what Exton has done as a "deed of slander"(5.6.35) rather than as a murder. This odd remark closely resembles what the Queen says to the Gardener upon confronting him in 3.4: "Thou old Adam's likeness, set to dress this garden,/How dares thy harsh rude tongue sound this unpleasing news?"(3.4.73-74) And just as the Queen berates the Gardener, so, referring to Cain rather than to Adam, does Henry berate Exton:

The guilt of conscience take thou for thy labor,
But neither my good word nor princely favor.
With Cain go wander thorough shades of night,
And never show thy head by day nor light.
(5.6.41-44)

At the end of 3.4, after the Queen and her ladies have departed, the Gardener remarks:

. . . here in this place
I'll set a bank of rue, sour herb of grace.
Rue, even for ruth, here shortly shall be seen,
In the remembrance of a weeping queen.
(3.4.104-07)

At the end of 5.6 Henry turns to his gathered men and addresses them in rueful terms and, like the Gardener, with the promise of a penitent gesture:

I'll make a voyage to the Holy Land,
To wash the blood off from my guilty hand.
March sadly after, grace my mournings here,
In weeping after this untimely bier.
                                    (5.6.49-52)

The third act ends in a private garden; the play ends in the public world. The main point to be made is that the garden scene expresses the reaction of the heart (the Queen) and the reaction of the hand (the Gardener) to the news of the fall of Richard. To the Queen's sorrow and anger are added the Gardener's joy and penance: sorrow, joy, anger, penance. After Richard has been deposed (act 4), divorced from his Queen (5.1), and murdered by Exton (5.5), the last scene of the play expresses the reaction of the head (the King) to the news of the public reprisals and then to his confrontation (to put it that way) with King Richard. In the last scene Henry expresses joy and sorrow and anger and penance. Thus, by considering the final scene as an extension in time of the garden scene and by perceiving that Henry's reaction combines and utilizes the earlier reactions of the heart (the Queen) and of the hand (the Gardener), we are enabled to understand more clearly both Shakespeare's intention and his meaning at and by the end of this early, great play.

NOTE

1. Three unnamed women and three unnamed men are in the garden scene. Except for some silent lords, Hotspur, and Henry IV, all of the men in 5.6 are named. The patterns in both scenes are unmistakable and must be deliberate.

4

Richard II and *1 Henry IV*:
An Enlarged Context

The historical saga chronicled by Shakespeare in his two tetralogies begins after the death of one Gloucester, Thomas of Woodstock, and ends after the death of another Gloucester, Richard III. In both *Richard II* and *Richard III* a Henry succeeds a Richard as King of England. Not surprisingly, as Geoffrey Bullough has noted, the two plays are comparable.[1] Nor is it surprising that *Richard II*, the play most crucial to our understanding of this cycle of history plays, would have its value enhanced by every enlarged context. It is therefore instructive to consider *1 Henry IV* as a special kind of sequel to *Richard II*, as its companion play, as its complement, as its counterpart: the political and moral imbalance caused by the deposition and the murder of Richard II in the first play of the full sequence is set right by the son, the future Henry V, in the very next play.

In the first scene of *1 Henry IV*, the King remarks:

> O that it could be prov'd
> That some night-tripping fairy had exchang'd
> In cradle-clothes our children where they lay,
> And call'd mine Percy, his Plantagenet!
> Then would I have his Harry, and he mine.
> (1.1.86-90)

In their only interview or private meeting in the two plays, King Henry addresses his dissolute son in this surprising way:

> As thou art to this hour was Richard then
> When I from France set foot at Ravenspurgh,
> And even as I was then is Percy now.
>
> (3.2.94-96)[2]

In the next-to-last scene of *Richard II* Richard is killed by order of Henry;[3] in the next-to-last scene of *1 Henry IV* Percy or Hotspur (who has been equated with Bullingbrook) is killed by Prince Harry (who has been equated with dissolute Richard): once Richard in the person of the Prince kills Henry in the person of Hotspur, the world that has been turned upside down in *Richard II* is righted. Having distanced himself from the guilt-ridden court, Prince Harry on the battlefield first saves his father's life and then kills Hotspur. These two actions certify the Prince as the legitimate son and heir, as the Prince of Wales, and serve to redeem the King and his court from the guilt and shame of having murdered the rightful ruler.

In all of his plays Shakespeare can be trusted to employ three related parables or systems or tropes: the body trope, the family trope, the play-acting or stage trope. The body trope—in its essential form of the head, the heart, and the hand—is particularly in evidence in *Richard II*: the head thinks; the heart feels; the hand acts.[4] In *Richard II* the primary emphasis is on the head and the heart. The first half of the play (up to the end of 3.3, where Richard acknowledges to Bullingbrook that he must go to London and give up the crown) dramatizes Richard's failure as head: he is wanton in his disregard for others; he underestimates the Bullingbrook threat to his crown. The second half of the play dramatizes King Henry's failure as heart. As his final comment indicates, he is the victim of the murder he desperately desired:

> I'll make a voyage to the Holy Land,
> To wash this blood off from my guilty hand.
>
> (5.6.49-50)

In *1 Henry IV* the emphasis is no longer on the head and the heart, as in *Richard II*, but is on the hands—on the two heedless and heartless members of the new generation; on the son of King Henry and the son of Northumberland, King Henry's erstwhile chief lieutenant; on Prince Harry and Harry Percy, Hotspur. The significant point is that, if the two plays are considered together, the dramatic emphasis neatly shifts from the head to the heart to the hand.

In much the same way, the symbolic location of the developing action moves by firm stages from the garden to the prison to the tavern to the battlefield. The strangest scene in *Richard II* is the allegoric garden scene, 3.4. The metaphor of England as a garden, which old John of Gaunt asserts in a panegyric in 2.1, is dramatized at the end of the third act as the garden trope: England is a garden; its king is a gardener. As a result of the Queen's rebuke, the Gardener turns from blunt awareness to pity and repentance. He comes to realize something he didn't know or understand. The behavior of the Gardener at the end of act 3 is much like the behavior of King Henry, the Gardener-King, at the end of the play: he also repents. The Gardener responds to the Queen; Henry responds to the King.[5]

The second location of major symbolic significance is the prison. In his only soliloquy in the play Richard considers England or his world, not as a garden, but as a prison. In this scene, 5.5, just before strange music interrupts his heartfelt introspection, Richard comments:

> But what e'er I be,
> Nor I, nor any man that but man is,
> With nothing shall be pleas'd, till he be eas'd
> With being nothing.
>
> (5.5.38-41)

The dramatization of the prison trope, which includes Richard's soliloquy, ends with his murder at the hands of Exton:

> As full of valure as of royal blood!
> Both have I spill'd; O would the deed were good!
>
> (5.5.113-14)

At the end of 3.4 the Gardener expresses his pity; at the end of the next-to-last scene, 5.5, Exton expresses his grief-stricken guilt; at the end of the play Henry expresses his heartfelt repentance. The main point is that by the end of *Richard II* the prison trope applies, not just to Richard, but to Henry. Now he is the one imprisoned in England: he will never make a pilgrimage to the Holy Land; he will sadly follow after Richard.

The third location of major symbolic significance is the tavern, which is introduced in the second scene of *1 Henry IV* and dramatized most fully in the elaborate 2.4, the quintessential tavern scene. This location or setting is the habitation of Prince Harry or Hal, as he is known in this underworld.[6] As Hal recognizes, tavern life is a waste of time, a place of idleness, of "playing holidays"(1.2.204). The garden is an unsophisticated answer; the prison is an unsatisfactory solution or an impasse; the tavern contains the solution, a way out of the impasse. It is the dwelling place of the young man who, on the death of his father, will become Henry V. The chief denizen of this wasteful world, Hal's shameless mentor, is Falstaff, a foul-mouthed old man, totally without faith or trust or honesty. He is the head without the heart; he is the body without the soul that should inhabit it. Unlike a gardener or a prisoner, Falstaff appropriates someone else's place for his own ends. Rather than working in it, as a gardener must, or being constrained by it, as a prisoner is, Falstaff makes this place of indulgence his unsavory home. To Hal the tavern has been a learning place. He has become so proficient "that [he] can drink with any tinker in his own language during [his] life"(2.4.18-20). But Hal now realizes that he has nothing more to learn from the tavern, which is as corrupt as the court.

The fourth location of major symbolic significance is the battlefield, the setting for the third and fourth scenes of act 5. It is the location needed by the heir apparent.[7] The character of main thematic importance is no longer Richard II or the Gardener or Henry IV or Hal but Prince Harry. As a testing place, it provides the opportunity that the Prince must seize if he is to do what in 3.2 he promised his father he would:

> I will redeem all this on Percy's head,
> And in the closing of some glorious day
> Be bold to tell you that I am your son,
> When I will wear a garment all of blood,

And stain my favors in a bloody mask,
Which washed away shall scour my shame with it.
(3.2.132-37)

On the battlefield Hal is reborn as the Prince of Wales. To him blood is a badge of honor, not, as to his father at the end of *Richard II*, a sign of shame and guilt; the Prince can wash his shame away; the King cannot rid his hands of guilt. Both would agree that the battlefield rewards victory at any cost: ". . . For nothing can seem foul to those that win"(5.1.8). The end crowns all. The business of the battlefield is death.[8] And the battlefield, like the court and the tavern, is a place of deceit, falsehood, and treachery, where many men march in the King's coats and where someone like Falstaff can be rewarded for something he didn't do.

* * * * *

In the two plays, considered together, one kind of symbolic action is supplanted by another kind: the action of the head and the heart gives way to that of the hand; the garden and the prison change into the tavern and the battlefield. In *Richard II* the symbolic action is vertical rather than horizontal, a rise and a fall, an up and a down. The play is replete with small examples of the general principle. In 1.3 Richard stops the trial by combat between Mowbray and Bullingbrook by throwing down his warder; in act 4, right before the deposition of Richard, seven gages are thrown down; in 5.3 the Duchess, Rutland, and York kneel to King Henry and then stand up. A pair of scales gives this up-and-down action metaphoric and symbolic value: Richard is in one scale; Bullingbrook is in the other. As we might expect, the Gardener provides the mixed, valorized metaphor: when one scale is down, the other is up; Bullingbrook "weighs King Richard down"(3.4.89). At his deposition Richard employs an elaborate, extended version of the same figure. Richard takes hold of one side of the crown; Bullingbrook is bid to take hold of the other side. Richard then likens the crown to a deep well: Richard is in one bucket; Henry, the other. When one bucket is down, "full of tears"(4.1.188), the other is up, "dancing in the air"(4.1.186). The

basis of the metaphor is dramatized in 3.3 when Richard appears
"on the walls" and then comes down to the base court in order to
acknowledge to Bullingbrook that he knows he must go to London.
The point is that the symbolic action, along with its commentary,
is emphasized in three consecutive, mid-play scenes: 3.3; 3.4; 4.1.
In the next-to-last scene (5.5), as he is struck down, Richard
expresses the thematic imperative:

> Mount, mount, my soul! Thy seat is up on high,
> Whilst my gross flesh sinks downward, here to die.
>   (5.5.111-12)

The body of the dispossessed king must fall in order for the soul
to rise. But the play itself ends, not with a vertical, up-and-down
movement, but with a horizontal or lateral movement. At the end
of the play, because of the fall of Richard's body and the rise of
his soul, Henry IV, the living king, is pulled in two ways at once:
he wants to go to the Holy Land to save his guilty soul; he is
forced to remain in England to secure his uncertain crown. Henry
IV doesn't go up or down; he ends the play by following after the
dead Richard.

The pervasive symbolic action of being called in two ways at
once is dramatized in *1 Henry IV* in a seemingly trivial episode in
2.4, the crucial tavern scene. While Hal tries to get Francis, a
drawer, to answer his quick questions, Poins, off stage, keeps
calling the drawer, ostensibly for service. Hal does not give the
drawer time to answer any question, and Poins insistently
continues to call. When the vintner appears and reprimands Francis
("What, stand'st thou still, and hear'st such a calling?"[2.4.81-
82]), Francis goes to see what Poins wants.[9] England is a tavern,
and Francis is a parodic double for Richard II, who went to fight
the Irish kerns rather than to remain in England. Francis is a
double for Henry IV, who wants to go to the Holy Land but who
must remain in England. Francis is a double for Hotspur, whose
wife wants him to remain at home but whose "honor" calls him to
battle. Francis is a double for Hal, in, for instance, 3.3, where he
is torn between the Hostess's appeal for justice and Falstaff's claim
of friendship. Francis is a double for Henry V, who will insist on
going to France rather than remaining in England. The point is that

a central symbolic action is the lateral one of a public person's being called in two ways at once, of his not responding, and then of his responding to a call.

The second major symbolic action in *1 Henry IV* is also presented as trivial action in 2.4, the tavern location, and it also involves Francis, the drawer, who represents rulers or putative rulers. At the beginning of the scene Hal tells Poins that he is going to ask Francis to what end he gave him some sugar. Then Hal gives the sugar to Poins (". . . to sweeten which name of Ned, I give thee this pennyworth of sugar"[2.4.22-23]). Thus the symbolic action is the lateral one of handing something from one person to another. To Francis the sugar has heartfelt symbolic value: he gives it to Hal. Hal doesn't value the gift as a gift: to him it is only a pennyworth of sugar, and he has no reluctance in giving it away. In addition, the gift decreases in value as it is handed on. On one level the sugar represents the money that Falstaff steals from the true men and that Hal steals from Falstaff. On another level the sugar represents the crown: Richard gives it to Henry, who will pass it on to his son. Receiving the crown from his father, Henry V will hand it on to his son, Henry VI.

In *Richard II* the dominant image is that of a pair of scales in which Henry is weighed against Richard: the demands of the heart are set over against the demands of the head. To Richard the crown is a valuable commodity, a deep well. In *1 Henry IV*, where the emphasis has passed to the hand, the crown (insecure and uneasy on its wearer's head) has become devalued: it is now just a commonplace commodity, money or a pennyworth of sugar. Falstaff has no illusions about it. But in a stricter, more immediate sense, the action involving Francis and the sugar serves as a version of, or a gloss on, significant action in the last two scenes of the play, on the battlefield and afterwards. It serves to encourage us to devalue what would otherwise be considered to be important or noble.

After Prince Harry has killed Hotspur, Falstaff rises from apparent death, picks up the body of Hotspur and, after a brief time, throws it down, thus replicating the essential up-and-down action of *Richard II*: the risen Falstaff lifts up Hotspur and then sends him crashing down; the body rises and falls. Falstaff outrageously claims to have killed Hotspur, and, incredibly, the

Prince allows the claim to stand. The symbolic point is that in giving Hotspur to Falstaff, the Prince is repeating the action of giving the money back to the true men or of giving the sugar to Poins: ". . . to sweeten which name of [Falstaff] . . ." (2.4.22). On the battlefield the dead Hotspur becomes a gift, and Prince Harry keeps it briefly and then gives it away: it is of little value, food for worms, like honor that died on Wednesday.

The last scene of the play presents another version of the same symbolic action. Just as on the battlefield the Prince gives Hotspur to one John (Falstaff), so, after the victory, he gives his other antagonist, Douglas, to another John (Lancaster). Douglas is like money or a pennyworth of sugar. The Prince gets Douglas from the King, gives Douglas to Lancaster, and tells his brother to release Douglas. Although the action is charged with political significance, it is the sugar all over again. The Prince's action here is as cold and heartless as it was with Francis in the tavern and with Hotspur on the battlefield. The Prince asks the King to grant a request that, given the Prince's public behavior on the battlefield, the King cannot refuse. In giving Douglas to Lancaster, the Prince is putting himself between the King and his younger brother, John. His action certifies his regained position. As the Prince of Wales he can make a demand upon the King, and then he can order his brother to perform a specific deed.

Like the money and the sugar, Hotspur and Douglas pass through the hands of the Prince. He has reconciled the action of being pulled in two ways at once by establishing for himself the middle position of being able to receive and then to give. And what he has done is to reverse on the battlefield the order of the two Francis episodes as they occur in the tavern. In a reduced form, it is what he will do as the successful Henry V: once he secures the crown ("No king of England, if not king of France!"[Hen V 2.2.193]) at the Battle of Agincourt and then marries Kate, he will—at the height of his power and his glory—die and thus pass on the crown to his saintly son, Henry VI. And, as the first tetralogy has already dramatized, blood and death will follow.

NOTES

1. Geoffrey Bullough. *Narrative and Dramatic Sources of Shakespeare* (London: Routledge and Kegan Paul, 1960), 356.

2. As everyone knows, Shakespeare changed the age of Hotspur from being the same as that of Henry Bullingbrook to being roughly that of the Prince.

3. In the Folio only five scenes are in act 5.

4. See William B. Bache, *Design and Closure in Shakespeare's Major Plays* (New York: Peter Lang, 1991), 119-172.

5. See the preceding chapter on *Richard II*.

6. Warren J. MacIsaac says that Falstaff's tavern name for the Prince is Hal. "After his victory over Hotspur, the Prince is either 'Harry' or the 'Prince of Wales,' whether in response or address" ("A Commodity of Good Names." *Shakespeare Quarterly* 29 [1978]: 417-419.)

7. Henry V will use the battlefield to establish himself as king in *Henry V*.

8. For a discussion of the Prince as a businessman see Roy Battenhouse, "Falstaff as Parodist and Perhaps Holy Fool." *PMLA* 90 (1975): 32-52.

9. For other discussions of the Francis episode see the following: John Shaw, "The Staging of Parody and Parallels in *1 Henry IV*." *Shakespeare Survey* 20 (1967): 61-73; J. D. Schuchter, "Prince Hal and Francis: The Imitation of an Action." *Shakespeare Studies* 3 (1967): 129-137; Sheldon Zitner, "Anon, Anon: Or, A Mirror for a Magistrate." *Shakespeare Quarterly* 19 (1968): 63-70; Mark Rose, *Shakespearean Design* (Cambridge, MA: Belknap P, 1972), 72.

5

All's Well That Ends Well:
The Significance of the First Scene

All's Well That Ends Well seems best regarded as a companion piece to *Measure for Measure*: the two titles are the most dialectical ones in the canon.[1] *Measure for Measure* deals with employing craft to counter vice, justice to offset injustice, corrected and instructed love to replace self-love or vanity.[2] *All's Well* proffers the thesis that a good end justifies an evil means, that deception may be necessary to retain or sustain honesty, that a sweet present can emerge out of a bitter past. In *Measure for Measure* the Duke uses the office of friar to promote a rescuing bed-trick; in *All's Well* Helen uses the role of wife to produce an honorable bed-trick. At the time of the mid-play treachery, the interceding Duke is the explicit brother and the implicit father; Helen intercedes as the explicit pilgrim and the implicit wife. The Duke has to gain the approval of Isabel and Mariana; Helen has to win the aid of the Widow and Diana.

Measure for Measure concerns a corrupt Viennese society; *All's Well* deals with a debased French court and an inconclusive war. *Measure for Measure* shows the effect of the church (the Duke as friar; Isabel as prospective nun) on an uninstructed world; *All's Well* shows the effect of an exceptional woman, whose actions are sanctioned by the older generation, on a diseased court and a corrupt husband: the only church person in the play is Helen in the guise of pilgrim. In *Measure for Measure* the business is for the Duke to come forward as himself; in *All's Well* "The business is for Helen to come hither" (1.3.96-97). Like *Measure for Measure*, *All's Well* is concerned with "A showing of a heavenly effect in an earthly actor" (2.3.23-24).

One reason that "The verse of *All's Well That Ends Well*—compressed, elliptical, abstract, often tortuous and obscure—is very different from the fluid, concrete, and playful language of the early comedies"[3] is that *All's Well* presents a desperate, irredeemable world. Helen can cure the King's fistula, but she cannot save him from death. Unlike Benedick or Orlando, Bertram is not corrected or transformed by love. Angelo of *Measure for Measure* can at least feel remorse because of his sinful act. As a human being, Bertram is unconscionable and despicable. Helen can rescue the rash, stupid Bertram from ignominy, but she will never be able to make him a reliable husband and father:

> I have to-night dispatch'd sixteen businesses,
> a month's length a-piece, by an abstract of success:
> I have congied with the Duke, done my adieu with his
> nearest; buried a wife, mourn'd for her, writ to my
> lady mother I am returning, entertain'd my con-
> voy, and between these main parcels of dispatch
> [effected] many nicer needs. The last was the greatest,
> but that I have not ended yet.
>
>   (4.3.85-92)

It is this monster, proud of having wantonly deflowered a maid, that will be forced in the last scene of the play to accept the remarkable "dead" wife that he disdained and meant to betray. He is far worse than the mean-spirited Claudio of *Much Ado*.

Othello, which was written about the same time as *Measure for Measure* and *All's Well*, makes extensive use of Shakespeare's familiar strategy of character doubles: Brabantio, Cassio, Iago, and Roderigo are, in various ways, doubles for Othello; Bianca and Emilia are immediate doubles for Desdemona. In *Measure for Measure* Angelo and the Duke are doubles, as are Isabel and Mariana. In *All's Well* Bertram and Parolles are doubles, as are the Countess and the Widow, as are Diana and Helen. In a larger sense, Bertram, who discards Helen, is like Angelo, who discards

Mariana; Diana is like Mariana. Parolles can be compared to Iago; Helen as wife can be compared to Desdemona. In act 5 of *Measure for Measure* Angelo, like Bertram, is publicly revealed to have been treacherous; in act 5 of *Othello* Iago is publicly discovered to have been an unconscionable villain. But, in act 4, rather than in act 5, of *All's Well*, Parolles is publicly revealed to be an incorrigible coward, liar, and traitor. Parolles's disgrace precedes Bertram's.

Shakespeare's usual practice is to present the crisis of the play in the next-to-last scene of act 3: in 3.3 of *Othello* occurs the obligatory confrontation between the principal antagonists, the plot-necessary confrontation between Othello and Iago. Since the third act of *Measure for Measure* has only two scenes, it is 3.1 that presents the obligatory first meeting between the Duke and Isabel: out of this crucial interview will arise the bed-trick. *All's Well* modifies the general procedure by having the obligatory Bertram-Helen meeting take place in the third-from-last (rather than the next-to-last) scene of act 3, and, properly speaking, it is not a confrontation scene. The Widow, Diana, and Helen, as well as others, watch Bertram, Parolles, and some soldiers pass by. Out of this scene will come the bed-trick. In all three instances (*Othello*, *Measure for Measure*, *All's Well*) the participants of the obligatory crisis scene are responsible for fourth-act action. The chief difference is that in 3.5 of *All's Well* all of the characters (rather than just some of them) needed by the plot are on stage. This fact serves to explain why *All's Well* needs two choric, end-of-third-act scenes instead of the customary one.

In the choric 3.4 of *Othello* Desdemona's role as wife and Emilia's double role as Iago's wife and Desdemona's friend are tested; then Cassio gives the fateful handkerchief to the new Bianca. In the choric 3.2 of *Measure for Measure*, where the Duke is confronted in turn by Elbow-Pompey, Lucio, Escalus-Provost-Mistress Overdone, the Duke's offices as brother in the church and father of the city are tested. In the first of the two choric scenes of *All's Well*, 3.6, Bertram and two French lords agree to "let [Parolles] fetch off his drum"(3.6.19-20); Parolles will then be captured and made to confess. In 3.7 Helen persuades the Widow to permit Diana to participate in the bed-trick. Thus Parolles and Diana are the agents (one, unwilling; the other, willing) of two deceptions: the first will reveal the true nature of a bound and blindfolded Parolles to Bertram; the second will enable Helen to consummate her marriage. All of the characters of 3.6 and 3.7 will be instrumental in carrying out in act 4 the two plot-necessary deceptions.

It is instructive that 4.2 ends with Diana's ten-line soliloquy, her only one in the play:

> Since Frenchmen are so braid,
> Marry that will, I live and die a maid.
> Only in this disguise I think't no sin
> To cozen him that would unjustly win.
>
> (4.2.73-76)

As we ought to expect, the next scene, 4.3, ends with Parolles's eleven-line soliloquy, his second in the play:

> Who knows himself a braggart,
> Let him fear this; for it will come to pass
> That every braggart shall be found an ass.
> Rust sword, cool blushes, and, Parolles, live
> Safest in shame! Being fool'd, by fool'ry thrive!
> There's place and means for every man alive.
> I'll after them.
>
> (4.3.334-40)

The play may proceed to its now-destined but still-surprising conclusion.

Although it is Shakespeare's practice to establish the essential nature of the main characters in the first act of a play, he rarely begins with a scene designed to display the nature of such a main character. *Troilus and Cressida*, another play contemporaneous with *All's Well*, is an exception. It begins with the elaborate establishment of essential character. The first two scenes present the main characters of the love plot: Pandarus is with Troilus in 1.1; Pandarus is with Cressida in 1.2. Both scenes are heavily expositive. The first scene is the essential Troilus scene; it concentrates on his initial plight (to go to battle or to pursue Cressida); he is on stage throughout the scene; he delivers a soliloquy. The second scene is the essential Cressida scene; it concentrates on her initial plight (to listen to Pandarus and surrender herself to Troilus or not); she is on stage throughout; she delivers a scene-ending soliloquy. The ensuing Troilus-Cressida action is an extrapolation of the first two scenes; the first two scenes of the play are a condensation, a digestion, a shorthand version of the full Troilus-Cressida action. The main function of these first two scenes is not just to foreshadow future action.

Although the strategy is not so readily apparent as it is in *Troilus and Cressida*, the first scene of *All's Well* is also an essential-character scene: it concentrates on Helen's initial plight (being hopelessly in love with the departing Bertram); she is on stage throughout the scene; she has two soliloquies.[4] The ensuing action is an extrapolation of the scene; 1.1 is a condensation, a digestion, a shorthand version of the plot. The scene itself has two parts: the departure of Bertram and Lafew for Paris, followed by a soliloquy; Helen's discussion with Parolles, followed by a soliloquy. In this regard the scene is a version of one of Shakespeare's usual designs for a complete play: the first three acts; the final two acts. As we expect, most of the exposition is in the first part of the scene. Here we learn that Bertram's father has just died and that the new count has been summoned to Paris by the king. We hear that Helen, the only daughter of a famous, now-dead physician, has been adopted and reared by the Countess. We learn from the Countess that Helen "derives her honesty, and achieves her goodness"(1.1.46-47). We are told that Helen's grief is over her father. In the first soliloquy we discover that her tears were really prompted by the departure of Bertram: he is so far above her that her love seems hopeless.

The second part of the scene is radically different in tone and emphasis from the first. At the end of the first soliloquy Helen remarks, ". . . my idolatrous fancy/Must sanctify [Bertram's] reliques. Who comes here?"(1.1.97-98) And onto the stage comes, not one of Bertram's reliques, but the embodiment of that which goes with Bertram. Parolles's sudden, first appearance elicits Helen's aside:

> One that goes with [Bertram]. I love him for his sake,
> And yet I know him a notorious liar,
> Think him a great way fool, soly a coward;

> Yet these fix'd evils sit so fit in him,
> That they take place when virtue's steely bones
> Looks bleak i' th' cold wind. Withal, full oft we see
> Cold wisdom waiting on superfluous folly.
>
> (1.1.98-105)

Helen discloses to us the essential nature of Parolles before he says a word. But not till 4.3 will this nature be made clear to Bertram. The main sense of this obscure-seeming aside seems to be something like the following: being a liar, being a fool, and being a coward are so much a part of Parolles's make up that these qualities occupy the place that virtue should hold; being deprived of their proper place, the "steely" bones of virtue are exposed and neglected. In addition, we are told that wisdom waits on folly, rather than the other way around.

As we might well expect in a Shakespeare play, Helen's aside is echoed in the end of Helen's second, scene-ending soliloquy, as if to emphasize that Helen is also a kind of double for Parolles:

> The King's disease—my project may *deceive* me,
> But my intents are *fix'd*, and will not leave me. [italics added]
>
> (1.1.228-29)

Since Helen first addresses Parolles in the scene as "monarch," we may perhaps surmise that, in addition to his being seen as a double for the King, Parolles is meant to be seen not only as the embodiment of Bertram's evils but also as the realization of the King's embodied disease, a symbolic fistula. But the main point is that the evils that are fixed in Parolles give way to the intentions (to win Bertram by curing the King) that are fixed in Helen. The play's argument then is not only that the deception, folly, and cowardice (which are embodied in Parolles) must be brought into the open, recognized, and condemned but also that the virtue and wisdom (embodied in Helen), which are now cold and useless, must be brought by Helen's intentions, first, to the court and then back to Rossillion. Isabel in *Measure for Measure* must be called away from the nunnery in order to become a true sister to Claudio and Mariana and a daughter to the friar. Helen must leave the cloistered Rossillion and move to the "learning place" that is the court in order to become a physician to the King and a wife to

Bertram. Like Isabel, Helen must enter the world if she is to correct and instruct it. After Helen's intentions are realized, Parolles's fixed evils must perforce be publicly disclosed.

The second part of 1.1 functions as a step-by-step pregnant summation of the Helen-Diana-Bertram-Parolles action that will be later dramatized. Helen's responses to Parolles mark the development. For instance, Parolles says, ". . . away with [virginity],"(1.1.132) and Helen responds, "I will stand for't a little. . . "(1.1.133). Helen will not surrender her virginity yet. At the end of another attack on virginity, Parolles again says, "Away with 't!"(1.1.149) Helen responds this time with a question: "How might one do, sir, to lose it to her own liking?"(1.1.150-51) Though Parolles's response is as expected, he three times uses a mild oath that is also the proper answer to Helen's question: "Marry . . . marry . . . marry"(1.1.152,162,163). Parolles ends this passage with a question of his own, "Will you anything with it?"(1.1.163-64) This is Helen's reply:

> Not my virginity yet: [. . . .]⁵
> There shall your master have a thousand loves,
> A mother, and a mistress, and a friend,
> A phoenix, captain, and an enemy,
> A guide, a goddess, and a sovereign,
> A counsellor, a traitress, and a dear;
> His humble ambition, proud humility;
> His jarring concord, and his discord dulcet;
> His faith, his sweet disaster; with a world
> Of pretty, fond, adoptious christendoms
> That blinking Cupid gossips.
>
> (1.1.165-75)

The long, elaborate list (to which we seem meant to add "adoptious christendoms") is meant to be used by us as a choric document of major importance. It is designed to enable us to understand the manifold symbolic significance of the moment that Bertram impregnates Helen: "*There* shall your master have. . ."[italics added](1.1.166). The list is difficult, but we have little trouble seeing how and why the various roles accrue to Helen at and after the consummation of her marriage: she is mother, mistress, friend, phoenix, captain, etc. And we readily understand

how and why "Little Helen's"(1.1.188) action in the night involves
others: the mother may refer to the Widow or the Countess; the
goddess to Diana; the sovereign to the King.

The reference to christendoms and Cupid looks forward to
Helen's stumbling remark that she wishes Bertram well:

> ['Tis pity] That wishing well had not a body in 't,
> Which might be felt, that we, the poorer born,
> Whose baser stars do shut us up in wishes,
> Might with effects of them follow our friends,
> And show what we alone must think, which never
> Returns us thanks.
>
> (1.1.180-86)

In terms of the referential nature of the scene, the body refers to
the baby Helen will be carrying: the plural pronouns refer not just
to the various roles in her elaborate list but, more simply, to Helen
and her child. Helen now wants her wishes to have a baby; in time
Helen and her embodied child will follow their friends (as they do,
from Florence to Marseilles to Rossillion) and will bring to
Bertram the thankless answer to his impossible *never*. Helen will
be the obedient wife: she will have done what her husband,
Bertram, demanded in his unconscionable letter to her in 3.2:

> When thou canst get the ring upon my
> finger, which never shall come off, and show me a child
> begotten of thy body that I am father to, then call me
> husband; but in such a 'then' I write a 'never.'
>
> (3.2.57-60)

At the end, although Helen has not really fulfilled the conditions
of the letter, she says she has:

> And, look you, here's your letter. This it says:
> "When from my finger you can get this ring,
> And [are] by me with child, etc." This is done.
> Will you be mine now you are doubly one.
>
> (5.3.311-14)

Helen does not have a child to show Bertram; she is being duplicitous, though necessarily so. The underlying significance of what the end will be is uncovered in Helen's aside in 1.1 ("Yet these fix'd evils are so fit in him/That they take place when virtue's steely bones/Looks bleak i' th' cold wind. Withal, full oft we see/Cold wisdom waiting on superfluous folly" 1.1.102-05.) We can always read *take place* in the usual sense of *occur*: the fixed evils occur at the same time that bones look bleak in the cold wind. Since at the end of the play Parolles is rescued by Lafew ("Good Tom Drum, lend me a handkercher. So, I thank thee; wait on me home. I'll make sport with thee"[5.3.321-23]), his fixed evils, rather than being exorcised, will be in place ("Being fool'd, by fool'ry thrive!/There's place and means for every man alive"[4.3.338-39]). While lying, folly, and cowardice are alive and well, Helen's child, which may perhaps be stillborn, will be just "steely" bones. Deadly divorce between Bertram and Helen will have taken place. And the cold wisdom of Lafew, Helen, Bertram will continue to wait on the superfluous folly of Parolles, Bertram, Helen.

In 1.1 a page now enters and calls Parolles by name for the first time in the play: "Monsieur Parolles, my lord calls for you"(1.1.187). In the subsequent exchange between Helen and Parolles, "under Mars"(1.1.192,193,194,196) is mentioned four times. Like *Troilus and Cressida*, the twin subjects of *All's Well* are love and war. In both plays love is spoken of in martial terms. For instance, the earlier discussion of virginity in the first scene of *All's Well* is presented in this way: "Man is enemy to virginity; how may we barricado against him?"(1.1.112-13) In addition, we can see at the end of 1.1 a veiled reference to the Mars-Venus-Vulcan story, in which War and Love are caught in a net by the deceived husband, Vulcan.

But the most crucial significance of the iterated "under Mars" is the following notion: that which is out of sight or *under* ("The wars hath so kept you under . . ."[1.1.195)) will *mar* the future. As Parolles says earlier, "Man, setting down before you, will undermine you and blow you up"(1.1.118-19). That which was *under* Bertram, both socially and at the time of conception, will destroy both Bertram and Helen. Helen, who was *under* Bertram, both in her own estimation (see the first soliloquy) and at the moment of conception, will *mar* their future. Parolles's almost last words to Helen in 1.1 are these: "Get thee a husband, and use him as he uses thee"(1.1.214-15). This advice quite accurately describes what Helen has done at the end. And if we look all the way back to the first line of the play, we can see pregnant significance in regard to the essential Helen even there: "In delivering my son from me, I bury a second husband"(1.1.1-2). When her stillborn child is delivered, her marriage to someone who has been "doubly one"(5.3.314) will die.

NOTES

1. For a discussion of some of the comedies as a social tetralogy, see *Design and Closure*, 20-23.
2. See *Design and Closure*, 97-113.
3. See Anne Barton's introduction in The Riverside *All's Well*, 502.
4. Joseph G. Price, *The Unfortunate Comedy* (U of Toronto P, 1968). See pp.137-145 for a discussion of the first scene. Joseph Westlund, *Shakespeare's Reparative Comedies: A Psychoanalytic View of the Middle Plays* (Chicago: U of Chicago P, 1984). See pp. 128-133 a for discussion of the first scene. Westlund makes some worthwhile, useful observations, but he is hostage to his patronizing thesis.
5. See note in The Riverside *All's Well* (506). Also see the Arden edition of *All's Well* for the following:

> The break in sense and metre here is usually said to be
> due to textual corruption. It may be so, but Helena is
> "fooling the time" (like Desdemona in *Oth.*, 2.1): the
> words that pass have (for her) a deeper frame of
> reference than Parolles can understand; in this context
> abrupt transitions of thought may be expected. Will
> you anything with it (your virginity)? says Parolles.
> "No," replies Helena (in effect), "I shall not change
> my virginity." Suddenly, with only a *yet* to bridge the
> gap, she starts to talk about the court and its cult of
> love. It is probable that Shakespeare expected his
> original audience to understand the connection that is
> suppressed, for it is hard to imagine that Helena's
> refusal to trade on her virginity leads to the sense that

others elsewhere may be less scrupulous, which leads directly to her evocation of the amorous dialect of the court. The reason why Helena suppresses the intermediate idea is also fairly obvious: the words would be too intimate to be spoken to Parolles—perhaps too intimate to be spoken at all. Throughout this scene broken and ambiguous language is characteristic of Helena, though nowhere else are her ellipses as harsh as here. (13)

6

Readjustment in *Much Ado About Nothing*

As a play draws to a close, Shakespeare takes the time to proffer to us a world as it is being readjusted. The changing world, altered by force of circumstance and the decisive action of some of its inhabitants, functions as a foil for the celebration (marriage in a comedy) or the calamity (death in a tragedy) that signifies a Shakespeare conclusion. In two of the great early comedies (*As You Like It* and *Twelfth Night*) the signal of readjustment is the return (in act 5) of the Duke, who has been absent since act 2; in the other great comedy (*Much Ado*) the Leonato of 5.1, though he is not a duke and has not been absent, seems much different from the way he was. In three of the great tragedies (*Hamlet, Macbeth*, and *King Lear*) the signal of change is the return (after long absence) of the transformed hero: Hamlet returns in 5.1; Macbeth in 5.3; Lear in 4. 6. In the other great tragedy (*Othello*) the hero, though he is not royal and has not been absent, is much different in 5.2 from the way he was. In these comedies the principal agent of readjustment is the young man who will become a significant husband: the converted Orlando, the real Cesario (Sebastian), the transformed Benedick. But then, to a considerable extent, the world of each play is readjusted into being what it was.

In the first of the four scenes of act 5 of *Much Ado* (a street scene) Benedick fulfills the promise made to Beatrice in the church scene (4.1) to challenge Claudio to a duel. The second scene takes place in Leonato's orchard, where Benedick tells Beatrice that he has challenged Claudio; the third scene takes place in the churchyard, where Don Pedro and Claudio hang an epitaph on Hero's tomb and "sing it to her bones"(5.1.285); the fourth scene takes place in Leonato's house, where, after the women are unmasked, the play concludes in a festive dance. The act's 332-line first scene, which has at its center the encounter between the transformed Benedick and his erstwhile companions, is the definitive scene of readjustment in Shakespeare comedy.

The scene itself has five parts: an interchange between Leonato and his brother, Antonio; a confrontation between these two old men and the newly arrived Don Pedro and Claudio; Benedick's challenge to Claudio as well as his avowal to discontinue Don Pedro's company; the admission of guilt by Borachio, one of the apprehended villains; the return of the vindicated Leonato, now accompanied by the Sexton. Scrutinizing these various parts of 5.1 enables us to uncover the corruption, deceit, and subversion that suffuse the action. Indeed the self-interest (commodity) or self-love that motivates these men is both oppressive and desperate. Dogberry's absurd speech about the offenses of the bound Borachio and Conrade serves to ventilate the nature of masculine ill will:

> Marry, sir, they have committed false report;
> moreover they have spoken untruths; secondarily,
> they are slanders; sixt and lastly, they have belied a
> lady; thirdly, they have verified unjust things;
> and to conclude, they are lying knaves.
>
> (5.1.215-19)

Even the now-admirable, transformed Benedick is not without self-interest and deception. In the church scene he allows himself to be manipulated into becoming Beatrice's needed instrument for getting revenge against Claudio. Receiving a specific charge from Beatrice in 4.1, he carries out his promise to her in 5.1: he is obedient to her will; he agrees to become her sword. It should be noted, however, that Benedick performs in 5.1 as he does because he has not been deluded by Don John: he didn't witness the assignation in the night. Yet, even though he is certain that Hero is alive, he delivers a false challenge: "You have kill'd a sweet lady, and her death shall fall heavy on you"(5.1.148-49).

In the church the Friar counseled deception:

> So will it fare with Claudio:
> When he shall hear she died upon his words,
> Th' idea of her life shall sweetly creep
> Into his study of imagination,
> And every lovely organ of her life
> Shall come apparell'd in more precious habit,
> More moving, delicate, and full of life,
> Into the eye and prospect of his soul
> Than when she liv'd indeed.
>
> (4.1.222-30)

But the Friar's prediction in 4.1 about Claudio's future behavior turns out in 5.1 to be untrue: Claudio, as well as Don Pedro, remains callous, heartless. Their attitude toward Benedick is unchanged from what it was in 3.2, before they were deceived by Don John. In 5.1, when they stumble upon Leonato and Antonio, they are really looking for Benedick: they want to entertain themselves at the expense of a lovesick fool. They discover that a sincere Benedick can deliver a serious challenge. As Don Pedro makes clear to Leonato, he feels only mild regret about the dead Hero:

> My heart is sorry for your daughter's death;
> But on my honor she was charg'd with nothing
> But what was true, and very full of proof.
>
> (5.1.103-05)

Once Borachio confesses, the manner of Don Pedro and Claudio abruptly changes. Now Claudio announces that Hero's "image doth appear/In the rare semblance that I lov'd it first"(5.1.251-52). Only after being convinced that Hero is innocent does Claudio feel remorse.

Before hearing the Friar's counsel in 4.1, Leonato declares that if Don Pedro and Claudio have wronged Hero's honor, they "shall well hear of it"(4.1.192). After hearing the Friar's counsel, Leonato remarks, "Being that I flow in grief,/The smallest twine may lead me"(4.1.249-50). Still, when Leonato next appears (5.1), we are shocked to hear his excessive upset and his immoderate grief. Now Leonato is so grief-stricken and so wildly out of control that his brother, Antonio, is afraid that he will kill himself. But when Antonio concludes that Leonato should "bend not all the harm upon yourself;/Make those that do offend you suffer too"(5.1.39-40), Leonato sensibly responds: he will make Don Pedro and Claudio suffer. Like Beatrice at the end of the church scene, Leonato does not intend to forgive a grievous wrong: he doesn't want to see if time will bring Claudio to repentance. Like Beatrice in 4.1, Leonato wants a friend (Antonio) to become instrumental in achieving revenge. For a main structural point is that the interview between Beatrice and Benedick at the end of 4.1 has been translated by Shakespeare into the Leonato-Antonio exchange at the beginning of 5.1. Like Benedick with Beatrice, Leonato tries in vain to silence an importunate friend (Antonio).

But why is Leonato so grief-stricken and angry? Why is he so importunate for revenge? Although it is true that at first he reacted strongly to his daughter's guilt and shame, he ought to be comforted that Hero is alive. But perhaps, like Beatrice in 4.1, he now feels that the treatment of Hero in the church was so unforgivable that the ones responsible must be punished at once. But then, after Hero is declared innocent (5.1), why is he so impatient to have her *marry* Claudio? Isn't Leonato's violent anger too quickly forgotten? Was his anger a sham? Should a brutish Claudio be so easily forgiven *and* rewarded? Was Claudio's sin just a matter of mistaking?

The beginning of the play helps us fathom Leonato's seemingly erratic behavior. Then Leonato didn't care whether Hero married Don Pedro or Claudio: he just wanted her to marry someone important and rich. In part his upset in the church was that Hero was *not* going to marry Claudio: he has lost a rich son-in-law. Thus at the beginning of 5.1 he is upset largely because Hero is unmarried and banished. He is afraid that she has no viable future. But once Hero is declared innocent, a marriage can again take place. In the church Leonato's expressed position was that Hero was foul and unclean. Perhaps the real reason that he manipulates Claudio in 5.1 into marrying Hero in the guise of his niece is that he wants the marriage to take place before some other news comes out, especially if Hero really is unchaste and if *that* is the new news. In some sense then Leonato is still trying to get rid of an unmarriageable daughter. He even bribes Claudio by telling him that his niece is the sole heir of Antonio and himself. Unlike Beatrice, who is sure of Hero's innocence, Leonato knows no such thing. He probably believes that Hero is at best untrustworthy.

In their discussion at the beginning of 5.1, we expect Antonio to remind his brother that Hero is, after all, alive: everything has not been lost; Leonato has no need to kill himself. But the reason that Antonio does not provide this observation is that he believes Hero is dead. Unlike Leonato and Benedick, when Antonio says that Hero is dead, he means it. He wasn't in church; he isn't in on the secret. As we may well imagine, Leonato's manipulation of Antonio utilizes a deception: he needs Antonio in order to vent his grief and to help him confront *two* villains: Don Pedro and Claudio. Still, that Antonio does get carried away in his supportive zeal is amazing.

And the beginning of the play again helps us to understand Antonio's behavior: in 1.2 for the only time in the play mention is made of Antonio's son. Since we know (4.1) that Leonato has only one child and since we can be quite sure that Antonio's daughter (Leonato's niece) is just a made-up element in an intrigue, it seems certain that Antonio wants to fight either Don Pedro or Claudio because, believing that Hero is dead, he has every reason to expect his son to be Leonato's sole heir. Thus Antonio's strange behavior in support of his brother's cause is just another matter of self-interest and deception. Antonio wants Leonato to believe that he has an upstanding brother. As it turns out, Antonio's list of names ("Boys, apes, braggarts, Jacks, milksops"[5.1.91]), which he applies to Dan Pedro and Claudio, describes all of the men in the scene, with the possible exception of Benedick and the Sexton.

Brought before Don Pedro and Claudio in 5.1, Borachio confesses:

> What your wisdoms
> could not discover, these shallow fools have
> brought to light, who in the night overheard me
> confessing to [Conrade] how Don John your
> brother incens'd me to slander the Lady Hero,

> how you were brought into the orchard, and saw me
> court Margaret in Hero's garments, how you dis-
> grac'd her when you should marry her. My villainy
> they have upon record, which I had rather seal
> with my death than repeat over to my shame. The
> lady is dead upon mine and my master's false accusa-
> tion; and briefly, I desire nothing but the reward of
> a villain.
>
> (5.1.232-44)

If we remember the inception of the intrigue (1.3), we can see that
Borachio is now not being accurate or candid. For instance, it is
just not true that Don Pedro incensed Borachio to slander Hero.
Borachio told Don John that he, Borachio, had overheard Don
Pedro's plan to woo Hero for himself and then to give her to
Claudio. Don John wanted to do mischief, and he was eager to use
Borachio's information, but his malice was directed, not against
Hero, but against Claudio: "That young start-up hath all the glory
of my overthrow. If I can cross him any way, I bless myself every
way"(1.3.66-68).

When Leonato comes on stage with the Sexton and the proof
that Hero was unjustly accused, Borachio declares, "If you would
know your wronger, look on me"(5.1.262). He alone killed the
innocent Hero. After shifting much of the blame onto Don John
and then implicating Don Pedro and Claudio in a deception,
Borachio now offers himself as a convenient scapegoat: wanting to
manipulate Don Pedro and Claudio, he now declares that he was
solely responsible for the death of Hero. By shielding Don Pedro
and Claudio from further blame and censure, by providing them
with some cover and a victim, Borachio is putting these new
masters in his debt. In effect he is demanding from them "the
reward of a villain"(5.1.243-44). And when Leonato wants to
pursue the matter by bringing Borachio face to face with Margaret,
Borachio modifies his prior confession to Don Pedro and Claudio:

> No, by my soul [Margaret] was not [guilty],
> Nor knew not what she did when she spoke to me,
> But always hath been just and virtuous
> In any thing that I do know of her.
>
> (5.1.300-03)

Borachio is again trying to keep hidden what ought to be brought into the open. As Dogberry puts it, "I leave an arrant knave with your worship"(5.1.321).

Upon being given money for his bumbling service, Dogberry responds to Leonato, "God save the foundation!"(5.1.318) The behavior of the men in 5.1 (the foundation scene on which the ensuing concord rests) is in dire need of something like God's help: we have just witnessed what godless, self-centered men are capable of doing. Dogberry wanted money as a reward. We applaud Benedick's proposal to Beatrice in 5.2 to "Serve God, love me, and mend [wrong]"(5.2.93). We are glad that Don Pedro and Claudio in 5.3 have proclaimed Hero's innocence and do publicly ask for pardon at the tomb of the supposedly dead Hero. We are pleased that the two couples in 5.4 will be joined in holy matrimony. But we cannot be happy that Claudio and Hero, rather than Benedick and Beatrice, will be the leaders of the reestablished society. We do not trust the self-centered Leonato and the heedless Don Pedro. Don John will return, with his malice. The readjustment scene of *Much Ado* has gone beyond just sweeping the dust behind the door, as the end of *A Midsummer Night's Dream* puts it. Here those who should be severely corrected and instructed are forgiven, pardoned, even rewarded. Sin and vice are ignored or overlooked. Of the men only Benedick has been transformed. In the last scene Claudio is as crude as ever. Self-interest still seethes beneath the even tenor of their ways and guarantees that the future society will prove as unstable as the old.

7

Despair and Shakespearean Affirmation:
Twelfth Night

One of the most famous passages in all of Shakespeare is Jaques's disquisition on the ages of man in *As You Like It*, 2.7: "All the world's a stage,/And all the men and women merely players"(2.7.139-40). As soon as Jaques completes his list of roles that a man plays during a lifetime, Orlando enters with Adam in his arms and in effect responds to Jaques's simple, negative declaration. More pungently stated, Jaques's comment that life is meaningless is rejected or refuted by Orlando's acute, timely demonstration of what man must do for man: rescue and save him. Orlando will prove to be a true brother to Oliver, a needed husband for Rosalind, a prospective father—roles not mentioned in Jaques's male catalogue.[1]

A comparable famous passage occurs in 3.1 of *Measure for Measure*. The Duke in the guise of friar counsels the doomed Claudio to be "absolute for death"(3.1.5): "Thou has nor youth nor age,/But as it were an after-dinner's sleep,/Dreaming on both"(3.1.32-34). As soon as he concludes his description of the dismal truth about life, Isabel, Claudio's sister, comes on stage with these words: "Peace here; grace and good company!"(3.1.44) The Friar's reasonable but brutal contention that life is meaningless is rejected or rebuked by Isabel's grace and goodness. She will become a reliable sister to Mariana, a needed wife to the Duke, a prospective mother. Her future actions in the play will refute and repudiate the reduced truth that the Duke has just declared to her brother. Orlando and Adam are made welcome in *As You Like It*; Isabel is bid "very welcome"(3.1.49) in *Measure for Measure*. In 5.5 of *Macbeth*, the usurper, delivers a comparable, even more famous passage:

> Life's but a walking shadow, a poor player,
> That struts and frets his hour upon the stage,
> And then is heard no more. It is a tale
> Told by an idiot, full of sound and fury,
> Signifying nothing.
>
> (5.5.24-28)

Like the two passages cited above, this expression of the meaninglessness of existence, prompted by the news that his wife, the Queen, is dead, is followed at once by the arrival of someone he doesn't expect. A messenger comes on stage to report a miracle: Birnam Wood is moving. Macbeth's reasonable conclusion that life is a meaningless tale is offset or countered by the sudden announcement of something amazing.

All three famous passages owe their thematic significance to a similar textual strategy: a statement of despair is immediately followed by an unexpected entrance of someone who provides a rebuke to the despair, a contradiction of it.[2] But this new person has not heard the statement of despair. What this new person represents or signifies or states will be dramatized within the next two hundred lines: Orlando will become a lover, hanging poems from trees; Isabel will agree to obey the Friar and to save Mariana and Claudio; Macbeth, who hears rather than brings (as in the other two instances) the new news, madly decides to forsake his secure castle: "At least we'll die with harness on our back"(5.5.51). He is unwilling to give in to despair.

A similar famous passage is Hamlet's first soliloquy, 1.2:

> O that this too too sallied flesh would melt,
> Thaw, and resolve itself into a dew!
>
> (1.2.129-30)

As soon as Hamlet ends his long expression of suicidal despair, Horatio, Marcellus, and Barnardo arrive: "Hail to your lordship!"(1.2.160) They have seen, as he has not, the ghost of Hamlet's father. Hamlet's self-centered despair is corrected by his recognition, prompted by Horatio's news, that he must seek out and listen to the ghost of his dead father. As son and prince, his obligation is to something greater than himself; the news censors his despair and directs his behavior as son and prince.

Another more or less famous passage is Edgar's soliloquy, at the beginning of act 4 of *King Lear*. After being left behind by the rescuers of Lear, Edgar remarks:

> Welcome then,
> Thou unsubstantial air that I embrace:
> The wretch that thou hast blown unto the worst
> Owes nothing to thy blasts.
>
> (4.1.6-9)

Like the central or first person on stage in each of the other examples, Edgar speaks in a despondent, hopeless way. Yet the sight of an unexpected Gloucester, the now-blind father, is a new fact, a kind of rebuke. The world is worse than Edgar thought:

> World, world, O world!
> But that thy strange mutations make us hate thee,
> Life would not yield to age.
>
> (4.1.10-12)

Like Hamlet, Edgar is corrected by the awareness that he as a son must serve the needs of a helpless father. He overcomes his despair in order to rescue and to save the blind old man: his father thus provides him with the opportunity of service, a way out of the impasse of pernicious despair.

It is a measure of the difference between a Shakespeare comedy and a Shakespeare tragedy that Jaques or Duke Vincentio speaks philosophically to some other person about the meaningless nature of the world and that Macbeth, Hamlet, or Edgar speaks to himself about his loss and suffering in a world that has become meaningless. But all five situations depend upon the imagery that is expressed openly in *As You Like It*, "All the world's a stage"(2.7.139): the Duke is playing the role of friar; Macbeth famously exploits a theatrical metaphor; Hamlet is forced to "seem" at court; Edgar has been forced to disguise himself as a madman. The counter to each of these five men, as well as to the situation he finds himself in, is the rebuke or the obligation that a higher awareness gives to a lesser reality. In these instances Shakespeare insists upon a greater obligation and a profounder morality than that of one's duty to one's self, even to one's suffering self. In a play-world context Shakespeare repudiates the ignominy of spiritless despair.

We, the audience, know more than Jaques or the Duke or Macbeth or Hamlet or Edgar does. We have seen Orlando as Adam's friend; we know that Isabel has left the convent and has met with Angelo; we know that Malcolm has ordered each soldier to bear a bough of a tree; we have seen the Ghost; we have witnessed Gloucester's eyes being put out. Jaques, the Duke, Macbeth, Hamlet, and Edgar are surprised by the new arrival. We are not, and we should not be. Shakespeare's design is such that our context must be enlarged and enlarging.

* * * * *

Twelfth Night ends with Feste singing a song of despair, with its reference at the end to the stage:

> When that I was and a little tine boy,
>   With hey ho, the wind and the rain,
> A foolish thing was but a toy,
>   For the rain it raineth every day.
>
> But when I came to man's estate,
>   With hey ho, etc.
> 'Gainst knaves and thieves men shut
>   their gate,
>   For the rain, etc.
>
> But when I came, alas, to wive,
>   With hey ho, etc.

> By swaggering could I never thrive,
>   For the rain, etc.
>
> But when I came unto my beds,
>   With hey ho, etc.
> With toss-pots still had drunken heads
>   For the rain, etc.
>
> A great while ago the world begun,
>   [With] hey ho, etc.
> But that's all one, our play is done,
>   And we'll strive to please you every day.
> (5.1.389-408)

In her introduction to The Riverside *As You Like It* Anne Barton notes that Orlando and Adam enter after Jaques's ages-of-man speech. Old Adam is "the living image of all that Jaques has left out of his type picture . . . the tenderness of Orlando, as well as the respect paid Adam by Duke Senior, ridicules Jaques' despair"(367-68). *Ridicules* is the wrong word. In her introduction to The Riverside *Twelfth Night* Barton makes the following comment:

> Like Jaques' summary of the seven ages of life
> from cradle to grave, Feste's account of man's
> inexorable progress from a child's holiday realm
> of irresponsibility and joy into age, vice,
> disillusionment, and death draws upon an old,
> didactic tradition. Its basic pessimism is informed
> and sweetened, however, not only by the music to
> which it is set, but by the tolerance and
> acceptance of Feste himself. Precisely because of
> his anonymity and aloofness in the play now
> ended, he can be trusted to speak for all mankind,
> and not simply for himself. There is nothing that
> can be done about those harsh facts of existence
> to which Feste points, any more than about the
> wind and the rain. They must simply be endured.
> Like childhood happiness, all comedies come to
> an end. The great and consoling difference lies in

> the fact that one can, after all, as Feste points out,
> return to the theatre: and there, "we'll strive to
> please you every day." (407)

If we have succeeded at all in demonstrating Shakespeare's insistence upon the dangerous folly of just accepting the harsh facts of existence, it is supererogatory to declare that we have little in common with Barton's patronizing, dismissive attitude toward Feste and his final song, her attitude toward Shakespeare comedy, her attitude toward Shakespeare. *Twelfth Night* appears only in the Folio; its scenes and acts are clearly designated. Of Shakespeare's eleven epilogues (if *Two Noble Kinsmen* is included) only one of them is also a song. Of all the other plays only *Love's Labor's Lost* has a song or songs so close to its end. Only *Twelfth Night* begins and ends with music.[3] *Twelfth Night* is the only Shakespeare play with a double title, *Twelfth Night, or What You Will*, and the last line of its epilogue ("And we'll strive to please you every day"[5.1.408]) offers to give us what we want. Although *Twelfth Night* is a time of festivity, it precedes or introduces Epiphany, as Shrove Tuesday precedes Ash Wednesday. As if to emphasize its wider significance, the first stanza of the song appears in *King Lear*, 3.2, where it is also sung by a fool.

Throughout the play Shakespeare aligns Feste with other characters. In her first appearance in the play, 1.2, Viola says, "I can sing,/And speak to [Orsino] in many sorts of music/That will allow me very worth his service"(1.2.57-59), but she doesn't sing; she is replaced as the singer of *Twelfth Night* by Feste. In 1.5 Feste demonstrates to Olivia that she, not he, is the fool. In 2.3 Maria says that Feste will join Toby and Sir Andrew in the garden to watch Malvolio being tricked by a letter: "I will plant you two, and let the fool make a third"(2.3.173-74). But Feste is not in that scene. Fabian, a new character, replaces him. In 4.2 Feste puts on the gown and the beard of the curate and, as Sir Topas, replaces the real priest or father and, besides speaking in his own person, counsels the imprisoned Malvolio. In act 5 Orsino sends Feste to fetch Olivia; he returns, not with Olivia, but, much later, with Toby. Feste shouts the significant beginning of Malvolio's letter, "By the Lord, madam"(5.1.292), and is replaced by Fabian as the public reader of Malvolio's letter. Fabian, rather than the expected

Feste, is sent to bring back the "notoriously abus'd"(4.2.87-88) Malvolio.

Only Feste moves freely among the various worlds of the play. As the emissary of Orsino, Viola as Cesario moves through the various worlds, but she runs into difficulties, which are at last resolved by the advent of Sebastian, whom she has been imitating. During the play Feste has an encounter or a confrontation with almost all of the other main characters: Maria, Olivia, Toby, Sir Andrew, Viola as Cesario, Sebastian as Cesario, Fabian, Orsino, Malvolio. With these characters Feste functions as someone to be employed or used: he exacts money for his services from Toby, Sir Andrew, Viola, Sebastian, twice from Orsino. Feste is also a reference or a corrective figure, a touchstone, the residual force, man alone. Feste does not confront either Viola as Viola or Sebastian as Sebastian; Feste never confronts the Captain, the true friend of Viola, or Antonio, the true friend of Sebastian; Feste never confronts Sir Topas, the priest or father, though he does badly imitate him in 4.2.

The point is that Shakespeare keeps Feste apart from the real Viola and the real Sebastian, the unexpected brother and sister thrown up by the sea, the strangers responsible for redeeming the sick, willful society of Illyria. He is kept apart from their friends, the Captain and Antonio, and their selfless service. He is kept apart from the father, the real Sir Topas, before whom Olivia and Sebastian plight their troth. Indeed in act 5, while on stage the enlarged family is working its way into being, Feste is absent: he does not witness and cannot know that which is designed to repudiate self-centered melancholy. Feste cannot be expected to understand and value that which he has not seen or heard or felt. He consequently puts his faith in the accumulation of money, in wealth, the polar opposite of love.

The textual strategy with which this chapter began is more in evidence in *Twelfth Night* than it is in any other play in the canon. Again, a character expresses negation and despair; an unwitting character or characters come on stage and in effect challenge that despair; the ensuing affirmation or enlarged response is then dramatized. In *Twelfth Night* the affirmation or gain is not immediate; rather, it is at the service of evolving human concord. For instance, in the first scene of act 1, Orsino is at an impasse:

he loves Olivia; she doesn't love him. Onto the stage to begin 1.2 comes Viola, who, like Olivia, has just lost a father and a brother but who, unlike Olivia, is not submerged in grief. Viola will resolve Orsino's plight through selfless service and love. Viola wants to serve Olivia as Viola, but since she cannot, she will serve Orsino as Cesario: she moves beyond herself. Her impasse of being in male attire will be resolved by Maria and Toby, who begin 1.3: they will serve to discredit Malvolio and two other "suitors," Sir Andrew and Cesario. At the end of 1.5 Olivia, like the Orsino of the first scene, finds herself in the impasse of loving an unresponsive person, Cesario. Sebastian, the real Cesario, the answer to Olivia's plight, comes on stage at once, in 2.1; however, his thematic service will not be needed until act 4.

A remarkable feature of *Twelfth Night* is that the Clown begins each of the last three acts. Act 3 begins with a confrontation between the Clown and Viola as Cesario; act 4 begins in exactly the same way, with the Clown confronting Cesario, but now the person he thinks is Cesario is really Sebastian; act 5 begins with the Clown confronting Fabian. After his initial confrontation with Viola as Cesario in act 3, the Clown disappears from the act: he does not witness Malvolio as a madman being led away; he does not see Sir Andrew and Cesario as discredited cowards. In act 4, after his initial confrontation with Sebastian as Cesario, the Clown disappears from the scene; he reappears in 4.2 with the central members of the subplot: Maria, Toby, and the imprisoned Malvolio. In the last scene of act 4 Sebastian is prepared to marry Olivia; and the Priest, the good father, is then introduced. The main point is that, except for the encounters with Cesario (first Viola and then Sebastian) and then (early in act 5) with Orsino, the Clown in the final three acts is either absent from the stage or relegated to the subplot.

In 2.3 the Clown asks Toby and Sir Andrew whether they would like to hear a love song or a song of good life. They choose a love song, for, as Sir Andrew says, he cares not for good life. And thus the related major point is that the subplot is preoccupied with self-love, self-gratification. As the very next song, in the very next scene, 2.4, demonstrates ("Come away, come away, death"[2.4.51]), Orsino as well as Olivia is obsessed with the wantonness of despair and with the indulgent melancholy generated by self-centered love. The subplot world, which is unaware of anything beyond itself, is punished for its miscalculation. The main-plot world is redeemed by Olivia's and Orsino's final acceptance of selfless love in the persons of the Captain, Antonio, Sebastian, and Viola. Thus the new lesson of love enables the initially sick world of Illyria to become a human community: love and duty are shored against its ruins.[4]

On the easiest, conventional level the Clown sings the final song as a representative of the acting company: "And we'll strive to please you every day"(5.1.408) is what he tells the audience on behalf of his compeers. Barton's further point is that he sings, not for himself, but for all mankind. But since at the end of the play none of the five members of the subplot (Maria, Sir Andrew, Toby, Malvolio, Fabian) is on stage and since the Clown knows little or nothing about the five makers of concord (the Captain, Antonio, Viola, Sebastian, Sir Topas) and since the Clown has not been on stage to witness the affirmation dramatized by the public acceptance of Sebastian by Olivia and of Viola by Orsino, the Clown would seem to be singing from the perspective of the group he is now associated with, the members of the absent subplot. Like these others, he cares not for good life; to him life offers nothing to counter the wind and the rain. The Clown has come to stand, not for mankind, but for the faithless, spiritless subplot or underworld, the unredeemed world. And the reduced truth of the epilogue underscores the underworld threat to future concord: Maria is not even present in act 5; Sir Andrew has lost everything and gained nothing; Toby will not easily forgive Sebastian's abuse;[5] Fabian's last speech is a lie; Malvolio wants revenge. The Clown's song emphasizes the danger endemic to any human community.

But the Clown's despair is also a function of our affirmation. For as a person who can still sing about the sad history of his life, he is existential man, man deprived of any human community, man without spiritual certainty, man unaware of the new lesson of love. His stated position is like that of Jaques, the Duke, Macbeth, Hamlet, and Edgar in the episodes cited. The main difference is that in the other examples affirmation is dramatized after the expression of despair; in *Twelfth Night* dramatized affirmation comes before the despair. Since, like *As You Like It* and *Measure for Measure*, *Twelfth Night* is a comedy, the despair is philosophic rather than dramatic. But coming as it does at the end of the performance and in the form of a song and with a reference to the play in its last stanza, it is the same textual strategy carried to its logical conclusion. We have participated in *Twelfth Night*, and as a kind of congregation we ought to be able to counter and to rebuke spiritless despair. Collectively we are about to turn our backs on the Clown and his song as we leave this secular church and go our separate ways.

NOTES

1. See in particular the essays on *As You Like It* and *Twelfth Night* in *Design and Closure*, 45-96.

2. Strictly speaking, this isn't true in *As You Like It*: Orlando enters earlier in 2.7 with his sword drawn; he is expected to return.

3. Kenneth Muir, *Shakespeare's Comic Sequence* (Liverpool: Liverpool UP, 1979), 92.

4. Barbara K. Lewalski comments: "The dual nature of Christ as human and divine, and the two modes in which his role was executed—his humiliation as suffering servant and his exaltation as divine being—were constantly emphasized in Epiphany sermons . . . " ("Thematic Patterns in *Twelfth Night*," *Shakespeare Studies* 1 [1965], 176). She then adds, "In *Twelfth Night* Viola's role alludes to the human dimension, Christ's role as patient servant, willing sufferer, model of selfless love" (177).

5. As, in another context, Anne Barton expresses it, "At precisely this point, as the two broken revellers are being helped away in a state of debility and antagonism, Shakespeare exchanges prose for verse and radically alters the scene" ("'As You Like It' and 'Twelfth Night': Shakespeare's Sense of Ending," *Stratford-upon-Avon Studies* 14 [1972], 170).

8

Recapitulative Lists

As we have seen, in 3.3 of *Richard II*, as soon as Richard comes down to the base court and, confronting Bullingbrook, acknowledges that he must go to London in abject defeat, the famous garden scene is presented.[1] The design of this choric scene is clear and decisive. Three nameless ladies come on stage (the Queen exchanging remarks with one of her ladies as the other stands silently by); when three nameless men enter, the three ladies retire (the Gardener exchanging remarks with one of his men as the other stands silently by); the Queen comes forward, confronts, and berates the Gardener for his impertinence; she and her ladies leave the stage; the rebuked Gardener remarks:

> . . . here in this place
> I'll set a bank of rue, sour herb of grace.
> Rue, even for ruth, here shortly shall be seen,
> In the remembrance of a weeping queen.
> (3.4.104-07)

At the beginning of 3.4, the Queen, disconsolate over her husband's misfortune, speaks to her ladies: "What sport shall we devise here in this garden/To drive away the heavy thought of care?"(3.4.1-2) Playing bowls and dancing are mentioned but rejected by the Queen. Telling either joyful or sorrowful tales will bring more sorrow. One of the ladies says that she will sing, and, if that will not help, she will weep. The Queen responds, "And I could sing, would weeping do me good,/And never borrow any tear of thee"(3.4.22-23).

Having replaced the Queen as the center of concern, the Gardener speaks to his men:

> Go bind thou up young dangling apricocks,
> Which like unruly children make their sire
> Stoop with oppression of their prodigal weight;
> Give some supportance to the binding twigs.
> Go thou, and like an executioner
> Cut off the heads of [too] fast growing sprays,
> That look too lofty in our commonwealth:
> All must be even in our government.
> You thus employed, I will go root away
> The noisome weeds which without profit suck
> The soil's fertility from wholesome flowers.
> (3.4.29-39)

The Gardener and his man now consider the equation between the kingdom and the garden, between the king and the gardener. If the king were to behave like a gardener, all would be well. The impertinence of these two men prompts the Queen's rebuke and the Gardener's remorse.

The pattern is that of two lists in a single, choric scene: one list, made up of five items, is given by two women; another list, made up of three items, is given by a man. The Gardener's list to his men is a kind of work order for all three men: binding up the "apricocks"; cutting off the heads of sprays; rooting out noisome weeds. The first list has to do with the Queen and her ladies, who have come to the garden distraught with care and sorrow; the second list has to do with the Gardener and his men, who have come to keep or to put the garden in repair. The first list is a statement of the communal, womanly attempt to deal with the Queen's unhappiness caused by the fall of King Richard; the second list is a statement of what the Gardener and his men must do in taking care of the garden. The passing of power from one king to another is delayed by (and for) a choric ventilation of the garden trope.

In *Richard II* the choric garden scene (3.4) takes place immediately after Richard acknowledges to Bullingbroke his loss of power. In *Much Ado* the first half of the choric, unfolding "Watch" scene (3.3) takes place at the same time that crucial plot action (the deception of Don Pedro and Claudio by Don John, Borachio, and Margaret) is taking place off stage. In 3.4 of *Richard II*, except for the Queen, all of the characters are on stage for the first and only time in the play; in 3.3 of *Much Ado*, except for Borachio and Conrade, all of the characters are on stage for the first time. Like that of the choric 3.4 of *Richard II*, the design of 3.3 of *Much Ado* is clear and decisive. Communally, Dogberry and Verges ineptly charge the Watch with "proper" behavior; they leave the stage and are replaced by Borachio and Conrade; the Watch overhears Borachio's confession and arrests both Borachio and Conrade. After eavesdropping, the Queen in *Richard II* comes forward and makes her presence felt; after eavesdropping, the Watch comes forward and makes its presence felt. The Queen rebukes the Gardener; the Watch arrests the two villains.

Dogberry tells the Watch to "comprehend all vagrom men"(3.3.25), to "bid those that are drunk get them to bed"(3.3.43), to "if you do take a thief . . . let him show himself what he is, and steal out of your company"(3.3.59-60). Verges then remarks, "If you hear a child cry in the night, you must call to the nurse and bid her still it"(3.3.65-66). Dogberry ends the charge: ". . . you, constable, are to present the Prince's own person"(3.3.74-75). Thus the charge to the Watch is made up of a list of five items: vagrom men or vagrants, drunkards, a thief, a child who has a nurse, and the constable as Prince. In terms of groups and then individuals, this five-item list can be seen as a synopsis of the plot action of the play: soldiers come to Messina as vagrants; they become drunk with self-love or commodity; a thief (Don John) is allowed to steal away; Hero, like a child, cries in the night and awakens the nurse (Beatrice); the constable, who arrests the wrongdoers, presents or represents the Prince. The five items of this list should be perceived as roughly corresponding to the five acts of the play.

In the second half of the scene Borachio's question to Conrade contains another list in the form of three similes:

> Seest thou not, I say, what a deformed thief
> this fashion is, how giddily 'a turns about all
> the hot-bloods between fourteen and five-and-thirty,
> sometimes fashioning them like Pharaoh's soldiers
> in the reechy painting, sometime like god Bel's
> priests in the old church-window, sometime like
> the shaven Hercules in the smirch'd worm-eaten
> tapestry, where his codpiece seems as massy as
> his club?
>
> (3.3.130-38)

Like the first list in the scene (from vagrants to the constable as Prince), the second list moves from the group to the individual: soldiers, priests, Hercules. In terms of the first list the thief, Don John, turns good men (Don Pedro and Claudio) into villains; in terms of the second list the thief, fashion, turns the hot-bloods into soldiers, priests, Hercules. In the second half of the play, because of Don John and Borachio, the soldiers go to the church (4.1), where, after Hero is defamed, Friar Francis offers his temporizing advice and where Benedick is fashioned into a hero by Beatrice. Moreover, the Watch performs the soldierly function of capturing Borachio and Conrade; like priests, the members of the Watch are instrumental in producing Borachio's public confession (5.1); their function as soldiers and priests gives way to Benedick's function as Beatrice's hero. In terms of the play the first list ends with an unlikely constable as Prince; the second list ends with an unlikely Benedick as Hercules.

The listed groups and individuals in 3.3 of *Much Ado* can thus be translated into a two-fold version of the action of the play: the lists function as a synoptic chorus. Although the choric lists in 3.4 of *Richard II* are of activities rather than of groups and individuals, the lists are patently synoptic: the first, on-going, "female" action is described as bowling, dancing, telling tales, singing, and weeping; the second, on-going, "male" action is described as a binding up, a cutting off, a rooting out. In *Much Ado* the first list deals with activities in the full play, of vagrants, etc.; the second list deals primarily with activities in the second half of the play, of soldiers, etc.

The main reason for the emphasis on activities rather than on groups and individuals is that, as the beginning of a long series of history plays, *Richard II* is concerned with on-going forces or activities. As a self-contained comedy, *Much Ado* has a firm, deliberate conclusion: it ends with the prospect of two happy marriages and with the reconciliation implicit in a stately dance. The end of *Richard II* is conclusive to *Richard II* but not to the cycle of history plays. Groups and individuals, naturally of relevance in a comedy, give way in a series of history plays to activities produced by political behavior. Still, a central point is that the lists in 3.4 of *Richard II* are also directed toward activities at the end of the play. King Henry both sings and weeps. After the garden scene, having bound up, cut off, and rooted out, Henry can now be the legitimate Gardener-King, the father of the renowned Henry V.

Again, except for the Queen in 3.4 of *Richard II* and Borachio and Conrade in 3.3 of *Much Ado*, no major character is on stage during these choric scenes. But Prince Harry as Hal is on stage throughout the main choric scene of *1 Henry IV*, the long tavern scene, 2.4. This scene is a choric recapitulation of the career of the boy who will become the famous king, Henry V. This large-scale recapitulative purpose is at some odds with the localized choric purpose of double lists, as exemplified in *Richard II* and *Much Ado*. This is at least part of the reason that only the first of the expected lists (of five items) occurs in 2.4, and it comes, not in the middle, but at the end of the scene. The second list (of three items) occurs at the beginning of the next scene, with, as expected, a new set of characters.

At the end of 2.4 Hal tells Peto to read the papers that have been found in the pockets of the sleeping Falstaff. Peto reads the following five-part list:

Item, a capon	2s. 2d.
Item, sauce	4d.
Item, sack, two gallons . . .	5s. 8d.
Item, anchoves and sack after supper .	2s. 6d.
Item, bread	ob.

(2.4.535-39)

This is a list of the consumables that Falstaff has put on his bill: the various items almost certainly have not been paid for. He has simply appropriated the items, turning them into himself before they were properly his. Earlier in the scene Falstaff plays the part of the king and then the part of the son: he exchanges roles with the madcap prince. The tavern has replaced the court. King Henry IV has taken his title of King of England, but he hasn't paid for it: he has appropriated it, pouring it into himself before it was properly his. The choric function of the first list in *Richard II* and *Much Ado* encourages our perception here that this first list is a synopsis of the action of *1 Henry IV*. The capon may symbolize the initial impotence of Falstaff, the King, and the Prince; sack is also a word for rape and pillage; anchovies, which increase the thirst for sack, may refer to those things, such as the rash behavior of Hotspur, that encourage wanton behavior; the little bit of bread may indicate the truth about the consequences of savage behavior on the battlefield: "O monstrous! but one half-pennyworth of bread to this intolerable deal of sack!"(2.4.540-41)

As in *Richard II* and *Much Ado*, after the first list, a new group of characters appears, and a second list occurs. But in *1 Henry IV* the new characters are in a separate scene, 3.1. The general similarity between the two scenes is clear: in both 2.4 and 3.1 an old man (Falstaff or Glendower) tells fantastic lies; a young man (Hal or Harry Hotspur) rebukes him. Not surprisingly then, the second list (3.1) is also presented on a piece of paper, the map that the Archdeacon has divided into three parts. Mortimer (the man designated by Richard as his heir) is given England; Glendower (Mortimer's father-in-law) is given Wales; Hotspur is to receive Scotland, the land he has already sacked. Following the example of the usurper Henry IV, these rebels intend to steal England, Wales, and Scotland from the new king: to them the entities are consumables, things to appropriate before they are properly theirs. After the interview between the King and his son in 3.2, Prince Harry must do as he has promised and kill Hotspur. At the end of *1 Henry IV*, with Scotland secured, the King and the Prince "will towards Wales,/To fight with Glendower and the Earl of March [Mortimer]"(5.5.39-40). As in the other two plays under consideration, the second list in each instance (binding up, cutting off, rooting out; soldiers, priests, Hercules) bears directly upon the action in the second half of the play, but, because of the on-going historical enterprise, part of the list (Wales, England) in the play involves action beyond the scope of *1 Henry IV*: Glendower and Mortimer will not be seen in this play after this scene.

The other two choric scenes (3.4 of *Richard II*; 3,3 of *Much Ado*) end with a confrontation (the Queen confronts the Gardener; the Watch confronts Borachio and Conrade); in *1 Henry IV* the obligatory confrontation (between the Prince of Wales and Hotspur) is put off until the end, on the battlefield, where, after confronting and killing Hotspur, the Prince delivers the following pronouncement:

> Fare thee well, great heart!
> Ill-weav'd ambition, how much art thou shrunk!
> When that this body did contain a spirit,
> A kingdom for it was too small a bound,
> But now two paces of the vilest earth
> Is room enough. This earth that bears [thee] dead
> Bears not alive so stout a gentleman.
> If thou wert sensible of courtesy,
> I should not make so dear a show of zeal;
> But let my favors hide thy mangled face,
> And even in thy behalf I'll thank myself
> For doing these fair rites of tenderness.
> Adieu, and take thy praise with thee to heaven!
> Thy ignominy sleep with thee in the grave,
> But not rememb'red in thy epitaph!
>
> (5.4.87-101)

At the end of 3.4 of *Richard II* the Gardener promises to make the penitent gesture of setting "a bank of rue, sour herb of grace . . ./In the remembrance of a weeping queen"(3.4.105-07). Here, performing "fair rites of tenderness"(5.4.98), the Prince covers Hotspur's mangled face with his "favors." In *Richard II* and *Much Ado* the rebuke is overheard (by the other gardeners; by the members of the Watch); in *1 Henry IV* the speech, which is only in part a rebuke, is also overheard: the supposedly dead Falstaff eavesdrops upon the Prince's quasi-soliloquy. The situation in 5.4 echoes and mirrors the end of 2.4: there Falstaff is lying on stage asleep; here he is lying on stage pretending to be dead. In 5.4 Falstaff rises and stabs Hotspur in the thigh before brazenly proclaiming that he, not the Prince, has killed Hotspur. Like the

Prince, Falstaff thanks himself. Hotspur's pitiful ambition, having been acknowledged and rebuked by the Prince, is appropriated by the lying Falstaff for his own grace: "Thus ever did rebellion find rebuke"(5.5.1).

The second list (England, Scotland, Wales) comes to prominence in *Henry V*, the end of the tetralogy. There the new king controls factionalism at home and consolidates his new position as king of England by gathering his divided forces and going to war against the common enemy: "No king of England, if not king of France!"(2.2.193) At Harfleur, the King's valiant soldiers are from England (Gower), Scotland (Jamy), Wales (Fluellen), Ireland (Macmorris). The great nation that the insurgents in 3.1 of *1 Henry IV* wanted to sunder is reunited in France.

At the beginning of act 5 of *Measure for Measure*, the Duke appears in his own person at the city gate. At the end, after all of the disclosures have taken place, the revealed Duke, now back in his useful garb as friar, delivers the final speech:

> She, Claudio, that you wrong'd, look you restore.
> Joy to you, Mariana! Love her, Angelo!
> I have confess'd her, and I know her virtue.
> Thanks, good friend Escalus, for thy much goodness,
> There's more behind that is more gratulate.
> Thanks, Provost, for thy care and secrecy,
> We shall employ thee in a worthier place.
> Forgive him, Angelo, that brought you home
> The head of Ragozine for Claudio's,
> Th' offense pardons itself. Dear Isabel,
> I have a motion much imports your good,
> Whereto if you'll a willing ear incline,
> What's mine is yours, and what is yours is mine.
> So bring us to our palace, where we'll show
> What's yet behind, that['s] meet you all should know.
>   (5.1.525-39)

At the end of the play the returned Duke confronts all of the other main characters, who have gathered together. His fifteen-line speech has three parts. In the first part the Duke addresses five people by name, ending with thanks to Escalus and (employing the regal we) thanks to the Provost. In the one-sentence second part the Duke turns back to Angelo, repeating his name and Claudio's and introducing the name of Ragozine. In the third part the Duke turns to Isabel, whose name is introduced: now the *us* or *we* refers to the Duke as Duke as well as to the Duke and Isabel as a couple. They will lead the way into the city and then to the palace.

In both *Richard II* and *Much Ado* the three parts of the full pattern are clearly distinguished (a list by the ladies, a list by the Gardener, a confrontation between the Queen and the Gardener; a list by Dogberry and Verges to the Watch, a list by Borachio, a confrontation between the Watch and the villains). In *1 Henry IV* these choric parts are integrated into the plot and are thus, in and by themselves, not readily seen as a pattern (Falstaff's list on consumables, the map of Great Britain, the confrontation between Prince Harry and Hotspur). In *Measure for Measure* the smoothly integrated parts are not at once distinguished as a pattern, but the guiding principle seems to be that of lists (five names and then three): Claudio, Mariana, Angelo, Escalus, Provost; Angelo, Ragozine, Claudio. The lists are not of activities (*Richard II*) or of individuals and groups (*Much Ado*) or of consumables and territories (*1 Henry IV*) but of the characters (except for Ragozine) on stage. Again, the lists are not treated as lists or dramatized, as they are in the preceding plays. And the lists come at the conclusion of the action, almost like an epilogue, with a choric appeal to the audience. As in the earlier plays, eavesdropping occurs, but now it has become public disclosure, with the audience as eavesdropper. A related point is that the Duke's concluding speech ends, not just this particular play, but the comedic tetralogy.

Still, the first list can be perceived as a synopsis of the action from the Duke's perspective: the action begins with Claudio's being punished for the sin of fornication; as 3.1 and 4.1 make clear, the Duke as friar has been doing what he can to comfort Mariana's "brawling discontent"(4.1.9); Angelo's importunate desire enables the Duke as friar to use craft against Angelo's vice; for a proper ending the Duke must rely on the good offices of Escalus and the Provost. The second list, which as in the other plays concerns second-half action, refers to Angelo's breaking his vow to Isabel; to the good fortune of Ragozine's death and to the

Provost's delivering Ragozine's head to Angelo; to the release of Claudio.

The third part of the pattern, the confrontation, becomes here the turning of the Duke to Isabel. This confrontation, different in nature from the other ones, is still a natural consequence of the first two lists. Isabel's heartfelt service to Mariana in the scene itself secures for her the roles of sister and wife and then the office of duchess: she is rewarded, not rebuked. The complications have been resolved. Although not verbalized, a rebuke (as a didactic function) is made after the procession of actors has emptied the stage: the audience is being mocked by two empty chairs.[2]

Measure for Measure and *Othello* were written about the same time (1604), have in common a main source (Cinthio), and are clear in structure and direct in intention. The last scene of each play is dominated by its chief character; each last scene proceeds by means of disclosure; each draws to an end with a long speech by the protagonist. Othello's last speech is an ostensible five-part list:

> I pray you, in your letters,
> When you shall these unlucky deeds relate,
> Speak of me as I am; nothing extenuate,
> Nor set down aught in malice. Then must you speak
> Of one that lov'd not wisely but too well;
> Of one not easily jealous, but being wrought,
> Perplexed in the extreme; of one whose hand,
> Like the base [Indian], threw a pearl away
> Richer than all his tribe; of one whose subdu'd eyes,
> Albeit unused to the melting mood,
> Drops tears as fast as the Arabian trees
> Their medicinable gum. Set you down this;
> And say besides, that in Aleppo once,
> Where a malignant and a turban'd Turk
> Beat a Venetian and traduc'd the state,
> I took by th' throat the circumcised dog,
> And smote him—thus.
>
> (5.2.340-56)

Confronting the five men in front of him, Othello is not being compellingly honest: Desdemona is the one who loved not wisely but too well. Othello bemuses his onstage audience so that he can provide himself with the opportunity to kill himself with an unexpected knife: he wants to join Desdemona on the marriage bed. Still the first four items do serve to describe himself: he did throw a priceless pearl away. His reenactment of a bloody event (Set you down this;/And say besides, that in Aleppo once . . . . [5.2.351-52]) connects the present moment to a past occasion. The list of five items is complete: *one, one, one, one, once*. And the last scene discloses five deaths (Desdemona's, Brabantio's, Emilia's, Roderigo's,[3] Othello's). And the five men addressed by Othello signify the development of the action: Iago began the intrigue; prior to this scene Montano appeared only in act 2; Cassio turned to Desdemona for help in act 3; Lodovico, the Duke's representative, was introduced in act 4; Gratiano, who represents Brabantio, is introduced in act 5.

To these series of five-item lists is added the surprising other list: three bodies on the marriage bed. This list concerns action in the second half of the play as well as the action in the final scene. Desdemona's value is restored by Emilia, who redeems herself by turning against her husband and telling the truth; Othello justifies and sacrifices himself. Of the five deaths only three occur on stage: Desdemona's, Emilia's, Othello's. Three of the named men on stage have been wounded: Montano by Cassio (2.3); Cassio by Iago (5.1); Iago by Othello (5.2). After the death of Othello, three sacrifices are hidden from the five men on stage by a drawn curtain, thus dramatically separating the dead list from the living one.

The lists that are presented in the middle of *Richard II* or *Much Ado* or *1 Henry IV* summarize plot action; they present the audience with two related plot lists in a symbolic setting or, in *1 Henry IV*, symbolic settings. In each instance the first list is concerned with full plot action; the second list deals primarily with upcoming action. The characters of concern in the first list are balanced or countered by the characters of concern in the second list. But each pair of lists in these plays (activities in *Richard II*; groups and individuals in *Much Ado*; consumables and territories in *1 Henry IV*) constitutes a symbolic, thematic emphasis. The audience seems meant to use these double lists in order to certify a recapitulative understanding. Meaning is gathered and localized.

In *Measure for Measure*, where the main male character is also the person of secular authority, the recapitulative lists come at the end of the action; they come in the form of names, each one indicative of a plot performance. At the symbolic setting of the city gate the audience seems asked to contemplate the future of the Duke and Isabel. In *Othello* the lists are not of activities or of groups and individuals or of consumables and territories or of names, but of the alive and dead persons on stage. This recapitulative procedure of gathering together the living and the dead is characteristic of Shakespeare tragedy.

Here, for example, the audience is thrust back upon an elaborate two-fold consideration of the protagonist, Othello, vis-à-vis the play. We are mocked or rebuked by the curtain that divides from our view the burdened bed. The play ends, not with a couple, as *Measure for Measure* does, but with two men (Cassio and Lodovico), who speak the final words. The key point is that *Othello*, like *Measure for Measure*, concludes with a five-point list, a three-point list, and a kind of confrontation. *Measure for Measure* ends with the head (the Duke) and the heart (Isabel); *Othello* ends with the head (Lodovico) and the hand (Cassio).

Perhaps because of its thematic similarity to *1 Henry IV* (a kinsman has killed the king and usurped the throne), the full pattern of recapitulative lists is unmistakably presented in *Macbeth*. In addition, when *Hamlet*, *Macbeth*, and *King Lear* are considered as a trilogy, the Porter-of-Hell-Gate episode in *Macbeth* is its central choric event. The plot event that prompts the choric episode is the murder of the rightful king. Duncan is murdered, and the Porter is introduced. The pattern of lists is the same as in the other plays, but it has been modified, reversed. A character new to the play, the Porter of Hell Gate, enters to begin 2.3. Responding to the knocking at the south entry, the drunken Porter, as he crosses the stage, addresses in turn the three unseen guests who, he imagines, are seeking to come in: a farmer, an equivocator, an English tailor. Macduff, who has yet to speak a word in the play, and Lennox are then admitted by the Porter.

Responding to a question by Macduff, the Porter says that drink provokes "nose-painting, sleep, and urine" (2.3.28). Given Shakespeare's usual practice, we assume that both of the three-item lists (farmer, equivocator, English tailor; nose-painting, sleep, urine) refer to the action of the full play. But the second three-part list seems also to refer to current action off stage: Macbeth and his wife are washing away blood; Macbeth has just murdered sleep; the wine of life has just been turned into something else. The Porter then gives a list that makes clear the five ways that drink equivocates with lechery: ". . . it makes him, and it mars him; it sets him on, and it takes him off; it persuades him, and disheartens him; makes him stand to, and not stand to; in conclusion, equivocates him in a sleep, and giving him the lie, leaves him" (2.3.32-36). This series of double actions, the result of the murder of Duncan, is a choric description of second-half action.

As in *1 Henry IV*, the confrontation between designated opposites (Prince Harry-Hotspur; Macbeth-Macduff) is delayed until the end. As in *Othello*, the play ends with the final comments by the head (Lodovico-Malcolm) and the hand (Cassio-Macduff). And as in *Measure for Measure* and *Othello*, the play ends with a mocking reminder (two empty chairs; the severed head of Macbeth).

NOTES

1. For some typical treatments of the garden scene, see E. M. W. Tillyard, *Shakespeare's History Plays* (New York: Collier Books, 1962), 283-285; Harold Goddard, *The Meaning of Shakespeare* (Chicago: U of Chicago P. Phoenix Books. Vol. 1. 1962), 160; H. M. Richmond, *Shakespeare's Political Plays* (New York: Random House. Studies in Language and Literature, 1967), 130-131.

2. See W. Moelwyn Merchant, *Shakespeare and the Artist* (London: Oxford UP, 1959), 229-232.

3. In 5.2 Cassio remarks, " . . . and even but now [Roderigo] spake/(After long seeming dead)"(5.2.327-28).

9

Roles and Offices

Feste's song at the end of *Twelfth Night* briefly chronicles a man's progress through life, from little boy to man to married man to old man. Jaques's ages-of-man speech in *As You Like It* catalogues the life of man: infant, schoolboy, lover, soldier, justice, pantaloon, child. The significant familial roles of father and husband are not mentioned in this list, but Duke Senior, a father, is on stage at the time, and Orlando, a future husband, will at once come back on stage. Still, so far as it goes, Jaques's ages-of-man catalogue captures a valid truth.

In 3.2 of *As You Like It* Rosalind as Ganymede informs the lover Orlando of the various ways time affects a young maid, a priest, a rich man, a thief, and a lawyer: time goes too slowly for a maid about to be married; time goes too quickly for a thief on his way to the gallows. In 4.1 Jaques distinguishes eight kinds of melancholy: a scholar's, a musician's, a courtier's, a soldier's, a lawyer's, a lady's, a lover's, and a traveler's. As acts 3 and 4 indicate, ability, circumstance, disposition, gender, and time serve to expand and qualify the roles played by man as described by Jaques in 2.7. In *As You Like It* there is little tension between roles: Orlando is a soldier *before* he is a lover, but he is not torn between being a lover and being a soldier, as, for example, Troilus in *Troilus and Cressida* is. And since Orlando has no office, he is not torn between a role and an office, as Troilus is. In *As You Like*

It neither Duke Senior nor Duke Frederick is torn between his role as brother or father and his office as duke.

In *A Midsummer Night's Dream* roles help to make clear the crucial play-acting trope. "Hempen home-spuns"(3.1.77)—Quince the carpenter, Bottom the weaver, Flute the bellows mender, Snout the tinker, Snug the joiner, Starveling the tailor—rehearse and then enact the little Pyramus and Thisby story to and for an onstage courtly audience. Everyday workers undertake disproportionate roles: Bottom is Pyramus; Flute is Thisby; Snout is the Wall; Snug is the Lion; Starveling is the Moon or Moonshine. Hippolyta, the only woman in the onstage audience to comment on the Pyramus-Thisby performance, grows weary of the moon and acknowledges the silliness of the foolish actors, but she is also aware that the Pyramus-Thisby story has merit and that imagination is needed to "mend" the inept performance and thus to preserve its meaning and significance.

If they were properly attentive, the two sets of young lovers (Hermia and Lysander; Helen and Demetrius) ought to perceive that the Pyramus-Thisby story has relevance to their recent experience: they too had to deal with an impediment or obstruction (a Wall), a force (a Lion), and an illusion (Moonshine). Theseus, however, cannot know that the performance he is so patronizing toward is a version of what will result from his marriage to Hippolyta (which is being celebrated): the Phaedra-Hippolytus disaster. We, the audience, have no trouble extending the relevance of Pyramus-Thisby to Theseus-Hippolyta as well as to Theseus-Phaedra. And since we have just watched the action in the night, we can also accommodate the relevance of Pyramus-Thisby to the forest couples: Oberon-Titania; Bottom-Titania.

Thus *A Midsummer Night's Dream* depends for its meaning upon the Pyramus-Thisby complex of roles. Demetrius's comment near the end of the onstage performance is instructive: "A mote will turn the balance, which Pyramus, which Thisby, is the better: he for a man, God warr'nt us; she for a woman, God bless us"(5.1.318-20). We ought to see various other men in the play as being Pyramuses and various other women as being Thisbys. And it is generally true in Shakespeare that we, the audience, are granted men and are blessed with women: men are the head; women are the heart.

In a broader sense, *Romeo and Juliet* and *Antony and Cleopatra* can be seen as being versions of the Pyramus-Thisby story: each play has its lovers, its Wall, its Lion, its Moonshine. The Pyramus type (Romeo, Antony) dies before the Thisby type (Juliet, Cleopatra). Pyramus, Romeo, and Antony kill themselves while under a misapprehension; a bereft Thisby, Juliet, and Cleopatra refuse to go on living. And we are further encouraged to see the full pattern of the Pyramus-Thisby performance (two lovers, Wall, Lion, Moonshine, and the attendant choric comment [by Quince, Theseus, Demetrius, Lysander, Hippolyta]) as being a general pattern of a Shakespeare play.

Measure for Measure, the play that concludes Shakespeare's comedic tetralogy (*Much Ado, As You Like It, Twelfth Night, Measure for Measure*), best illustrates the function of roles and offices in Shakespeare: the primary roles are those of the family; the primary offices are those of a rigid city-state, dukedom, or kingdom. *Measure for Measure* makes definitive use of the offices of both church and state: the Duke, the father of Vienna, operates under the guise of friar, the brother in the church. Initially, the Duke leaves his office in order to better understand the office of duke and in order to test the behavior of his upright replacement, the self-righteous Angelo. As the action unfolds and difficulties perforce develop, the Duke could at any time reassume his neglected office of duke. Instead of dropping his assumed mask, the Duke continues to submit himself to the office of friar.

In *Romeo and Juliet* Friar Lawrence is faced with a dilemma: soon after Romeo and Juliet are married, Romeo is banished, and Juliet is ordered by her father to marry Paris. Friar Lawrence does all that his office as a brother in the church permits: he gives Juliet temporizing advice together with a potion that, once taken, will delude others into believing that she is dead. In *Much Ado* Friar Francis is faced with a comparable dilemma: having been discarded by her prospective husband, Claudio, Hero collapses. Friar Francis does all that he as a church brother can: his temporizing advice is that others be allowed to believe that Hero is dead; Claudio will then rack the value of Hero and love her more than before. In *Measure for Measure* Friar Lodowick is also faced with a puzzling dilemma: Angelo has insisted that, if Claudio, Isabel's brother, is to be saved from death, Isabel must surrender her virginity to him, Angelo. Friar Lodowick does all that he as a friar can: his temporizing advice is for Mariana, Angelo's forsaken betrothed, to substitute for Isabel at an assignation.

The limited power of Friar Lawrence leads to the suicide of both Romeo and Juliet; the weak advice of Friar Francis is immediately offset by Beatrice's trapping Benedick into agreeing to kill his best friend, Claudio; the use of craft against vice by Friar Lodowick results in Angelo's becoming more wicked than the Duke could have imagined. But the efforts of these three friars have not been in vain. Because of Friar Lawrence's advice, Romeo and Juliet rise above themselves to become exemplars of romantic love: they would rather kill themselves than live in a meaningless world. Friar Francis's advice prompts Beatrice to insist on immediate action against Claudio; by so doing she provides Benedick the needed occasion to prove himself worthy of her love. Friar Lodowick's advice enables Isabel to become a true sister to Mariana and a true daughter and then wife to the Duke; the friar's advice manages to save the lives of both Claudio and Angelo. Unlike the end of *Romeo and Juliet* and *Much Ado*, the successful conclusion of *Measure for Measure* depends upon the leader of the society, the Duke. Having been instructed in the office of friar, he will marry Isabel and become an exemplary brother-husband-duke.

In the last scene of *A Midsummer Night's Dream* the function of roles is explored; in 2.1 of *Measure for Measure* the tension between an office and a role is clarified. Elbow, an inept constable, brings Pompey, a bawd, and Froth, a foolish gentleman, before Angelo, the Duke's surrogate. Elbow's incompetence combined with Pompey's slipperiness obscures the facts of the simple case presented to Angelo. Rather than rendering a judgment, impatient Angelo surrenders the case to his deputy, Escalus. In effect then Angelo duplicates the Duke's behavior at the beginning of the play. Froth is reprimanded by Escalus; Pompey is warned and released; Elbow is told to bring the names of six or seven suitable replacements for the office of constable to Escalus's house.

Elbow's erratic behavior is a direct result of his plight: his pregnant wife has been insulted and slandered; he has arrested the two men who were mistreating his wife. Elbow is at once a constable, a husband, a prospective father. His office as constable is compromised by his unsuitability for his office and by his role as husband-prospective father. This little conflict between the office held and the role occupied by this ignorant man results in the neglect of *his* office by Angelo and in no proper resolution of the case. The Elbow situation is a parody of the main plot: Elbow stands for the Duke or Angelo; Pompey stands for the Duke as friar; Froth stands for Claudio or Angelo; Elbow's wife stands for Juliet or Isabel or Mariana. By the end of this comedy and indeed of the tetralogy, roles will be assigned, and offices will be properly filled: the Duke and Isabel will then be better able to rule Vienna.

* * * * *

It sems useful to consider Hamlet in the company of other young men, each the center of attention, in other Shakespeare plays. Hamlet has much in common with Romeo and Troilus. A young sensualist, Romeo is in love with Rosaline but forgetful of her as soon as he sees Juliet, the only daughter of the hated Capulets. Romeo is so impetuous and mercurial that he can kill Tybalt, his new kinsman, between the time he marries Juliet and the time he consummates that marriage. The sensualist becomes a murderer, quick to kill, quick to commit suicide.

Troilus and Hamlet more or less conform to the Romeo type, a sensualist who becomes murderous. Troilus is more willful than Romeo, more vain, more hypocritical. Unlike Romeo, he is a soldier, a son with siblings; a prince, one among many. He is not married and he does not commit suicide, but he concludes that he will "Never go home, here starve we out the night"(5.10.2). Hamlet's position is more poignant: he is an only son and an only prince. He is charged by the ghost of his father-king to kill his uncle-king. Impetuous like Romeo but less volatile, Hamlet is more volatile than Troilus. An aborted sensualist, the unmarried Hamlet turns murderous toward Polonius, Ophelia's father, and toward Rosencrantz and Guildenstern, his erstwhile friends. Hamlet is more intellectual and more sensitive than either Romeo or Troilus. And since his case is more extreme and since his role of deprived son and his office of revenging prince are more demanding, he is more melancholy. His end is also a kind of suicide.

Romeo and Troilus are lovesick: the great change that takes place in their lives is caused by their thwarted love for Juliet and Cressida. Romeo and Troilus could have been saved by their full acceptance of the role of husband: as soon as he is married, Romeo kills Tybalt and is banished; as soon as Cressida surrenders to Troilus, she is allowed by Troilus to be taken to the Greek camp.[1] Hamlet is a prospective lover. While Ophelia is alive, we *hear* (2.1) but do not see Hamlet (as we do Romeo and Troilus) as a distraught lover. The first time we see Hamlet with Ophelia (3.1) he, like a brutal lover, berates and rejects her. It is true that Hamlet is distraught by Ophelia's death in the graveyard scene (5.1). Marrying Ophelia may have saved Hamlet, but then his desgnated role of obedient son and his restrictive office of revenging prince never allow him to become a husband.

Hamlet may also be compared with two other disaffected young men, Prince Harry of *1 Henry IV* and Edmund of *King Lear*. Unlike Romeo and Troilus, they are not romantically inclined and then romantically thwarted. Each of these three young men (Harry, Edmund, Hamlet), a son at odds with his father (unlike Romeo or Troilus), is introduced in the second scene of each play. In that scene Harry has a soliloquy; Edmund has three soliloquies; Hamlet has a soliloquy and a four-line soliloquy-like reflection at the end.

A kind of prodigal son like Hamlet and Edmund, Prince Harry has lost his place at court to his brother, John. Sick of a life of self-indulgence, he decides in his soliloquy in 1.2 to wait for the proper occasion: "Redeeming time when men think least I will"(1.2.217). And when that time comes on the battlefield (5.4), Harry refers to himself as the Prince of Wales four separate times. His "real" name, Harry Monmouth, is mentioned only twice in the play, both times by Hotspur, once in 5.2, once in 5.4. The name Harry Monmouth (see *2 Henry IV* and *Henry V*) designates his role as the king's son; the title Prince of Wales designates his office as heir to the throne. Killing Hotspur restores the office of Prince of Wales to the cool, amoral Harry Monmouth, who is finally acknowledged as having taken back what he has neglected.

At the beginning Edmund has no role or office: "He hath been out nine years, and away he shall again"(1.1.32-33). As a bastard son, he is amoral, with just cause. In his first soliloquy he announces his intention of making Nature his goddess and of rising to power by duping his superstitious father and his weak, legitimate brother. In 3.5 Cornwall rewards the duplicitous Edmund with the office of Earl of Gloucester. The lust of Goneril and Regan propel this new earl toward the office of king. In the last scene of the play Regan creates Edmund her "lord and master"(5.3.78). Illegitimate and never a husband, he ends as he began, with nothing: "The wheel is come full circle, I am here"(5.3.175).

Hamlet is not cold and calculating like Harry or Edmund. Thrust into an impossible situation, for which he is singularly unprepared, he vacillates, for he hasn't become hardened like either of the other young sons. Compared to the relatively simple plight of Harry or Edmund, Hamlet's plight, since it narrowly concerns his private role and his public office, is extremely difficult and dangerous. As the older Hamlet's agent or hand, Hamlet struggles desperately between what his head tells him and what his heart feels. We hear his deep chagrin at the beginning of his first soliloquy as he, in a characteristic vein, contemplates suicide:

> O that this too too sallied flesh would melt,
> Thaw, and resolve itself into a dew!
> (1.2.129-30)

Unlike Harry or Edmund, he doesn't seize the opportunity when he finds it: he comes upon the guilty king at prayer (3.3) and does not revenge his father's murder.

We can measure the difficulty of *Hamlet* by noting how complex 1.2 of *Hamlet* is compared to the comparable scene in each of the other plays. Harry or Edmund dominates his particular scene, 1.2: he is amorally concerned with what his position now is and what he hopes it will become. In contrast, 1.2 of *Hamlet* is primarily concerned with King Claudius, who announces that Hamlet is *the* son and will be *the* king. Harry knows his destiny too, but there is a vast difference between these two princes. In his soliloquy in 1.2 Hamlet refers to the older Hamlet as (unlike Claudius) an excellent king; in his scene-ending speech he is upset about his father's spirit. Hotspur names the prince Harry Monmouth; right before he leaps into Ophelia's grave in 5.1, Hamlet, for the first and only time in the play, names himself: "This is I,/Hamlet the Dane!"(5.1.257-58)

As You Like It is more ranging and complex than either *Much Ado* or *Twelfth Night*, the plays with which it is rightly associated, because its theme is more important, more pervasive, and more theoretical. Whereas the plot of *Much Ado* concerns the envy and malice that arise from being a social castaway, like Don John, and whereas the plot of *Twelfth Night* concerns the bad will generated by thwarted ambition and scorned desire, as signified by Malvolio, the plot of *As You Like It* concerns the melancholy and the morbidity produced by having lived in a desperate society, as evidenced by Jaques. Like *Hamlet, As You Like It* confronts self-centered melancholy, but, unlike *Hamlet*, it discounts it.

The young hero of *As You Like It* is like other Shakespeare young heroes. Initially, Orlando, like Harry, Edmund, and Hamlet, is a disaffected young man, but unlike these three he has no plan of action to correct his position. Like Romeo, he falls in love at once. Like Romeo and Troilus, he is impetuous and thoughtless. His father, like Hamlet's, is dead, but his enemy is just an envious older brother, not a usurping uncle. Orlando acts quickly, as the early Hamlet could have, but with immediate unhappy consequences: his initial behavior leads his older brother, Oliver, to plot to kill him. Unlike Romeo and Troilus and Hamlet, Orlando is saved by the girl he loves, Rosalind. Like the Duke in *Measure for Measure*, he will end as an instructed lover, a prospective husband, ready to fill the enlightened office of duke.

As You Like It is like *Hamlet* in its emphasis on play-acting. The center of *Hamlet* is the Mousetrap. In *As You Like It* a main reason for the preoccupation with roles rather than with offices is that, except for the first act and two short scenes thereafter, the action takes place in the forest of Arden, a green world, where offices are of little consequence. Only Duke Frederick, the usurper at court, is obsessed with his office. Duke Senior in the forest puts the best face he can on having lost his office. Rowland, Orlando's father, had no office. Nor does Oliver, though he is thrust out of doors by Duke Frederick and is in danger of losing all he has. The play ends happily not only because Orlando overcomes himself but also because Oliver and Frederick are converted. Orlando will become the duke because he will marry the only daughter of the reinstated duke.

In 3.1 of *Hamlet*, after Hamlet rejects her and departs, Ophelia addresses him in what may be called a soliloquy:

> O, what a noble mind is here o'erthrown!
> The courtier's, soldier's, scholar's, eye, tongue, sword.
> (3.1.150-51)

The appellations for Hamlet by the distraught Ophelia are three of the eight roles mentioned by Jaques in his disquisition on melancholy in 4.1 of *As You Like It*. In a manner of speaking, Hamlet's attributes (eye, tongue, sword) replace Jaques's kinds of melancholy. Ophelia's point is that Hamlet used to be a courtier, a soldier, a scholar. It is therefore remarkable that it is precisely these roles and these attributes (a courtier with his tongue, a soldier with his sword, a scholar with his eye) that are prominent in the last scene of *Hamlet*. Hamlet acts like a scholar with Horatio, like a courtier with Osric and (before the duel) with Laertes, and like a soldier in the duel and after it: "Let four captains/Bear Hamlet like a soldier to the stage"(5.2.395-96). At the end of the play three named men are left alive on stage, and they can be designated by their roles: Osric, the courtier; Fortinbras, the soldier; Horatio, the scholar.

* * * * *

Since the movement of a Shakespeare comedy is toward marriage (or as in *All's Well* or *Cymbeline* or *The Winter's Tale* toward the re-establishment of marriage), it relies on familial roles (brother, sister, father, husband, wife, though rarely mother) both for its complication and for its resolution as an enlarged family. And since a comedy proceeds to its good end by means of assumed roles and deception and play-acting, it relies for its successful conclusion on such "reduced," assumed roles as Portia's judge or Viola's Cesario or the Duke's friar. And since a comedy insists upon the necessity of social order, it employs roles as social types: the soldier, the lover, the social outcast (Don John), the ambitious steward (Malvolio), the jaundiced philosopher (Jaques). Though an ordered society will require properly filled offices, office in a comedy is of secondary importance. The figure of authority, usually a duke, is often not even on stage during the third and fourth acts. In *Measure for Measure* the Duke as duke is on stage only at the beginning and the end; Leontes in *The Winter's Tale* is absent in act 4; Prospero is absent in act 2 and most of act 3. The main point is that the figure of authority is always on stage at the end, when social order is restored and when he is most needed.

Each of the four great tragedies—*Hamlet, Othello, Macbeth, King Lear*—is preoccupied with its hero: he is the center of attention. He is on stage in every act: each tragedy ends, not, as in a comedy, with marriage, but with the death of the hero and the death of others, followed by a glimpse of a reduced social order. As these heroes are betrayed, as they suffer and endure, we are meant to see at last "the cinders of [their] spirits/Through th' ashes of [their] chance"(*Ant* 5.2.173-74). These tragedies are predicated upon the tension between roles (son, husband, father) and offices (prince, general-governor, usurper, king). But the main tactics of Shakespeare comedy are still employed, though realistically presented, dramatically justified, and life-threatening. In fact, these tragedies rely for choric purposes on that staple of Shakespeare comedy, the clown or fool: Polonius, the Gravedigger, Yorick, Osric in *Hamlet*; the Clown in *Othello*; the Porter in *Macbeth*; the Fool in *King Lear*. What needs to be emphasized is that in a tragedy a clown or a fool is rarely a surprise: except for the unexpected Clown in *Othello*, we expect a king to have a counselor or a fool; a great house would have a porter; a gravedigger will be necessary.

Halfway through each tragedy an act of violence occurs: Hamlet kills Polonius; convinced that his wife is unfaithful, Othello strikes Desdemona; although Fleance escapes, Banquo is killed; Gloucester is blinded. Thereafter the world of the hero changes. During a Shakespeare comedy a character moves from role to role under slight urgency: Viola becomes Cesario; Benedick and Orlando turn from soldier to lover; the Duke assumes the role of friar. These cool changes are at the service of the thought of the play: as the action moves toward renewal, suffering is put in the context of thematic control. The hero and heroine in a comedy rely on the service of others for the play's successful conclusion: they depend on outside help. The mid-play change in the tragic hero is the product of betrayal, of violence and death: as his world changes, he is forced back upon himself; he is reduced to the roles imposed on him.

Although *Macbeth* depends on the same last-act strategy used in *Richard III* and *Richard II* (alternating scenes of both claimants to the crown [Richard III and Richmond; Richard II and Bullingbrook; Macbeth and Malcolm]) and although *King Lear* has (for special reasons that have to do with Lear as father) a last act with a long middle in which Lear and Cordelia are absent, all four tragedies rely on the same device of imposed roles at the end. And in each instance these roles are reached through the agency of a scene that presents the woman central to the welfare of the hero; she is presented in a reduced and imposed role: in 4.5 of *Hamlet* Ophelia is mad maid, forsaken by the lover who killed her father; in 4.3 of *Othello* Desdemona, like Ophelia, sings the song of a distraught maid forsaken by her mad lover; in 5.1 of *Macbeth*, having been forsaken by her ("Some say he's mad"[5.2.13]) husband, Lady Macbeth, with her eyes open but their sense shut, relives the horrors of her past; in 4.7 of *King Lear* Cordelia, now just a kind daughter, rejoins her lost father, who has been mad.

In a Shakespeare comedy the principal woman or the heart continues to serve her future husband and to save society. In a Shakespeare tragedy, after the mid-play violence and change, which signals the death of the head, and after the consequent death of the woman or heart, the hero is presented in the role of a not-extraordinary man or hand. It is always a surprise to anyone reading *Hamlet* for the first time to realize in act 5 that Hamlet is thirty years old, not twenty or so. And it is a source of amazement that Hamlet, who is so shaken by Ophelia's death in 5.1, can be almost at once calm and philosophical: in this last scene he never even mentions Ophelia. Ophelia may, but we don't, think of Hamlet as a soldier; we don't expect Laertes to be the better duelist.

Hamlet, upon his return to Denmark at the beginning of act 5, is presented in a series of reduced roles. In act 5 Hamlet is successively a clown (with the gravedigger and Yorick), a distraught lover (with the dead Ophelia), a scholar (with Horatio), a courtier (with Osric and Laertes), a soldier (with Laertes and Claudius and to Fortinbras). Looking at the last scene a little more closely, we may further say that Hamlet is a brother with Laertes and a schoolboy (she offers him her napkin to rub his brow) with Gertrude.

In the last scene *Othello* enters as a priest and a bridegroom; to Emilia he is a gull and a dolt; to Gratiano a nephew; to himself a deceived fool. He ends by presenting himself in a catalogue of reduced roles:

> Then must you speak
> Of one that lov'd not wisely but too well;
> Of one not easily jealous, but being wrought,
> Perplexed in the extreme; of one whose hand,
> Like the base [Indian], threw a pearl away
> Richer than all his tribe; of one whose subdu'd eyes,
> Albeit unused to the melting mood,
> Drops tears as fast as the Arabian trees
> Their medicinable gum.
>
> (5.2.343-51)

In act 5 Macbeth is a dwarfish thief to Angus; later he is a "scholar," a soldier in his armor, a bear, a hell-hound, a coward, an "apparition." At the beginning of act 5 King Lear is a courtier and a scholar to Cordelia; to each other Lear and Cordelia are like spies and sacrifices; off stage Lear is like a soldier in killing the slave; at the end he is an old man, a father, even perhaps, like Cymbeline at the end, a mother. In these tragedies the roles the hero plays in his last act are not in conflict, one with the other: as his assured end approaches, the tragic hero moves from role to role. This procedure, not unlike a procession, is at the service of parading the various roles that go to make up the complexity of what he at one time was or could have been. Presented as they are, these roles help to clarify and to justify the past, which his office obscured.

The reduced hero reduces others. In *Macbeth*, for example, Malcolm is to Macbeth a boy; a frightened soldier is a cream-faced loon; the Doctor is of no use. To Lear the men on stage at the end are men of stones; he seems to identify them as a dog, a horse, a rat. The strange reference to Cordelia as a poor fool can be understood in this context. After the rust has been burnt off, the hero, in his heart-breaking recovery, is heartlessly realistic, even cruel: ". . . the readiness is all"(*Ham* 5.2.222). Just as his brutal progress has taught the hero the futility of office and the reality of roles, so Shakespeare teaches us that "All the world's a stage,/And all the men and women merely players"(*AYL* 2.7.139-40). It is a devastating lesson, redeemed by instructed love and perceived human duty.

NOTE

1. Vernon P. Loggins, *The Life of Our Design: Organization and Related Strategies in Troilus and Cressida* (UP of America, 1992), 39-50.

Part Two

10

The Redemption of Emilia

Richard Levin's incisive critique of those feminist critics of Shakespeare's tragedies who "assume that character and action exist for the sake of the thematic idea" (126) prompts us to examine the function and the significance of Emilia in *Othello*.[1] We are primarily interested in Emilia's plight as the wife of Iago and the companion of Desdemona: she becomes Desdemona's friend, defender, disciple. Although we do not share many of Levin's assumptions, beliefs, and convictions, we support his critical assertion that the "feminist branch of thematism," like other thematic criticism of Shakespeare, "does not work" (128).

Thematic criticism tends to falsify meaning by abstracting it. But a concern for Emilia's dramatized situation serves to correct and enhance the understanding of Emilia, of the other main characters of the play, of *Othello*, and even of the nature of Shakespeare tragedy. Shakespeare's dramatic method was designed not only to display characters in action but also to present those characters within clarified, prescribed patterns and systems. Note in particular Shakespeare's use of three-item and five-item patterns that serve to counter and to negate the charge of thematic "selectivity" (128) and of thematic "homogenization" (129). The immediate concern is Emilia and her structural (for want of a better word) position in *Othello*.

Dr. Johnson's observation that Emilia wears her mantle of goodness loosely but does not cast it off situates Emilia as normal, fallible woman. In the play she occupies this middle position, between the good Desdemona and the wicked Bianca. It should be said that a case can be made against Desdemona and a case made for Bianca, just as a case can be made for or against Emilia. Shakespeare was no sexist or primitive psychologist: he is always intent upon getting us to understand human beings and their behavior; he doesn't just praise or patronize or denounce. Women were treated less humanly then than they now are or than they should be, but that is not Shakespeare's fault. Nor is it his fault that his society (whether the one he was a part of or the one he depicts) is closed or, like a prison, enclosed. The structural point is that in the play Emilia is one of three kinds of women: the saint, the norm, the strumpet. In the play, apart from marriage, none of the women has a worthwhile future.

On another structural level, the play concerns three couples or three love relationships: Othello and Desdemona; Iago and Emilia; Cassio and Bianca. Since the marriage between Othello and Desdemona is precarious until the ironic end, their plot problem can be described as how and when their marriage will be consummated. Othello and Desdemona are thus increasingly preoccupied with their future. Iago and Emilia are increasingly preoccupied with their errant past. The play begins with Roderigo demanding the money and jewels (see 4.2.186) he gave Iago; Roderigo's persistence is turned by Iago into a vicious attack on Brabantio and Othello. Emilia's future is determined by her picking up the handkerchief dropped in 3.3, the seduction scene. Cassio and Bianca are preoccupied with their uncertain present: as soon as he has lost it, Cassio is importunate to get back the office of lieutenant; the besotted Bianca cannot live apart from Cassio. They are obsessed with the present.

Emilia is in eight of the fifteen scenes of the play. She is in only one scene in the first two acts, 2.1, the tempest scene; that first appearance, brief as it is, establishes the essential Emilia. She will thereafter struggle between her plight as Iago's wife and her duty to her beloved mistress, Desdemona. The dramatization of the struggle between Emilia's two roles will involve the sudden first appearance of Bianca, woman-as-strumpet, who will come on stage in 3.4, the handkerchief scene, right after Othello is convinced by Iago in the seduction scene that his wife, Desdemona, is a strumpet. Bianca is the personification of Othello's ugly conviction about his wife.

The concern of the episode in which Emilia first appears on stage, the tempest scene, is that of women. Having come through the tempest, Desdemona, Iago, Roderigo, and Emilia arrive on shore in Cyprus. Cassio addresses Desdemona:

> O, behold,
> The riches of the ship is come on shore!
> You men of Cyprus, let her have your knees.
> Hail to thee, lady! and the grace of heaven,
> Before, behind thee, and on every hand,
> Enwheel thee round!
>
> (2.1.82-87)

Almost at once Iago contradicts Cassio's elaborate praise of Desdemona as a lady by engaging her in a series of alehouse paradoxes, his hateful, denigrating, sexist jokes about women. Emilia has only three lines in the scene, all three in this episode, and each a response to her husband, Iago: "You have little cause to say so"(2.1.108); "You shall not write my praise"(2.1.116); "How if fair and foolish?"(2.1.135) The last line is the only interjection by Emilia or by anyone else during the alehouse-joke exchange between Iago and Desdemona.

There are five alehouse paradoxes: "If she be fair and wise"(2.1.129); ". . . if she be black and witty"(2.1.131); ". . . if fair and foolish"(2.1.135); ". . . foul and foolish"(2.1.140); "She that was ever fair, and never proud"(2.1.148). These paradoxes are miniature stories or parables. We may consider the middle one ("How if fair and foolish?"[2.1.135]) as being the one that best applies to Emilia: she asks the question. Iago's answer reveals his contempt for her; it also foreshadows her future: "She never yet was foolish that was fair,/For even her folly help'd her to an heir"(2.1.136-37). Emilia is both fair and foolish; her folly will result in a kind of heir or good consequence, not in a "most lame and impotent conclusion!"(2.1.161) Emilia will prove to be foolishly faithful to her lady, Desdemona, and she will end with that married couple on that fateful bed, hidden at last behind a curtain: "The object poisons sight"(5.2.364).

In the seduction scene Othello brushes away Desdemona's hand with its handkerchief, and the handkerchief falls; they then leave, and Emilia picks it up:

> I am glad I have found this napkin;
> This was her first remembrance from the Moor.
> My wayward husband hath a hundred times
> Woo'd me to steal it; but she so loved the token
> (For he conjur'd her she should ever keep it)
> That she reserves it evermore about her
> To kiss and talk to. I'll have the work ta'en out,
> And give't Iago. What he will do with it
> Heaven knows, not I;
> I nothing but to please his fantasy.
>
> (3.3.290-99)

As Desdemona's companion, Emilia knows how much the napkin means to her lady, but, as Iago's obedient wife, she is quite willing to filch it for her husband. This seemingly trivial theft, done with little malicious intent, will haunt Emilia. Thereafter she will have three interviews with Desdemona: in 3.4, the handkerchief scene; in 4.2, the brothel scene; in 4.3, the bedroom scene. As we might expect, it is structurally the middle interview that is most crucial.

The verbal play on the word *lie* in the interlude with the Clown that begins the handkerchief scene (3.4) alerts us to the presence of lies in the scene itself. First Desdemona and Emilia are with Othello; then they are with Iago and Cassio; then they are with Cassio; then they are alone. Othello charges the handkerchief with value by recounting the undoubtedly spurious history of it. He makes the handkerchief even more significant and valuable than Desdemona previously thought, and then he four times demands the handkerchief from Desdemona. When she fails to produce it and in effect lies, he leaves the stage, angry and upset.

And so, almost as soon as she has picked up the handkerchief, Emilia is presented with the opportunity of rectifying her no-longer-petty theft. She is given the chance of relieving her lady's plight by telling the truth. But she needn't tell the truth. She could tell a small lie and say that she thinks she has seen it somewhere; she could then ask Iago for it. But instead of doing something quietly sensible, she offers this rationalization:

> 'Tis not a year or two shows us a man:
> They are all but stomachs, and we all but food;
> They eat us hungerly, and when they are full
> They belch us.
>
> (3.4.103-06)

In addition to revealing a great deal about her marriage to Iago, these lines may indicate that Emilia also knows Othello quite well. But, beyond that, under the pressure of her feelings of guilt, she resorts to the understandable tactic of aligning herself with women against the enemy, men, and by so doing she offers another woman, Desdemona, a kind of sisterly comfort.

After Iago has left, the upset Desdemona remarks to her friend, "Alas the day, I never gave [Othello] cause"(3.4.158). Emilia responds:

> But jealous souls will not be answer'd so;
> They are not ever jealous for the cause,
> But jealous for they're jealous. It is a monster
> Begot upon itself, born on itself.
>
> (3.4.159-62)

The almost universally held belief that Othello is the jealous Othello can be traced directly to these lines and to similar ones by untrustworthy Iago in the seduction scene (3.3). Othello is upset, angry, but surely not jealous or not just jealous. The relevant point is that, again, Emilia is compensating for her feelings of guilt or for her recognition that she is not being so forthright as she should be. After all, what Emilia does is a common enough dodge. But it is also a startling illustration of how perceptive Shakespeare is about the way a wife in a male-dominated society can behave under stressful conditions. In the next scene Bianca, a whore, rejects with jealous anger the handkerchief given her by Cassio.

In the brothel scene (4.2) Othello questions Emilia, then treats her like a bawd; he orders her to stand guard outside the door; as he leaves the room, he rewards her with money. In a masterstroke of characterization, Emilia eavesdrops like a bawd upon Othello's heartless accusation of Desdemona as being a strumpet. Up to a brief time before (in the previous scene Othello strikes her), Desdemona has had no experience with physical abuse and little with verbal abuse. "A child to chiding"(4.2.114), Desdemona withdraws into herself. After Othello has left, Desdemona plaintively asks that Iago be brought to her. And then, with stunning, dramatic effect, she weeps and kneels for help from the very villain so accurately described by Emilia a few moments before. "Go in, and weep not; all things shall be well"(4.2.171), Iago says, but, as the rest of the scene demonstrates, Iago's expression of pity will have no consequence. Under pressure from the beaten, disgruntled Roderigo, Iago will proceed to convince his dupe, Othello, of the necessity of murdering Cassio and Desdemona at once.

Emilia goes from hardening her heart against men to hardening her heart against the one man who, by slandering Desdemona, has caused Othello to behave as he has. In the scene the handkerchief is never mentioned, and Emilia does not make the connection between Othello's behavior over the loss of the handkerchief then and his abusive behavior now. Nor does she seize upon her previous excuse that Othello is jealous because he is jealous, as if she knows now how flimsy that explanation was. She never guesses that the eternal villain could be her husband. In the judgment scene (5.2) Emilia finds it impossible to believe that her husband could be so villainous. The truth is that chance and circumstance help to make the self-centered Iago a murderous villain, someone destroyed at last by his fair, foolish wife.

With Desdemona, Othello's wife, standing by her side, Emilia makes the following incredible comment to her husband:

> Some such squire he was
> That turn'd your wit the seamy side without,
> And made you to suspect me with the Moor.
> (4.2.145-47)

The oblivious Desdemona, who will at once kneel to Iago, seems to hear only the comforting fury in Emilia's words but not the words. Emilia's comment reveals that she may indeed have had a love affair with Othello. But the main point is that Shakespeare is using here his pervasive strategy of words spoken but not listened to or heard by another person on stage, in this case Desdemona.

The last interview Emilia has with Desdemona is the touching one in which she helps her mistress prepare for bed. As Emilia helps undress her lady and helps her put on her nightly wearing, Desdemona sings Mad Barbary's song of willow. Then Emilia makes the next logical move in her series of reactions: from being against men to being against one man, she now takes the affirmative action of being for wives:

> Let husbands know
> Their wives have sense like them; they see, and smell,
> And have their palates both for sweet and sour,
> As husbands have. What is it that they do
> When they change us for others? Is it sport?
> I think it is. And doth affection breed it?
> I think it doth. Is't frailty that thus errs?
> It is so too. And have not we affections,
> Desires for sport, and frailty, as men have?
> Then let them use us well; else let them know,
> The ills we do, their ills instruct us so.
>
> (4.3.93-103)

Desdemona may have been oblivious before, but now she hears Emilia all too clearly. For what Emilia unwittingly does is to isolate the unhappy Desdemona from her only friend, Emilia. Desdemona does not understand; she cannot believe that any wife could or would commit adultery:

> Good night, good night. [God] me such uses send,
> Not to pick bad from bad, but by bad mend.
>
> (4.3.104-05)

The tone of *Othello* combines heartbreaking emotion and mocking irony. In the bedroom scene Desdemona is like an innocent bride waiting on her wedding night for the rape that will turn her into a wife. Othello comes to the wedding chamber in the judgment scene, a light in his hand, somber and serious, like a priest ready to perform the bloody sacrifice that will save

Desdemona's soul. At the end of the bedroom scene (4.3) Desdemona is isolated as expectant bride; at the beginning of the judgment scene Othello is isolated as priest-groom. As we have seen, Emilia has three interviews with her lady, Desdemona. Emilia also has three interviews with her lady's husband: in the brothel scene, before Othello treats Desdemona like a strumpet; in the judgment scene, after he has killed his wife; and, a little later, after Iago has mortally wounded her.

Emilia's movement in the second half of the play is marked by three preliminary confrontations. In the brothel scene, with the distraught Desdemona at her side, Emilia confronts Iago, the villain she actually describes in the scene but does not recognize; she denounces and rejects that unknown villain. In the street scene, 5.1, after Iago has wounded Cassio and "killed" Roderigo, Emilia confronts Bianca, the prostitute, and denounces and rejects her—an action that is the next logical move after the celebration of wives at the end of the previous scene. After Othello has killed Desdemona, Emilia confronts, denounces, and rejects the guilty Othello:

> O gull, O dolt,
> As ignorant as dirt! Thou hast done a deed—
> I care not for thy sword, I'll make thee known,
> Though I lost twenty lives. Help, help, ho, help!
> The Moor hath kill'd my mistress! Murther, murther!
> (5.2.163-67)

In the judgment scene, only Bianca (Desdemona as strumpet) and Roderigo (Othello as dupe) are absent. The scene itself has two main parts. The first part is concerned with Othello and Desdemona and then with Othello and Emilia. The second part is concerned with Othello and other men. At the end of the first half of the last scene, the obligatory public confrontation between the guilty, bereft, grief-stricken Emilia and her desperate, brutal, villainous husband at last takes place. "I charge you get you home"(5.2.194), Iago orders. There is every reason for Emilia to obey her husband: Desdemona is dead; Othello has been denounced; her husband is in great danger; if she speaks she will implicate herself; she must know that Iago will try to stop her. This is Emilia's response: "'Tis proper I obey him; but not now./Perchance, Iago, I will ne'er go home"(5.2.196-97). And then she confesses everything: nothing can stop her. Her actions are perfectly foolish and perfectly wonderful. And, as she should expect, Iago kills her for them.

And then, alone with Othello for the last time, she delivers her last speech:

> What did thy song bode, lady?
> Hark, canst thou hear me? I will play the swan,
> And die in music. [*Sings*] "Willow, willow, willow."
> Moor, she was chaste; she lov'd thee, cruel Moor;
> So come my soul to bliss, as I speak true;
> So speaking as I think, alas, I die.
>
> (5.2.246-51)

Her final speech redeems her squalid past. It is only right that she should emulate her precious lady. It is only proper that she not even mention her hateful husband. Her victory has been that of the soul over the body, that of the woman over the wife.

NOTE

1. Richard Levin. "Feminist Thematics and Shakespearean Tragedy," *PMLA* 103 (1988): 125-38. Also see Alberto Cacicedo's comments on *Othello* and Richard Levin's reply in "Forum," *PMLA* 103 (1988): 817-19.

11

The Plight of Coriolanus

To put it boldly, the critical response to *Coriolanus* hasn't been very profound or even very useful.[1] Usually dependable critics like Harold Goddard, Frank Kermode, Harry Levin, and Derek Traversi haven't been very successful at advancing our understanding and consequent appreciation of what is almost certainly Shakespeare's last tragedy. The perfunctory critic is taken with the influence of Plutarch or with Shakespeare as another Chapman or with Shakespeare's elitist politics or with Coriolanus's intransigent, violent nature or with Coriolanus as a mechanical man or with Coriolanus's domination by his mother, whom he certainly wishes to please. Chambers suspects that Shakespeare was suffering from what Huck Finn would call the fantods. Some estimable critics can't even decide what to call the play: to G. B. Shaw it is Shakespeare's finest comedy; to Kermode it is a debate; to Rossiter it is a history; to Campbell it is a satire; to Eliot it is one of Shakespeare's assured successes.

The simple truth is that *Coriolanus* is a typical Shakespeare tragedy in design and structure and that it is a masterpiece, incisive, sophisticated, trenchant. It is true that as a tragedy it is harsh and political, that it is obsessed with Coriolanus (all of the other characters can't stop talking about him), that it doesn't have a substantive subplot, that the "choric" voice is not irreverent, pungent, or witty. On the plot level it isn't as interesting as the more famous tragedies. It isn't gripping like *Hamlet* or *Othello* or magnificent like *King Lear* or *Antony and Cleopatra*. We would perhaps all agree that it is a little strange, like *Timon of Athens*. But it is concerned, as the other tragedies are, with character formation and character disclosure. Coriolanus is complex—a round character, as Forster would say. And the tragedy is best approached through a consideration of Coriolanus's plight, for it is plight that creates the pervasive irony that distinguishes every character-oriented Shakespeare play.

Faced with an insurrection caused by a shortage of grain and aware that the "Volsces are in arms"(1.1.224), the Roman senate gives the unruly plebians food and empowers the citizens by appointing tribunes to represent their interests. Having been many times wounded in battle and having been twice rewarded with the oaken garland, Caius Martius is a certified protector of Rome and Romans, an ill-tempered, proud public servant. As Plato would say, Martius is qualified to rule because he knows that if he doesn't rule, someone less qualified will. And the only office he can aspire to in republican Rome is that of consul: he can't muscle his way, like Octavius Caesar, to power. And so, contemptuous of the whining plebians, angry at the undeserving citizens, dismissive of the opportunistic tribunes, dismayed by a senate foolish and frightened enough to reward a rebellion, distrustful of the cowardly patricians, Martius, a petulant, ill-used general, turns his attention elsewhere, to the outside enemy, the invading Volscians.

In the past he sought "danger where he was like to find fame"(1.3.13). In the coming fray his declared intention is to hunt and kill Aufidius, the leader of the Volscians; his undeclared ambition is to become a Roman consul. In 2.1, after Martius has become Coriolanus, his mother, Volumnia, comments, ". . . only/There's one thing wanting, which I doubt not but/Our Rome will cast upon thee"(2.1.200-02). Thus his brutal, vitriolic onstage behavior in the long first scene is churlish but understandable: his past service has not brought him the reward that he sincerely believes he has earned. He wants more fame and the power that should attend it.

In typical fashion the first scene presents Martius's public plight; the second scene introduces his chief enemy, the Volscian Aufidius; the third introduces the three women of the play, to whom Martius is, respectively, a husband, a son, a friend. In this scene, 1.3, Valeria's portrayal of Martius's namesake, his young son, makes clear one of the moods of the father:

> . . . [he has] such a confirm'd
> countenance. I saw him run after a gilded butter-
> fly, and when he caught it, he let it go again, and after
> it again, and over and over he comes, and up again;
> catch'd it again: or whether his fall enrag'd him, or
> how 'twas, he did so set his teeth and tear it. O, I
> warrant, how he mammock'd it!
>
> (1.3.59-65)

The gilded butterfly can be considered as the fame or the honor that the public Martius again and again catches and releases and, after "his fall enrag'd him"(1.3.63), finally destroys. And thus Valeria's vignette can be considered as a reduced statement or version of the father's behavior in the play: his wrath destroys his gain, the gaudy, flimsy prize with which he has been obsessed.

Until the last scene of act 1, Martius is *the* bloody man on stage. In 1.4, after he is shut inside Corioles, this is the stage direction: *Enter* MARTIUS *bleeding, assaulted by the enemy.*[2] In 1.5 Lartius remarks to his friend Martius, "Worthy sir, thou bleed'st"(1.5.14). In 1.6 Cominius, the lord general, says that Martius "does appear as he were flea'd"(1.6.22), "mantled"(1.6.29) in his own blood. In 2.2 at the Capitol, Cominius says that when Martius stopped the fliers at Corioles, ". . . from face to foot/He was a thing of blood"(2.2.108-09). There is then plenty of evidence that from 1.4 to the end of 1.9 Martius is blood covered: "Go we to our tent./The blood upon your visage dries, 'tis time/It should be look'd to"(1.9.92-94).

But Martius discounts the blood as being significant or meaningful. In 1.5 he tells Lartius that the blood is "not dangerous" to him. In 1.6 he says that he is "smear'd" with blood. In 1.8 he tells Aufidius, "'Tis not my blood/Wherein thou seest me mask'd"(1.8.9-10). In 2.1 we are informed that Martius received two wounds, one in the shoulder and one in the left arm. Yet, after the initial battle, when in 1.6 Martius joins Cominius in another part of the battlefield, he makes the following comment, "O! let me clip ye/In arms as sound as when I woo'd"(1.6.29-30). We must assume that Martius has not yet been wounded in the left arm: at least up to this point, his arms are sound.

When Martius meets Aufidius in 1.8, he declares that he will fight with no one else: *Here they fight, and certain Volsces come in the aid of Aufidius. Martius fights till they be driven in breathless*. Martius is not to be blamed that Aufidius is helped by his friends. The opposing leaders want to fight each other on equal terms: Aufidius ends the scene by denouncing the men who aided him. But the amazing thing is that, after a day of violent exertion, Martius can drive off at least three armed opponents. He doesn't perform like someone who has recently been wounded. Act 1.9 begins with a scene direction in which Martius is reported as entering *with his arm in a scarf*. The immediate assumption is that, a short time before, Martius was wounded in the onstage scuffle with the Volscians, yet there is no evidence in 1.8 that he was wounded there. More surprising still is the stage direction at the beginning of 1.10: *Enter* TULLUS AUFIDIUS, *bloody*. When and where was he wounded? Apparently not in 1.8.

There is no hard evidence that Martius was wounded in this day's battle. In 2.1 Volumnia says that before the present battle Martius had twenty-five wounds; in 2.3 Coriolanus says to himself in a kind of soliloquy that up to now he has had "Of wounds two dozen odd"(2.3.128). If he were recently wounded, the number should be twenty-seven. Although in a letter he reports to his mother that he has been wounded, there is no evidence that Volumnia ever sees the wounds. Virgilia actually denies that her husband has been wounded: "O no, no, no"(2.1.120).[3] No one is said to have treated the wounds. When Coriolanus enters in 2.1, his arm is apparently not in a scarf. In 2.3 Coriolanus tells some citizens that he will show them his wounds, but he never does so: their specific complaint is that they never get to see Coriolanus's wounds. But why, we may well ask, would Martius pretend to be wounded? And where does all the blood come from? Is Aufidius, his Volscian counterpart, also just pretending to be wounded? It is true that Martius does say, in 1.9, that his nose has been bleeding.

The specific speculation is that when Martius was inside Corioles, he employed the practice of Falstaff and his men, as reported in 2.4 of *1 Henry IV*, and tickled his nose with something like speargrass in order to make it bleed, and then he beslubbered himself with his own blood. Like bloody Prince Harry at Shrewsbury, Martius wants to give the appearance of one who has fought long and valiantly in a just cause.[4] Like Harry on the battlefield intent upon finding and destroying Hotspur, Martius on the battlefield is intent upon finding and destroying Aufidius: "He is a lion/That I am proud to hunt"(1.1.235-36). His reconfirmed or enhanced fame, he thinks, depends on his destroying his arch enemy or (as Harry calls Hotspur) his factor,[5] Aufidius, in single combat. That he fails in this quest, through no fault of his own, is part of the unexpressed regret he must feel after the battle, when the war is over. One certain irony is that, although he has not attained his stated goal of hunting Aufidius down, his honor and valor are celebrated, and he is rewarded with the surname Coriolanus. He feels guilty, if not ashamed; in light of his recent, offstage behavior, he doesn't deserve to be called Coriolanus.

Now there can be little doubt that Martius is a very brave and efficient warrior, a very good destroyer of men. There is no doubt that in the past he honorably sustained twenty-five wounds in fighting for Rome and Romans. But in this day-long battle he wants, for understandable but private reasons, to insure his fame and subsequent power: he can't trust the plebians, the tribunes, the patricians, or the senators to do anything for him. Beyond fighting with determination and bravery, what he can do or what he does do is to paint and smear himself with blood. He then intends to search out, find, and kill Aufidius. It is a major point that, even in the past on the battlefield, Martius was not above using craft or policy, for, as Volumnia remarks to him in 3.2, "I have heard you say/Honor and policy, like unsever'd friends,/I' th' war do grow together"(3.2.41-43):

> If it be honor in your wars to seem
> The same you are not, which, for your best ends,
> You adopt your policy, how is it less or worse
> That it shall hold companionship in peace
> With honor, as in war, since that to both
> It stands in like request?
>
> (3.2.46-51)

* * * * *

One of the strangest and most memorable episodes in the play takes place at the end of 1.9. After refusing princely gifts from Cominius (a refusal perhaps made for political reasons), Coriolanus begs a favor, which is readily granted.

> *Cor*. I sometime lay here in Corioles
> At a poor man's house; he us'd me kindly.
> He cried to me; I saw him prisoner;
> But then Aufidius was within my view,
> And wrath o'erwhelm'd my pity. I request you
> To give my poor host freedom.
> *Com*.   O, well begg'd!
> Were he the butcher of my son, he should
> Be free as is the wind. Deliver him, Titus.
> *Lart*.   Martius, his name?
> *Cor*.   By Jupiter, forgot!
> I am weary, yea, my memory is tir'd.
> Have we no wine here?
>
> (1.9.82-92)

The usual critical comment has to do with the part of the episode that Shakespeare invented: for Shakespeare to have Coriolanus forget the name of his poor host in Corioles is a shrewd disclosure of Coriolanus's character and personality.[6] Yes. But the unnoticed point is that Coriolanus is being politic. He intends to do here something similar to what Prince Harry does at the end of *1 Henry IV*: Harry asks the King to give him Douglas; Harry then tells his brother, John, to release Douglas. Harry wants to put himself metaphorically above his brother and in this way to reclaim and to re-establish his neglected office of Prince of Wales. Coriolanus seems to want Cominius himself to free the poor host: he perhaps wants to put himself above the lord general, the consul. But perhaps Coriolanus expects Cominius to "give" him the poor man; he would then tell Lartius to deliver the poor host to freedom: metaphorically he may want to put himself above his erstwhile friend and fellow leader, Lartius. As it happens, once Cominius gives Lartius the order to deliver the host, Coriolanus aborts his plan. He has been forestalled in his vain attempt to get Cominius to respond in a desired way.

But this involved answer is still only partial. Cominius has just declared that Martius should hereafter be called Martius Caius Coriolanus. After a *Flourish. Trumpets sound, and drums*, they all shout "Martius Caius Coriolanus!"(1.9.67) And then, twenty-seven lines later, Lartius calls the newly named Coriolanus "Martius." Coriolanus abruptly and deliberately forgets the name of the poor man. If Lartius can forget Coriolanus's new name, he can forget the host's. Coriolanus's comment "By Jupiter, forgot!"(1.9.90) may refer primarily to Lartius's forgetting or neglecting to use the surname Coriolanus, the confirmation of Martius's new, changed status.

But even this notion leaves the answer incomplete. Coriolanus is truly tired: it has been a day of great exertion and strain. Coriolanus has forgotten that he beslubbered himself with blood. Coriolanus suddenly remembers that he does not want the name of his poor host known because that knowledge may lead to the truth about his own bloody appearance. He does not want to sully his newly attained honor. And so he is quite willing to sacrifice a past benefactor in order to keep unblemished his new fame.

When Coriolanus next comes on stage (2.1), he, again crowned with the oaken garland, has Cominius and Lartius on either side of him, like aides-de-camp. The garment of blood has been replaced by clothing more suitable (no mention is made of the scarf) to his new role of victorious general. In the scene he is all but assured of becoming consul. In 2.2 he no longer wears the oaken garland; he enters 2.3 wearing the gown of humility that Roman custom dictates. It would discomfort any proud leader to have to pander for support to a group of poor men that he has publicly despised, but how much worse it must be for a Coriolanus to submit to the indignity of an outmoded custom and, further, to know that he hasn't really earned the office he is being given. But he wants the office and the power. From his perspective all three major roles (bloody soldier, public hero, humble solicitor) are, in a progressively more apparent sense, false: the first role has led to the second and thus to the third.

* * * * *

After speaking to some citizens in 2.3, Coriolanus, alone on stage, delivers his first soliloquy in the play. The thematic significance of the soliloquy is emphasized by Shakespeare's use of rhymed couplets:

> Better it is to die, better to starve,
> Than crave the hire which first we do deserve.
> Why in this woolvish [toge] should I stand here
> To beg of Hob and Dick, that does appear,
> Their needless vouches? Custom calls me to't.
> What custom wills, in all things should we do't,
> The dust on antique time would lie unswept,
> And mountainous error be too highly heap'd
> For truth to o'erpeer. Rather than fool it so,
> Let the high office and the honor go
> To one that would do thus. I am half through:
> The one part suffered, the other will I do.
>   (2.3.113-24)

The above quotation prompts a reminder about the nature of a Shakespeare tragedy.[7] It has two parts: the first three acts, the final two acts. Coriolanus's soliloquy in 2.3 is balanced by his soliloquy in 4.4. At the end of act 3 Coriolanus is banished from Rome; at the end of act 5 he is killed. Coriolanus has an interview with his mother in 3.2; he has an interview with his mother (now accompanied by Virgilia, Valeria, young Martius) in 5.3. In 3.3, when Sicinius calls him a traitor, Coriolanus becomes angry, loses control; in 5.6 Aufidius replaces Sicinius as the instigator of Coriolanus's wrath.

The action in the second half of a Shakespeare tragedy inverts or recapitulates or rehearses or translates first-half action. Thus, in order to understand it, the end of a Shakespeare tragedy must be considered as a version of the end of act 3, the end of the first-part action. At the end of act 3, Hamlet kills Polonius; at the end of act 5, he kills Laertes and Claudius. At the end of act 3, Othello leaves the stage convinced that his wife is a strumpet; at the end of act 5, Othello kills himself for believing that his wife was a strumpet. At the end of act 3, Gloucester's eyes are plucked out; at the end of act 5, Lear collapses with the dead Cordelia in his arms. In no other tragedy is the end of act 5 as a version of the end of act 3 more apparent or more meaningful than it is in *Coriolanus*.

One of the central, pervasive strategies in any Shakespeare play is the recapitulative point-of-view scene.[8] Such a scene is meant to be placed over against the play or used as a kind of gloss on the play: the scene clarifies the play; the play clarifies the scene. The point of view is determined by the character or characters who remain on stage throughout the scene. The last scene of act 3 of a Shakespeare tragedy is *not* from the perspective of the tragic hero.[9] Act 3.4 of *Hamlet* is from the point of view of Gertrude; 3.3 of *Coriolanus* is from the point of view of the tribunes, Brutus and Sicinius. Their limited, self-interested perception of *Coriolanus* is challenged and criticized by the reader's or the audience's informed awareness of Coriolanus's present plight.

Brutus and Sicinius think they know how proud Coriolanus is, how he hates to be checked or stopped, how easily he can become choleric and surrender self-control. And so they arrange for the citizens to take the hint for action from them. When Sicinius will say that Coriolanus should be banished or fined or sentenced to death, they should take up the cry, whatever it is. If Sicinius says "banished," they should shout "banished." When Coriolanus forgets his promise to act mildly, Sicinius and the citizens banish him. When he brusquely banishes *them*, the citizens rejoice. This then is the action of the scene from the perspective of the tribunes. It is true that Coriolanus isn't aware of the tribunes' specific plot against him in the scene or of the reaction of the crowd after his departure. But, again, the first half of the play is designed to enable us to go beyond the limited perspective of the tribunes. We must import to the scene Coriolanus's complex perception of his place in the world, as we have been encouraged to understand it.

Accompanied by Menenius and Cominius and "those senators/ That always favor'd him"(3.3.7-8), Coriolanus comes on stage and delivers a political speech that we can be certain he regards as public cant:

> Th' honor'd gods
> Keep Rome in safety, and the chairs of justice
> Supplied with worthy men! plant love among's!

> [Throng] our large temples with the shows of peace,
> And not our streets with war!
>
> (3.3.33-37)

The first senator responds with "Amen, amen"(3.3.37). Later on in the scene, when Coriolanus is under attack by the tribunes and the plebians, no senator raises a voice on his behalf. So much then for his friends in the senate and for their help.

Menenius comments to the plebians:

> Lo, citizens, [Coriolanus] says he is content.
> The warlike service he has done, consider; think
> Upon the wounds his body bears, which show
> Like graves i'th' holy churchyard.
>
> (3.3.48-51)

Coriolanus at once replies: "Scratches with briers,/Scars to move laughter only"(3.3.51-52). Understandably, Coriolanus is discontented and embarrassed by his friend's well-intentioned remark. But if Coriolanus has not been wounded on this battlefield, his scars are just scratches; if the good truth be known, they should cause laughter. The point is that he doesn't want anyone to "think/Upon the wounds"(3.3.49-50). Coriolanus's private discontent and uneasiness are furthered by Menenius's added comment: "Consider [Coriolanus] . . . like a soldier"(3.3.52-54). His battlefield success has been based on a kind of hoax; no one notices that he didn't succeed in hunting Aufidius down. But then it should be acknowledged that, if the plebians were to consider him as only a soldier, they ought to conclude that they may well someday need him.

Coriolanus is understandably upset and angry because, after giving him their voices for consul, they are now taking their voices back. The plebians are base, cowardly, untrustworthy. After Coriolanus has been sentenced to banishment, Cominius, meaning to be helpful, does what he can for the celebrated hero:

> I do love
> My country's good with a respect more tender,
> More holy and profound, than mine own life,

My dear wive's estimate, her womb's increase
And treasure of my loins; then if I would
Speak that—

(3.3.111-16)

Cominius's speech is broken off by the tribunes. They refuse to allow him to continue his appeal, and Cominius does not insist that he be heard: Coriolanus has been banished, and that's the end of that. To Coriolanus Cominius's speech, even if it were completed, would be just so much cant: Coriolanus knows that on the battlefield he was really putting his concern for self and family above his concern for Rome.

Coriolanus shouldn't have listened to his mother and Menenius to be mild; he cannot be pleased that the supportive senators remain silent; he regrets that Menenius and Cominius have foolishly tried to support his cause. And so he rejects the "common cry of curs"(3.3.120) of the plebians and the tribunes. Because they have banished him, he willfully banishes them *and* Rome, the city of his mother, his wife and child, his friends (Menenius and Cominius). His wrath overwhelms his pity, and he commits himself to an intransigent position. He cannot and he will not go back.

Typically, at the end of act 3 of a Shakespeare tragedy the end is assured: Juliet is isolated and alone; Hamlet is a murderer; Othello is convinced that his wife is a strumpet; Gloucester has had his eyes plucked out; Antony, having been defeated at Actium, rejoins Cleopatra. In 3.3 of this play Coriolanus's fate is secured. In the scene the declaration "It shall be so" is iterated seven times. The first senator's comment "Amen, amen." (so be it) reinforces the notion of inevitability. And this is the way it is at the end of the first half of a Shakespeare tragedy. The end of the second half of a tragedy draws upon, modifies, and transforms this end.

The scene also documents a profound, unexpected change in Coriolanus. He banishes Rome; he will turn his back on his birthplace and find "a world elsewhere"(3.3.135). In 3.1 he publicly rejects Sicinius's "shall": "Shall remain?/Hear you this Triton of the minnows? Mark you/His absolute 'shall'?"(3.1.88-90) In 3.3 Coriolanus privately refuses to accept the declaration "It shall be so." He will find a world where he can make his way; it will be, he thinks, a world utterly unlike this inhuman one. And he will go alone, like a lonely dragon. When in act 5 the appeals to Coriolanus come to save Rome, they will come in the proper sequence of significance and value: Cominius, Menenius, Volumnia (accompanied by Virgilia, Valeria, young Martius). The interesting point is that the order of the sequence then is exactly opposite to the order of the sequence in 3.2 and 3.3: Volumnia, Menenius, Cominius.

* * * * *

Act 4 opens with Coriolanus saying farewell to his primary supporters: Volumnia, Menenius, Cominius. Virgilia, his wife, is also present, though almost silent. We are surprised and at least momentarily pleased to find that Coriolanus has recovered his composure. As he tries to cheer up those he must leave behind, his behavior is now mild, quite civilized, affectionate: ". . . my sweet wife, my dearest mother, and/My friends of noble touch"(4.1.48-49). Don't fret; he will be all right: "I shall be lov'd when I am lack'd"(4.1.15). He seems to sincerely believe that, once he has left, Rome will rack his value and come to appreciate his worth. But, more narrowly, his comment would seem to imply that those who love him dearly now will love him more dearly when he is gone. But they won't hear from him, and he won't hear from them for a long time. The trenchant irony is that these four will trade upon his love for them when, because of him, Roman lives will be in great danger.

Coriolanus is on stage for the greater part of seven consecutive scenes (acts 2 and 3 and 4.1). After being absent for two scenes, he returns in 4.4, in appearance a completely different man, *in mean apparel, disguis'd and muffled*. We learn that he has been dwelling out of doors, "I' th' city of kites and crows"(4.5.43). The world elsewhere was not at all what he expected. As Aristotle observes, a person who can't live in society is either a god or a beast. Coriolanus couldn't live in Rome because he was too much like a god; now he cannot live in Rome because he is too much like a beast. Like Lear, who falls asleep on stage in 3.6 and who is absent until he returns in 4.6 as a mad king and the natural fool of fortune, Coriolanus returns to the action much changed. Coriolanus may not have been wounded in the earlier battle, but he has been much abused during his lonely banishment in the wilderness: his "mean" apparel signifies his emotional state. His new view of society, like Lear's and Timon's in act 4 of their respective plays, is harsh, radical, unrelenting, as Coriolanus's soliloquy in 4.4 makes clear:

> O world, thy slippery turns! Friends now fast sworn,
> Whose double bosoms seems to wear one heart,
> Whose hours, whose bed, whose meal and exercise
> Are still together, who twin, as 'twere, in love
> Unseparable, shall within this hour,
> On a dissension of a doit, break out
> To bitterest enmity; so, fellest foes,
> Whose passions and whose plots have broke their sleep
> To take the one the other, by some chance,
> Some trick not worth an egg, shall grow dear friends
> And interjoin their issues. So with me,
> My birthplace [hate] I, and my love's upon
> This enemy town. I'll enter. If he slay me,
> He does fair justice; if he give me way,
> I'll do his country service.

> (4.4.12-26)

The situation here reflects the situation in 2.3. At that time he wore the gown of humility, gave a soliloquy, and confronted nameless citizens; here he wears mean apparel, gives a soliloquy, and confronts nameless servants. In the first soliloquy he mentioned common men, Hob and Dick; here he speaks of friends and foes. There he said it would be better to die and starve rather than to go forward with the charade; here, after almost starving and dying, he is ready to go forward to betrayal and death. There he was forced to play a role determined by Roman custom; here he assumes a role that violates the behavior expected of a guest. His willfulness was muffled in 2.3; he is muffled in 4.4. The gown of humility enabled Coriolanus to become a consul of Rome in act 2 (and to lose that office in 3.3); the mean apparel enables him to become the chief enemy of Rome in act 4 (and to save it in act 5).

The tribunes affected Coriolanus's destiny in the first half of the play; Aufidius affects his destiny in the second half.

Act 3.3 is from the viewpoint of the tribunes; 4.4 is from the viewpoint of Coriolanus. And just as we seem meant to challenge and criticize the viewpoint of the tribunes there, so we seem meant to challenge and criticize the viewpoint of Coriolanus here. But Coriolanus is a very different man now. Still for Coriolanus to say that a dear friend can become in a trice a bitter enemy contradicts the statement made in 4.1 that extremities are "the trier of spirits"(4.1.4). There he goes on to tell his mother:

> You were us'd to load me
> With precepts that would make invincible
> The heart that conn'd them.
>
> (4.1.9-11)

Coriolanus's spirits have been smothered; his heart has proved to be not invincible. His wife's immediate response (her only words in the scene) to the above comment is "O heavens! O heavens!"(4.1.12) In 4.4 Coriolanus has turned his back on Rome, on his mother's precepts, on his wife's heaven. He seems to have forgotten and rejected everything except what his voyage in the world ("O world") outside Rome has taught him. He is a truly desperate man, ready out of mere spite to commit suicide or to betray his birthplace. He seems quite mad, like Romeo, Hamlet, Othello, Macbeth, Lear, Antony, and Timon in act 4 of their respective plays.

Act 4.3 is a brief, choric scene thematically designed to prepare us for a new Coriolanus. Two men, who appear only in this scene, meet on the roadway: a Volscian named Adrian and a Roman named Nicanor. Right before Coriolanus enters in mean apparel, we are told that his banishment from Rome has had the effect he desired, that now Coriolanus is "lov'd" because he is "lack'd": ". . . the nobles receive so to heart the banishment of that worthy Coriolanus, that they are in a ripe aptness to take all power from the people, and to pluck from them their tribunes for ever"(4.3.21-24). According to Nicanor, Rome is ripe for civil disorder. Nicanor has brought this intelligence so that the Volscians can make a new assault upon Rome: without Coriolanus an uneasy

Rome is vulnerable. The immediate point of the scene is to introduce a Roman traitor, someone willing to betray his country to its enemy for, so far as we can tell, no substantive reason, like money or power. Nicanor's case is a reduced version of Coriolanus's; Adrian's case is a reduced version of Aufidius's: each man accepts an enemy for the use he can make of him. Like Nicanor, Coriolanus wants to bring down Rome.

Another kind of choric response is activated by relating the action inside Aufidius's house in act 4 to action earlier in the play. In 1.9 when Lartius asks for the name of the poor host, the newly named Coriolanus responds:

> By Jupiter, forgot!
> I am weary, yea, my memory is tir'd.
> Have we no wine here?
>
> (1.9.90-92)

Both in 1.9 and in 4.4 Coriolanus is weary, worn out. Right after Coriolanus gives his soliloquy in 4.4 and leaves the stage, a servingman enters with the following remark: "Wine, wine, wine! What service is here?/I think our fellows are asleep"(4.5.1-2). Coriolanus says that his memory is tired; the servingman says that his fellows are asleep. Both Coriolanus (1.9) and the servingman (4.5) mention wine. In each instance the issue concerns an absent host. Both Coriolanus (1.9) and the servingman (4.5) are interested in service. As usual, the situations illuminate each other.

But let us stress the immediate situation in act 4. As soon as Coriolanus leaves the stage in 4.4, *Music plays*, for the first and only time in the play.[10] In Shakespeare music generally symbolizes (see 4.7 of *King Lear*; 5.3 of *The Winter's Tale*; 5.1 of *The Tempest*) concord and harmony. In Shakespeare wine is often a soporific (see *Twelfth Night*, *Macbeth* ["nose-painting, sleep, and urine"(2.2.28)], *Antony and Cleopatra*) or the symbolic equivalent of love and power (see *Othello* and *The Tempest*). We may suppose that in *Coriolanus* wine is first a restorative (1.9) and then a soporific (4.5). By means of the servingman Shakespeare seems to be encouraging us to awaken (see Ariel's song in 2.1 of *The Tempest*). One point is that we should use the servingman's question ("What service is here?") to ponder Coriolanus's just-

completed assertion, "I'll do his country service"(4.4.26).
Strangely the symbolic answer to Coriolanus's announcement of
his traitorous service is music or harmony, as his service is
ironically implemented in act 5.

* * * * *

As it draws to a close, a Shakespeare tragedy follows a certain,
clear procedure. Although somewhat modified (as must be
expected) in the not-quite-typical *Romeo and Juliet* and *Antony and
Cleopatra*, a Shakespeare tragedy proceeds to its end in three parts
or stages or steps: it moves, we may say, from the heart to the
hand to the head. As might be expected, *Othello* provides the best
illustration of the procedure. There the parts or stages or steps are
presented in terms of the three final scenes: the first of these
scenes (4.3) ventilates the plight of the heart as presented in the
bedroom scene in the persons of Desdemona and Emilia; the
second (5.1) ventilates the plight of the hand as presented in the
street scene in the persons of Iago and Roderigo; the third (5.2)
ventilates the plight of the head as presented in the judgment scene
in the person of Othello. Othello's fate as tragic hero encompasses
those of the subsidiary heart and hand.

Since Hamlet is a son and a prince, Macbeth a husband and a
usurper, Lear a father and a king, the procedure in each of these
tragedies is modified accordingly. In part, the end of *Coriolanus*
proceeds as it does because the tragic hero is a son, a husband, a
father, a friend. But the public Coriolanus is also a kind of prince,
a kind of usurper, a kind of king. The essential point is that the
procedure is not much different in *Coriolanus* from what it is in
Hamlet, *Macbeth*, *King Lear*. *Coriolanus* ends with four scenes:
a long 5.3 presents the heart; 5.4, 5.5 and the beginning of 5.6
present the hand; the rest of 5.6 presents the head. Thus, as in the
other tragedies, the action proceeds from the plight of the heart to
the plight of the various hands, to the plight of the head. It
culminates in the death of the head. Like the other tragic heroes,
Coriolanus commits a kind of suicide.

The long 5.3 is from the perspective of the friendly foes,
Coriolanus and Aufidius. Aufidius speaks only three times in the

scene: five lines, before the entrance of the women and young
Martius; one line ("I was mov'd withal"[5.3.194]), after
Coriolanus capitulates to the appeal of the heart; an aside ("I am
glad thou has set thy mercy and thy honor/At difference in thee.
Out of that I'll work/Myself a former fortune"[5.3.199-202]"),
near the end. For us, if not for Coriolanus, Aufidius is an ominous
presence: we have listened to his persistent animosity toward his
enemy in 1.2; 1.8; 1.10; 4.7. At least Coriolanus recognizes the
extreme danger of his heartfelt, willful action:

> O my mother, mother! O!
> You have won a happy victory to Rome;
> But, for your son, believe it—O, believe it—
> Most dangerously you have with him prevail'd,
> If not most mortal to him. But let it come.
>   (5.3.185-89)

Coriolanus is acutely aware that his onetime enemy, though now
a confederate, is monitoring the event, and he seems to be asking
Aufidius to "Stand to me in this cause"(5.3.199). Having exposed
his heart, he tries to retain his soldierly honor.

As we are led through the final three stages of *Coriolanus*,
individual perspectives are paraded forth. We readily identify
Volumnia's Coriolanus, Virgilia's Coriolanus, Valeria's
Coriolanus, young Martius's Coriolanus: we see the tragic hero as
son, husband, friend, father. Having considered him as a son
(5.1), Menenius now thinks of Coriolanus (5.4) as a dragon with
wings; Sicinius is deeply fearful of the new Coriolanus and then
relieved that Coriolanus has relented; Aufidius thinks of
Coriolanus as a danger and a threat, someone to be eliminated. In
5.6 Aufidius rightly calls Coriolanus a traitor, a boy, a braggart,
a villain. All of these "reduced" Coriolanuses are at the service of
insisting that we accommodate them all. Only the audience can do
that. Only we have heard the soliloquies in 2.3 and 4.4; only we
can be attentive enough to comprehend the nature and the purpose
of the final scene.

Like the last scene of the other tragedies, the last scene of
Coriolanus, 5.6, which is from the perspective of Aufidius, is a
public spectacle, devoid of asides and soliloquies. In 3.3 we are
meant to criticize the perspective of the tribunes by our instructed

awareness of Coriolanus's condition and plight; in 5.6 we must criticize the perspective of Aufidius by our advanced awareness of Coriolanus's more desperate plight. In 3.3 Coriolanus was accompanied by friends and supporters (Cominius, Menenius, senators); here he is alone among his enemies, the family and friends of people he has killed. In 3.3, though he was unaware of them, Coriolanus had options (to be fined, banished, killed); here he has no options: Aufidius intends to kill him. In 3.3 Coriolanus still believed that there was a world elsewhere; here he knows that that belief was only a foolish illusion. The iterated "It shall be so" of 3.3 has by now acquired an unrelieved sense of inevitability. All he has left is death. But he does what he can to control, to modify, and to change the end that Aufidius intends.

At the end of *Othello* the tragic hero seizes an opportunity, grants himself an occasion, and kills himself. In front of an audience of onstage men, Othello justifies his past behavior and then re-creates a past event and kills himself with an unexpected weapon. Othello judges himself and then sacrifices himself to his dead wife, the redemptive saint. Coriolanus—knowing the hopelessness of his position and repentant of his sin against his mother, wife, friend, child—willfully and deliberately baits Aufidius into action. He becomes a kind of conspirator. In 3.3 Coriolanus's anger, prompted by Sicinius, was real; here it is an act, a deliberate display, a conscious use of an episode from his past. Coriolanus is manipulating Aufidius in order to make himself a butchered Caesar. He is being politic. It is only appropriate that the specific event he invokes from the past is the one that earned him the surname Coriolanus:

> If you have writ your annals true, 'tis there
> That, like an eagle in a dove-cote, I
> [Flutter'd] your Volscians in Corioles.
> Alone I did it. "Boy"!

> (5.6.113-16)

And Aufidius, who intended to perform a justified assassination, is made to feel the guilt of a murderer: "My rage is gone,/And I am struck with sorrow"(5.6.146-47). His pity overwhelms his wrath.

NOTES

1. After reviewing the critical commentary on *Coriolanus*, we must say that it is worse than we expected, though Harold Goddard is always worth reading. The best single piece of criticism that we have come across, though it is severely limited, is by Joyce Van Dyke: "Making a Scene: Language and Gesture in 'Coriolanus,'" *Shakespeare Survey* 30 (1977), 135-146. But then we are concerned with meaning, not, as so many of the critics are, with significance.

2. The stage directions derive from the Folio.

3. It is true that Virgilia may just be expressing her wifely concern. Volumnia's response, however, is of interest: "O, he is wounded, I thank the gods for't"(2.1.121).

4. See *Design and Closure*, 145-164.

5. See *1 Henry IV* the Prince says the following: "Percy is but my factor. . ." (3.2.147).

6. See Harry Levin's Introduction to the Pelican *Coriolanus* (Baltimore: Penguin Books, 1956), 24.

7. For a more complete discussion of the nature of Shakespeare tragedy, see *Design and Closure*, 1-7.

8. See *Design and Closure*, particularly the chapters on *Hamlet* (189-215), *Macbeth* (217-40), and *Antony and Cleopatra* (295-326).

9. The last scene of act 3 (3.5) of *Romeo and Juliet* is from Juliet's perspective; the last scene of act 3 (3.13) of *Antony and Cleopatra* is from Cleopatra's perspective.

10. The play does contain drums and trumpets, a sennet, flourishes, and a dead march.

12

The First Scene of Act 2:
The Beginning of an Extended Episode

It seems quite clear that a Shakespeare play begins with the plot problem, however narrowly or widely it is described. Consider the very beginning of *Hamlet*, of *Macbeth*, of *King Lear*. A crucial piece of plot information is given at once: the ghost of the dead king has been seen; the witches are going to meet with Macbeth; King Lear is going to divide his kingdom. In the first act all of the characters who will be most closely involved in the ensuing action are introduced: in *Hamlet* these characters are Horatio, the Ghost, Claudius, Gertrude, Laertes, Polonius, Hamlet, Ophelia; in *Macbeth* they are Duncan, Malcolm, Macbeth, Banquo, Lady Macbeth, a silent Macduff;[1] in *King Lear* they are Gloucester, Kent, Edmund, Lear, Goneril, Regan, Cordelia, Albany, Cornwall, Edgar, the Fool. With exquisite care the first act of a Shakespeare play chronicles and dramatizes the essential plot problem and introduces all of the major characters.

Not surprisingly, the first scene of the second act of a Shakespeare play is also important.[2] But it presents what seems at first glance to be of only secondary consideration: it changes the first-act emphasis; it is a second beginning. In part the purpose of the first scene of act 2 seems to be to document the nature of the world beneath the plot-shaken world of the first act: it supplies needed, explanatory information. But the more important structural truth is that the first scene of act 2 is the first in a series of sometimes ranging but always causally related actions culminating at the end of act 3. Generally, acts 2 and 3 of a Shakespeare play function as a developed, extended episode.

The extended episode in *Hamlet* begins with Polonius on stage; it moves to the arrival of the players at court, the staging of the Mousetrap, and the reaction of the main characters to the Mousetrap; it ends with the murder of Polonius and the last appearance of the Ghost. The extended episode in *Macbeth* begins with Banquo and Fleance; it moves to the murder of Duncan and then Banquo; it ends (if the choric 3.6 and 3.7 are not considered) with the appearance of Banquo's ghost at the banquet. The extended episode in *King Lear* begins with Edmund; it moves to the arrival of Cornwall and Regan, then Kent and Oswald, then Lear and the Fool, then Goneril to Gloucester's castle and then to the discovery of Edgar as Tom on the heath outside the castle; it ends with Edmund's accompanying Goneril off stage and with Gloucester's eyes being plucked out on stage. In each of these three plays the extended episode begins with a character (Polonius, Banquo, Edmund) that motivates the action of the extended episode. It ends with the impact that that initial character has had on the extended and enhanced plot problem: Polonius is killed, and the Ghost appears; Banquo is killed, and the Ghost appears; Edmund is rewarded with the office of earl, and Gloucester, disgraced and victimized, is turned into a ghost of himself.

As a close thematic antecedent to these great historical tragedies, *1 Henry IV* also concerns itself with a kingdom in turmoil. As the beginning of its extended episode, 2.1 of *1 Henry IV* is interesting and pertinent. The action is simple, unvarnished, all in prose: two carriers meet in an innyard in the early morning and prepare to set off for London; they are joined by Gadshill, one of the instigators of a robbery (see 1.2), who tries to borrow the lantern of each carrier; he is then joined by the chamberlain, who confirms the information that a rich franklin will be traveling to London; Gadshill and his cohorts will rob the franklin and give a share of the money to the chamberlain.

In keeping with its blunt, untrammeled action, the scene has a clearly marked structure. Although his voice is heard, the ostler doesn't appear. The scene has only four characters: the two carriers, Gadshill, the chamberlain. The scene has three sections: after speaking to the offstage ostler, one carrier is joined by the other; Gadshill enters and speaks to the carriers; as the carriers leave, the chamberlain enters. When the carriers leave the stage, they take their lanterns with them, and thus the second half of the scene takes place in symbolic darkness. The extended episode will draw to a close in the last scene of act 3, when Falstaff, who helped steal the money from the true men, and Prince Harry, who (accompanied by Poins) then stole the money from Falstaff and his men, meet in the tavern for the last time, before setting off for the battlefield.

And so the seemingly unremarkable 2.1 of *1 Henry IV* is resonant with meaning and signifiance; it is symbolic. For the chamberlain, who ought to act like a responsible servant or steward, is betraying one of his guests to thieves, who are really not what they seem but "nobility and tranquility, burgomasters, and great oney'rs"(2.1.75-76). One thematic point in 2.1 is that the roles of true men and thieves are not distinct: ". . . *homo* is a common name to all men"(2.1.95). The tavern stands for the court; this particular house stands for the commonwealth: "This house is turn'd upside down since [Richard II] died"(2.1.10-11). By his actions at the end of the play Prince Harry will turn the commonwealth right-side-up. We further notice that time in the scene seems to go backwards: the first carrier says that it is four o'clock; when Gadshill enters, the carrier says that it is two o'clock. Gadshill and the chamberlain are in the dark: ". . . you are more beholding to the night than to fern-seed for your walking invisible"(2.1.88-90). By the end of the extended episode "The money is paid back again"(3.3.178). And by the end of the play Richard II in the person of Prince Harry will kill Bullingbroke in the person of Hotspur (see 3.2). As the structure of 2.1 seems to predict, the end of *1 Henry IV* reverses the end of *Richard II* by going backwards and redeeming the murder of a rightful king.[3]

When we turn to 2.1 of *Hamlet*, we note that, like 2.1 of *1 Henry IV*, its action is simple and uncluttered; its bipartite structure is distinct. As a subplot scene it deals with a devious functionary of a rotten institution: the chamberlain of a villainous house; the lord chamberlain of a villainous Denmark. A main difference between the two scenes is that two of the three characters in the *Hamlet* scene are major (Polonius and Ophelia) and that, like 1.3 (an Ophelia scene), 2.1 of *Hamlet* is an essential-character scene. One of the requisites of such a scene is that the relevant character remain on stage throughout the scene, as Polonius does.[4] In 2.1 of *Hamlet* we witness the behavior of a devious, suspicious, political, roundabout, platitudinous, opinionated, heavy-handed, old, forgetful, and loyal subject of a usurping monarch. As everyone acknowledges, the portrait of Polonius, both as an individual and as a type, is brilliantly executed.

And we readily see that this portrayal of Polonius serves to document the world beneath the shattering action of the first act of *Hamlet*. And if we are prepared to see the scene as being choric, we quickly note that "By indirection find direction out"(2.1.63) is the dominant mode of the extended episode: everything is roundabout, circuitous; nothing is done simply or directly; the characters proceed by indirection, like the curving of a bowling ball toward the jack. For the numerous activities ("gaming . . . drinking, fencing, swearing, quarrelling,/Drabbing"[2.1.24-26]) referred to in the first half of the scene relate to activities later in the extended episode (Hamlet will "fence" with Rosencrantz and Guildenstern; he will quarrel with Polonius) as well as to the activities of drinking and fencing in act 5. Or, in respect to the numerous games mentioned in the scene, Polonius, Claudius, and Hamlet will be like fishermen: Polonius wants to catch his son; Claudius wants to catch Hamlet; Hamlet wants to catch Claudius. Specifically, using "[a] bait of falsehood [to] take this carp of truth"(2.1.60) relates to 3.1, in which Claudius and Polonius employ Ophelia as bait to find out Hamlet's truth. The notion of a game like tennis alerts us to see that *Hamlet* is like a game of blindman's buff, an image reinforced by Ophelia's remark:

> That done, [Hamlet] lets me go,
> And with his head over his shoulder turn'd,
> He seem'd to find his way without his eyes,
> For out a'doors he went without their helps,
> And to the last bended their light on me.
> (2.1.93-97)

In addition, the notion that can be derived from her comment is that throughout the play Hamlet goes forward while looking backward at some object of veneration (Ophelia or the Ghost): he is so obsessed with the past that he does not see where he is going.

Thus if 2.1 of *Hamlet* is considered as being choric, we can understand the symbolic significance of Polonius's "He closes with you in this consequence"(2.1.45), which is iterated twice as "closes in the consequence"(2.1.51,52). At the end of 2.1 Polonius and Ophelia set off to tell Claudius the news of Hamlet's love-madness. The consequence of that action will be the murder of Polonius in 3.4: the extended episode will end in that consequence. Polonius's going with Ophelia to the king will *close in* or prevent any consequence other than the murder of Polonius. And, beyond the extended episode, the murder of Polonius will lead to (or *close in*) the suicide of Ophelia at the end of act 4 and the killing of Laertes at the end of act 5. Of major importance is the realization of a different kind of consequence: the murder of Polonius will turn Hamlet into a murderer like Claudius and will turn Laertes into an avenger like Hamlet.

In 1.3 Laertes declares to Ophelia that he will not become a libertine, and nowhere in the play is he presented as being profligate. In the graveyard (5.1) Hamlet wildly professes his love for the dead Ophelia, but nowhere *in the play* is he presented on stage as being lovesick. It is therefore surprising that the Laertes that Polonius has in mind in 2.1 is an incipient reprobate and that the Hamlet that Ophelia describes in 2.1 is a despondent, rejected lover. We may well say that Polonius is misrepresenting and slandering his son and that Hamlet was only play-acting in Ophelia's closet (Claudius will conclude in 3.1 that Hamlet is not lovesick); still it is very surprising that the Laertes and the Hamlet imaged in 2.1 are classic types, cliché figures. Is that what they basically are? Are we to conclude that the action of the extended episode will turn Hamlet from despairing lover into a murderer and will then turn Laertes from wastrel into an avenger? In his hesitation to kill his guilty enemy (Claudius) at prayer, Hamlet is morally too precise, as a lover would be; in his eagerness to kill his guilty enemy (Hamlet) even in a church, Laertes is morally brazen, as a reprobate would be. Thus one meaningful shock of

2.1, considered as a choric scene, is that these otherwise typical young men will *close in* the consequence of a slaughterhouse.

In design 2.1 of *Macbeth* is like 2.1 of *1 Henry IV*: each scene has four characters; each scene has two main parts. Banquo and Fleance come on stage; they meet Macbeth and a servant; Macbeth, left alone on stage, delivers a soliloquy.[5] Each scene takes place at night. Instead of two lanterns, the *Macbeth* scene has two torches. Like Gadshill and the chamberlain, Macbeth in the second half of the scene is in the dark. It is interesting that in the preceding scene Lady Macbeth refers to Duncan's two grooms as "his two chamberlains"(1.7.63). Both 2.1 of *1 Henry IV* and 2.1 of *Macbeth* begin with a time notation: "Heigh-ho! an'it be not four by the day, I'll be hang'd"(2.1.1-2); "How goes the night, boy?/The moon is down, I have not heard the clock"(2.1.1-2). As in 2.1 of *1 Henry IV*, time in the *Macbeth* scene seems to go backwards. In the first half of the scene it is after midnight; in the second half of the scene it is the witching hour: "Now o'er the one half world/Nature seems dead"(2.1.49-50). As in *1 Henry IV* the commonwealth that Macbeth is in the process of turning upside-down will be turned right-side-up by Malcolm and Macduff.

Act 2.1 of *Macbeth* is like 2.1 of *Hamlet* in its basic two-part structure and in its use of two main characters: Polonius and Ophelia; Banquo and Macbeth. The doubles Laertes and Hamlet are of primary concern in one scene; the doubles Banquo and Macbeth are of primary concern in the other scene. As in 1.3 Polonius is concerned about the welfare of his son; Banquo must be concerned about the welfare of his son. Both Reynaldo and Fleance are new to their respective plays. Hamlet behaves as he does at this time, so we are told, because of Ophelia; Macbeth behaves as he does in 2.1 because of Lady Macbeth. Hamlet goes blindly forward; Macbeth is led on by the fatal vision of a bloody dagger. As we expect, Banquo feels a "heavy summons"(2.1.6) but does not want to respond or give in to it; Macbeth answers the summons to murder Duncan when "the bell invites"(2.1.62) him. Act 2.1 presents the only view of a lovesick Hamlet; 2.1 of *Macbeth* presents the only view of an hallucinating Macbeth: the Ghost in 3.4 is real, though only Macbeth (like Hamlet in 3.4 of that play) sees him.

Unlike 2.1 of the other plays under discussion, 2.1 of *Macbeth* is one in a series of closely related scenes having to do with main plot, rather than with just subplot, action: Macbeth is present in 2.1. Still, this 2.1, like the other 2.1 scenes, changes or interrupts the flow of the action: we don't expect Banquo and Fleance. And, again, 2.1 of *Macbeth* is the beginning of an extended episode. In the scene the interchange between Banquo and Macbeth concerning the weird sisters makes it clear that (no matter what Macbeth says) both men are thinking about what the weird sisters have predicted: Banquo will be the progenitor of kings. The key feature of the 2.1 scene is that of props and attendant symbolic action: the torches, Banquo's sword, whatever it is that Banquo also gives Fleance ("Take thee that too"[2.1.5]), the diamond that Banquo received from Duncan and now gives to Macbeth as a gift for Lady Macbeth, the dagger that appears as a vision, the blood that apparently appears on the dagger, the dagger that Macbeth draws, the bell that invites him to murder Duncan. A related feature is that of Macbeth's allegorized image of himself as "wither'd Murther"(2.1.52).

At the end of his soliloquy in the preceding scene (1.7), Macbeth remarks, "I have no spur/To prick the sides of my intent, but only/Vaulting ambition, which o'erleaps itself,/And falls on the other—"(1.7.25-28)[6] And then Lady Macbeth appears. It is a commonplace of *Macbeth* criticism that Lady Macbeth is the spur that urges Macbeth on, as if he were a horse. Moreover, it seems useful to see Lady Macbeth as also "Vaulting ambition"(1.7.27). In part ambitious Macbeth is prepared to kill Duncan because he wants to satisfy his wife's ambition to become queen.[7] Applying this same choric strategy to 2.1, we may then say that when Banquo says, "Give me my sword"(2.1.9) and Macbeth appears, Macbeth should be seen as Banquo's sword. In killing Duncan, Macbeth will be acting as Banquo's sword: Macbeth must kill Duncan and become king before Banquo can become the progenitor of kings. Then Macbeth identifies himself to Banquo as "a friend"(2.1.11). In killing Duncan, Macbeth will unwittingly be befriending Banquo. Thus 2.1 enables us to envision Macbeth's symbolic progress in the play as moving from sword to friend to dagger to "wither'd Murther"(2.1.52) to "fatal bellman"(2.2.3).

Act 2.1 of *Hamlet* is a kind of continuation of 1.3: both scenes concern the subplot Polonius family. Act 2.1 of *King Lear* is a kind of continuation of 1.2: both scenes concern the subplot Gloucester family. Act 1.3 of *Hamlet* is from the viewpoint of Ophelia; 2.1 is from the viewpoint of Polonius. In *King Lear* both subplot scenes are from the viewpoint of Edmund. Reynaldo, in his only appearance in the play, begins the *Hamlet* scene; Curan, in his only appearance, begins the *King Lear* scene. In the *Hamlet* scene both Laertes and Hamlet may be misrepresented and slandered; in the *King Lear* scene Edgar is misrepresented and slandered. Like the other 2.1 scenes under discussion, 2.1 of *King Lear* has two main parts. In the first half Edmund, after speaking to Curan, calls forth Edgar and speaks with him; he then speaks with his father, Gloucester. In the second half of the scene Edmund and Gloucester welcome Cornwall and Regan to the castle.

Act 2.1 of *1 Henry IV* begins in the dark with one and then two lanterns; 2.1 of *Macbeth* begins in the dark with one and then two torches; 2.1 of *King Lear* begins in the dark; Gloucester will enter with torches. The action of the *King Lear* scene, however, does not go backwards: it goes forward at a steady pace. Edmund and Edgar draw their swords, and after Edgar has run away, Edmund wounds himself in the arm, drawing blood. This action closes in the consequence of the treatment of Gloucester in 3.7 and the deaths of Goneril and Edmund in the last scene of the play. The most notable feature of the scene is the change in deportment of Gloucester toward Edgar from the first half of the scene to the second. For Edmund the result of his actions in 1.2 and 2.1 (revealing Edgar's "evil" intentions) is to be taken into the Duke's service:

> For you, Edmund,
> Whose virtue and obedience doth this instant
> So much commend itself, you shall be ours.
> Natures of such deep trust we shall much need;
> You we first seize on.
>
> (2.1.112-16)

We have never intended to suggest that Shakespeare, the least slavish of writers, depended slavishly upon dramatic formulae for his plays. We have meant to indicate that it was a useful practice for Shakespeare to have principles of organization and structure at his service in much the way that a sonneteer uses the formal structure of a sonnet as a directive and a guide. The substantive point is that, if we are to understand Shakespeare, we must closely observe his explicit systems of dramatic organization. For Shakespeare, the most resourceful of writers, was intent upon being understood. We have elsewhere argued for the significance of Shakespeare's mutually inclusive systems: five acts; three stages; two parts. To consider acts 2 and 3 as an extended episode is not meant to deny or to denigrate the three readily perceived systems. It is simply to proffer an organizational refinement. After a concentrated first act, in which the plot problem is ventilated and the principal characters introduced, the next two acts lead up to the crisis of the play, which occurs near the end of act 3. It seems necessary and useful to consider these two acts as a kind of unit and to see the first scene of that unit as performing a significant choric function.

NOTES

1. According to the Folio, Macduff is on stage but silent in 1.4.

2. For instance, the following main characters are introduced in 2.1 of their respective plays: the King of France, the Dauphin, Constance, and Arthur in *King John*; York in *Richard II*; Duke Senior in *As You Like It*; Sebastian in *Twelfth Night*; the King of France in *All's Well*; Achilles, Ajax, and Thersites in *Troilus and Cressida*; Montano in *Othello*; Pompey in *Antony and Cleopatra*; the court group in *The Tempest*. The following choric events take place in 2.1 of various plays: Gaunt's panegyric on England in *Richard II*; the dance in *Much Ado*; the uses-of-adversity speech in *As You Like It*; the tempest in *Othello*; the spider-in-the-cup speech in *The Winter's Tale*.

3. For a more complete discussion of this phenomenon, see *Design and Closure*, 145-69.

4. See *Design and Closure*, 189-212.

5. See the stage directions in the Folio: *Enter BANQUO, and FLEANCE, with a Torch before him*; *Enter MACBETH, and a SERVANT with a Torch*.

6. Macbeth's "Vaulting ambition" will "fall" on the "other," Lady Macbeth.

7. See *Design and Closure*, 217-240.

13

Hamlet, *Macbeth*, and *King Lear* as a Trilogy

In spite of nagging textual problems and the efforts of chronic disbelievers, *Hamlet*, *Macbeth*, and *King Lear* must be regarded as exemplars of artistic achievement. Still, as with Shakespeare's two historical tetralogies or the set of Roman plays or the four comedies that may be considered as a sequence,[1] these three famous tragedies are not just better understood but considerably enriched when considered together as a kind of sequence or trilogy. They complement and supplement and reinforce one another. Each tragedy concentrates on a royal-family plight in the context of an outside political threat. Each protagonist has a single office and a single role: Hamlet as prince and son; Macbeth as usurper and husband; Lear as king and father.[2] All three dramatic masterpieces employ the same structural and thematic patterns and systems. A modification in a pattern or a system is in large part a consequence of the particular office and role each protagonist has and holds: prince-son; usurper-husband; king-father.

The *Macbeth* plot is closely comparable to the *Hamlet* plot: in *Hamlet* the king has just been murdered; in *Macbeth* the king will soon be murdered. A prince-son (Hamlet, Malcolm [the Prince of Cumberland]) is displaced as designated king by a usurper-husband (Claudius, Macbeth); the prince is then directly opposed to that interloper; the prince subsequently manages to destroy his enemy.

Because their worlds are vastly different and because the emphasis is on the office of prince and the role of son in the first play and is on the office of usurper and the role of husband in the second play, *Hamlet* and *Macbeth* are not usually perceived as being as comparable as they in fact are. In the much different world of *King Lear* the primary emphasis is on the king office (as the title of the play indicates) and the father role. Although the king is not murdered, he is displaced and pushed out of doors at the beginning. Unlike Hamlet or Macbeth, King Lear will be finally reinstated. The end of the play is meant to echo and mirror its beginning and to verify that Lear is again king and father: there can be, it seems, no other reason for the dead Goneril and Regan to be brought back on stage and their faces covered.

In *Hamlet* the prince-son neglects the ghost-father's urging to kill the usurper; in order to prove the truth of the charge made by the ghost-father, the prince arranges to observe Claudius's response to a "vision" of the recent past, and, now sure of the usurper's guilt, the prince can and does act; he, however, kills not Claudius, the usurper, but Polonius, the old father. Hamlet could have killed the "king" in 3.3; instead, he kills a defenseless old man-father in 3.4. In *Macbeth* the usurper-husband resists his wife's insistent urging to kill the king; then, after vacillating, he follows the vision of a bloody dagger and commits the repugnant deed of killing a defenseless old man-father-king. Whereas Hamlet feels no guilt at his haphazard murder of old Polonius, Macbeth is shattered by his murder of the king: "Had I but died an hour before this chance,/I had liv'd a blessed time"(2.3.91-92). Hamlet madly responds to the appearance of his father's ghost in 3.4; Macbeth madly responds to the appearance of Banquo's ghost in 3.4.

In 4.4, as Hamlet is on his way from Denmark to England, he concludes his last soliloquy in the play: "O, from this time forth,/My thoughts be bloody, or be nothing worth!"(4.4.65-66) In 4.1, as Macbeth ends his second and last encounter with the weird sisters, he remarks, ". . . give to th' edge o' th' sword/His wife, his babes, and all unfortunate souls/That trace [Macduff] in his line. No boasting like a fool;/This deed I'll do before this purpose cool"(4.1.151-54). We readily note how similar Macbeth's situation here is to Hamlet's: both men reach a grim determination to do a bloody deed; both then disappear for about a half-hour of stage time.³ Hamlet, we feel, ought to turn back and kill the usurper; Macbeth, we feel, ought to try to seek out and kill Fleance, the future father of kings. Neither acts in a way we might well expect; that is, neither does what he could do to serve his particular cause and to effect, from his perspective, a desired result.

Hamlet is frustrated by the sudden, unexpected "vision" of an assertive, direct, "honest" prince, Fortinbras;⁴ Macbeth is frustrated by the sudden, unexpected "vision" of a line of future kings of Scotland, the descendants of Banquo, the friend he has just had murdered. Out of their frustration, Hamlet, who has just murdered Polonius, and Macbeth, who has killed Duncan and has just had Banquo murdered, decide, right before they leave the stage, to act again, *now*: they respond to what they have just seen and heard with an expression of quick determination. But Hamlet and Macbeth do not act as or for themselves: they will not be directly involved in the violence that will shortly take place on stage.⁵

The fourth-act plight of Hamlet as frustrated prince-son and the fourth-act plight of Macbeth as frustrated usurper-husband will be resolved for them and by them when they return to the stage in act 5. There Hamlet will foolishly agree to engage in a duel with Laertes, the son of the man he recently murdered. Macbeth will foolishly leave the secure castle for the battlefield, where, as he should guess, he may well meet Macduff, the husband and father of the family murdered in 4.2. The death of Ophelia in part prompts Hamlet's final realization that ". . . the readiness is all"(5.2.222); the death of Lady Macbeth prompts Macbeth's final despair: "To-morrow, and to-morrow, and to-morrow. . . ."(5.5.19). While Hamlet is off stage, Laertes becomes the protege of Claudius; while Macbeth is off stage, Macduff becomes the protege of Malcolm.

Hamlet sees the resolute Fortinbras in 4.4; Macbeth sees the dispiriting apparition of a line of kings in 4.1; Lear visualizes the absent Goneril and Regan in 3.6. After "trying" Goneril and Regan for their crimes against him, Lear comments, "Make no noise, make no noise, draw the curtains. So, so; we'll go to supper i' the morning"(3.6.83-84). After a declaration of fierce determination against his evil daughters, Lear sleeps and then disappears. As in the other two plays, violence shortly follows. In *King Lear* this violence takes the form of Gloucester's eyes being plucked out in 3.7. In 3.6 Lear is frustrated. His daughters have escaped his wrath: he can put them on trial, but he cannot punish them. Lear's initial actions, we may say, have led to this frustration and to this exhaustion. In 3.6, almost as soon as Lear sleeps, Edgar delivers a soliloquy.

Like Hamlet and Macbeth, Edgar (instead of Lear) will fight a deadly swordfight against a protege: Edmund is the protege of "King" Cornwall.[6] At the end, like Hamlet and Macbeth, Edgar will be only a soldier, a hand, a sword. Hamlet will fight for his father, the elder Hamlet; Edgar will fight for his godfather, the elderly Lear. The main structural and thematic point is that the end of each play is implicit *in the moment* that Hamlet, Macbeth, or Lear makes a resolution or reaches a kind of conclusion and then leaves the stage. Lear, for example, is with his Fool in 3.6; he will be with his "poor fool"(5.3.306), Cordelia, at the end. He sleeps in the middle; he awakens to the heavenly Cordelia at the end of act 4; he will "sleep" again at the end of the play. Lear follows Cordelia, as Kent will follow Lear.

Once Hamlet in 4.4 decides on action and the shedding of blood, Ophelia, having been absent from the stage since the Mousetrap in 3.2, arrives back on stage, in 4.5, distracted and distraught: mad Ophelia, no longer human, is the failed instrument of Hamlet's rise from son-prince to husband-father-king. Once Macbeth in 4.1 decides to destroy Macduff's family, Lady Macduff and her son arrive on stage in 4.2 and are murdered: the dead mother and child represent or signify Macbeth's aborted future as husband-father-king. Between the time that Lear sleeps (3.6) and then arrives back on stage (4.6), his three daughters appear on stage in individual scenes: Goneril, in 4.2; Cordelia, in 4.4, Regan, in 4.5. Like Ophelia and Lady Macduff and, as we will discover, Lady Macbeth, Lear's three daughters have been forsaken; they are isolated and alone. In 4.2, after Edmund leaves her, Goneril is rejected by Albany, her husband; as we learn in 4.3, Cordelia has been "forsaken" by France, her husband, and will not be received by her father, the shamed Lear. Cornwall, Regan's husband, is dead; in 4.5 we learn that Regan is fearful that the absent Edmund is in love with Goneril.

Those women who are of primary importance to the son Hamlet, to the husband Macbeth, and to the father Lear come on stage after Hamlet, Macbeth, and Lear have left it. Once the murderous Hamlet and Macbeth decide to be again bloody and once Lear, unable to be bloody, sleeps—once these protagonists express a resolution and leave the action, a daughter, a wife, and three "separated" wife-daughters come on stage, bereft, forsaken, frustrated. Each of the women in *King Lear* combines the uncomplicated roles of the other plays: daughter in *Hamlet*; wife in *Macbeth*. We can also say that the fierce declarations of Hamlet (4.4) and Macbeth (4.1) indicate a kind of unawareness, a turning away from reason and thought, a deliberate rejection of the head, a falling asleep. We note that Lear awakens to Cordelia in the sublime 4.7 and that each of the other "prospective" kings (Claudius, Malcolm) also "awakens" in the last scene of act 4 of each play.

It is interesting that the last scene of act 4 of *Hamlet* (4.7) and of act 4 of *Macbeth* (4.3) and the next-to-last scene of act 4 of *King Lear* (4.6) are closely comparable. Indeed all three scenes employ the same design and are intent upon clarifying plot as well as theme. The two men who begin each scene remain on stage throughout the scene: Claudius and Laertes in *Hamlet*; Malcolm and Macduff in *Macbeth*; Gloucester and Edgar in *King Lear*. Thus, in each instance, the action may be said to be from a double perspective; moreover, each scene dramatizes both a changing and a developing relationship between the two men. Each scene begins with an importunate "outsider" (Laertes, Macduff, Edgar) trying to get the other man (Claudius, Malcolm, Gloucester), an authority figure, to see a situation from the outsider's perspective: the outsider depends upon and needs the complicity of the authority figure. Laertes wants revenge upon Hamlet; Macduff wants Malcolm to lead a force against the tyrant, Macbeth; Edgar wants to cure his father, Gloucester, of despair. Though absent, Hamlet is mentioned by name six times; though absent, Macbeth is mentioned by name five times; Lear is briefly on stage, though changed, and, though unnamed, is referred to as king, by himself or others, six times.

In each scene the men test each other. The initial appeal by the outsider is affected in the middle of the scene by the sudden appearance of one person (who enters and then leaves) and then, toward the end of the scene, of another person (who enters and remains).[7] In *Hamlet* a messenger arrives with a letter from the newly returned Hamlet; Gertrude arrives with the news of Ophelia's death. In *Macbeth* a doctor enters with news about the saintly English king; Ross arrives with the news of the death of the Macduff family. In *King Lear*, Lear, followed by the gentleman who is searching for him, enters as mad king; Oswald arrives with the deliberate intention of killing, not King Lear, but the blind father, Gloucester. Out of manipulation (Claudius manipulates Laertes; Malcolm manipulates Macduff; Edgar manipulates Gloucester) emerges the person who will be engaged in the plot-needed swordfight in the last scene: Laertes-Hamlet; Macduff-Macbeth; Edgar-Edmund. Thus these testing scenes serve the purposes of a manipulative usurper (Claudius), of a manipulative prince (Malcolm), of a manipulative son (Edgar), and of a devastated and devastating king (Lear).

Thematically, once Edgar has Goneril's letter and may proceed against Edmund (4.6), the reunion between the father-king (Lear) and the daughter-queen (Cordelia) can take place (4.7). The main point is clear. A son and a husband are provisional roles: Hamlet wanted to become Ophelia's husband; Macbeth needed to become the father of a legitimate heir. A prince and a usurper are provisional offices, held upon sufferance: Hamlet hoped to become king; Macbeth needed to secure his stolen crown. A king is what Hamlet and Macbeth wanted to become: a father is the head of a family; a king is the head of a state. The tension between father and king is more definitive and less endangered than that between husband and usurper. In 4.7, Lear, now in safe hands, regains the authority, dignity, and majesty of old man-father-king. In the last scene of the play (5.3) Edgar replaces Lear in the necessary, ritualistic, public trial-by-combat, not as a prince or as a usurper or as a future king, but as Lear's knight: "Ripeness is all"(5.2.11).[8] At the end of the first two tragedies the provisional Hamlet and Macbeth are necessarily destroyed; Lear dies, not as an insecure prince-son (Hamlet) or as an insecure usurper-husband (Macbeth), but as a restored king-father-old man. To the alliance (in 4.7 of *Hamlet*, 4.3 of *Macbeth*, 4.6 of *King Lear*) between the head (Claudius-Malcolm-Gloucester) and the hand (Laertes-Macduff-Edgar) comes news of the heart or news from the heart: Gertrude reports the news of the death of Ophelia; Ross reports the news of the death of the Macduff family; Oswald, who is willing to carry out the dictates of Goneril and Regan, delivers to Edgar Goneril's declaration of love for Edmund. Claudius uses the death of Ophelia to strengthen Laertes's resolve to kill Hamlet; Malcolm uses the death of the Macduff family to strengthen Macduff's resolve to kill Macbeth; Lear's mad behavior causes Gloucester to lose the heart re-instilled in him by Edgar. Having killed Oswald and having received Goneril's letter, Edgar must give up any further intention of service to his again-distraught father, as 5.2 makes clear. Out of necessity, Edgar will become *The Knight*, a cold man of justice, who will serve Lear's cause.

With Ophelia and Lady Macbeth dead (Ophelia is not even mentioned in 5.2; Lady Macbeth is not mentioned on the battlefield),[9] Hamlet and Macbeth have no future: each has been reduced to a hand or a sword, like Edgar. In *Hamlet* Shakespeare seems to separate the human role (son and lover in 5.1) from the public office (prince in 5.2). In *Macbeth* Shakespeare separates the human role (husband and disillusioned man in 5.3 and 5.5) from the public office (usurper and tyrant on the battlefield). Hamlet "dies" as son before he is killed as prince: "Good night, sweet prince"(5.2.359). Macbeth "dies" as husband before he is killed as usurper: "Lay on, Macduff,/And damn'd be him that first cries, 'Hold, enough!'"(5.8.33-34) But Edgar, having filled the role of knight and having attained the office of Earl of Gloucester, may have a political future, but not as king.[10] Gloucester becomes the necessary private sacrifice to Edgar's rise; Edmund, who has stolen the role of legitimate son and the office of usurper, becomes the means toward Edgar's redemption.

In *Hamlet* or *Macbeth* the protagonist is killed by the man, the manipulated "opposite," that the protagonist most offended. In *King Lear* the offended man, Edgar, lives on. In *King Lear* Shakespeare heightens the casual but bloody duel (*Hamlet*) and the bloody swordfight (*Macbeth*) into a post-battle trial-by-combat. The end of a murderous prince-son and the end of a murderous husband-usurper are subsumed at last by the sublime end of an old man-father-king. The strategies of the first two plays serve to clarify the more difficult strategies of *King Lear*. And the artistic result is that Hamlet and Macbeth become elaborated parables of arrested development (prince-son; usurper-husband) and that Lear becomes an elaborated parable of paradoxical fulfillment as a human being (old man), and the head of the family (father), as the proper representative of the state (king). Thus, *King Lear* is the logical, elaborate consequence of the artistic strategies of *Hamlet* and *Macbeth*.

NOTES

1. For a more complete statement of this issue, see *Design and Closure*, 13-23.

2. This issue is more fully dealt with in the general context of Shakespeare tragedy in *Design and Closure*, 173-86.

3. "Hamlet is not in the play for 502 lines; Macbeth is not present for 436 lines." See *Design and Closure*, 175.

4. Horatio gives a cogent explanation of Fortinbras's intentions in 1.1.79-107. See Claudius's comments on Fortinbras in 1.2.17-25.

5. Off stage Hamlet ordered the destruction of Rosencrantz and Guildenstern.

6. In 2.1 Cornwall "seizes upon Edmund" as a protege because of his "good" services to Gloucester against Edgar.

7. The Gentleman is also on stage: in trying to rescue Lear, he prompts Lear's departure.

8. In 2.1 we are told that Edgar was one of Lear's knights: he is Lear's only knight at the end.

9. Malcolm does mention the "fiend-like queen"(5.9.35) in his last speech.

10. But see F. T. Flahiff, "Edgar: Once and Future King," *Some Facets of "King Lear"* (Toronto: U of Toronto P, 1974), 221-37.

14

Shakespeare's Four Great Tragedies:
"'Tis Time to Look About"

Young Hamlet loves a maid, Ophelia; middle-aged Macbeth loves
a wife, Lady Macbeth; old Lear loves a daughter, Cordelia. The
beloved woman precedes the man in death; her death, unlike his,
is private.[1] This woman-man death pattern is also a feature in
Othello, the fourth of the great tragedies. Like Macbeth, Othello
is middle-aged, a husband and a general. At about the same time
in each tragedy, (near the end of act 4), Shakespeare dramatizes a
comparable situation. Each of four scenes (one from each play)
concentrates on the woman crucial to the well being and future of
the man she loves; each scene employs comparable dramatic and
poetic strategies; each scene is both choric and recapitulative.
Considered as a group, these heartfelt, evocative scenes enable us
to understand Shakespeare's intention in these complex tragedies:
they clarify individual, as well as collective, meaning.

   Act 4.5 of *Hamlet* has five parts: in a prologue Gertrude, a
gentleman, and Horatio discuss the distracted Ophelia; Ophelia
enters and sings snatches of song; Laertes enters and demands
vengeance; Ophelia re-enters and sings another song and
distributes flowers; in an epilogue Claudius and Laertes agree to
avenge Polonius's death. The perspective in the scene is that of
Gertrude, the only character to remain on stage: she sees and hears

everything that happens. In this scene Gertrude delivers her only
aside or soliloquy in the play:

> To my sick soul, as sin's true nature is,
> Each toy seems prologue to some great amiss,
> So full of artless jealousy is guilt,
> It spills itself in fearing to be spilt.
>
> (4.5.17-20)

As the only witness to Hamlet's killing of Polonius, Gertrude now
watches the effect of that murder on Polonius's two children:
Ophelia has been driven mad; Laertes is mad for vengeance.

Ophelia's behavior in the scene reminds Gertrude of her own
very different behavior after the sudden death of her husband as
well as perhaps reminding her of the behavior of the Player Queen
after the "death" of the Player King. Laertes's dangerous anger
should remind Gertrude of Hamlet's dangerous anger during the
only private interview in the play between the mother and her son,
in 3.4. As both mother to Hamlet and wife to Claudius, Gertrude
does what she can, both here and elsewhere, to be true to her son
and to protect her beset husband from frantic accusations:
throughout the play she tries to be a good mother and a good wife.

Gertrude must know that Ophelia is mad not only because
Polonius is dead and was too hastily buried but also because
Polonius was killed by Hamlet, the man Ophelia loves. And
Ophelia's "Saint Valentine's Day" song ("Let in the maid, that out
a maid/Never departed more"[4.5.54-55]) should strew the
dangerous conjecture in Gertrude's mind that Hamlet seduced
Ophelia and that she has become mad in part because she is
pregnant. The important point is that Ophelia's madness is more
understandable to Gertrude, the only other woman on stage, than
it is to anyone else. Laertes is distracted and wildly vengeful
primarily because of the murder of his father. Ophelia's twin
performances in the scene can be considered to be Gertrude's
private mirror and personal Mousetrap. The songs, the flowers
distributed ("There's rosemary, that's for remembrance; pray you,
love, remember. And there is pansies, that's for
thoughts"[4.5.175-77]) and Laertes's list ("O rose of May!/Dear
maid, kind sister, sweet Ophelia!"[4.5.158-59]) are choric and
recapitulative. At the end of act 4, Gertrude elaborately describes

Ophelia's strange death; in the next-to-last scene of the play (5.1), she strews flowers on Ophelia's grave: "Sweets to the sweet, farewell!"(5.1.243)

Like that of 4.5 of *Hamlet*, the design of 4.3 of *Othello* is simple and clear. Othello and Lodovico provide a prologue to the interchange between Desdemona and her gentlewoman, Emilia, who are on stage throughout the scene. Instead of being from the perspective of a wife-mother, as with Gertrude in *Hamlet*, the comparable scene in *Othello* is from the perspective of two wives: one (Desdemona), innocent; the other (Emilia), experienced. Like Gertrude, Emilia feels guilty: she filched the handkerchief that the now-abused Desdemona believes is lost. And, like Gertrude, Emilia is trapped in conflicting roles: she is both Desdemona's friend and Iago's wife. In 5.1 Gertrude will take refuge in public sympathy for Ophelia; Emilia here vehemently argues the case for neglected and abused wives. Like Ophelia, Desdemona is distracted and distraught: she too is beside herself; she too has been thrust back upon herself; she too sings a sad, significant song. Mad Barbary's song of "Willow" tells the tale of a maid who, like Ophelia and to some extent like Desdemona, has been forsaken by the man she loves.

The song is pertinent to Desdemona's present plight, but it is also indicative of what will happen to her later in the play. After Desdemona sings, "Let nobody blame him, his scorn I approve"(4.3.52), she interrupts herself with "Nay, that's not next"(4.3.53). And indeed "Let nobody blame him"(4.3.52) is not what follows in the play; it is out of place; she will approve his scorn at the end. And it will be Desdemona's very last words that echo the words in the song: "Commend me to my kind lord. O, farewell!"(5.2.125) The wedding sheets, the clothing Emilia helps her mistress remove, and Desdemona's nightly wearing are the main props in the scene. In *Hamlet* clothing is responsible for Ophelia's end (filled with water her clothing drags her to a muddy death); Desdemona is destroyed by a handkerchief and smothered with a pillow.[2]

Like the two scenes described above, 5.1 of *Macbeth* has a simple and clear design: a nameless doctor and a nameless gentlewoman serve as both prologue and epilogue to the spectacle of a sleepwalking wife, Lady Macbeth. The Gentlewoman is Lady

Macbeth's regular attendant; needing a reliable witness as well as a medical expert, she is responsible for the presence of the Doctor. As in 4.5 of *Hamlet* ("Pray you mark"[4.5.28]), reminders are given to pay attention to a strange performance: "Observe her, stand close"(5.1.20); "Hark"(5.1.32). Like Ophelia and Desdemona, Lady Macbeth has been forsaken by the man she loves (Macbeth has gone "into the field"[5.1.4]), and, like them, she is distraught and distracted, close to madness. Gertrude and Emilia are guilty; Lady Macbeth is guilt-ridden: she has "known what [she] should not"(5.1.46) and has been a willing accomplice to murder. The need to have light constantly by her and the compulsive rubbing of her hands verify her weakness and her despair. In her broken, interrupted "soliloquy" she recalls and recapitulates the major events of her recent past: "Yet who would have thought the old man to have had so much blood in him"(5.1.39-40); "The Thane of Fife had a wife"(5.1.42); "Banquo's buried"(5.1.64); ". . . there's knocking at the gate"(5.1.66-67).

On the basis of procedures followed in the other scenes under discussion, the Folio text of 4.7 of *King Lear* should include material found in the quarto: a doctor, like the one in the comparable scene in *Macbeth*, should be present; 4.7 should conclude with a conversation between Kent and a gentleman. If quarto material is incorporated into the Folio text, the scene has a prologue (with Cordelia, Kent, the Doctor, and the Gentleman) and an epilogue (with Kent and a gentleman). Each of the other scenes under consideration has two women on stage; this scene has only one, but since faithful Kent is on stage throughout the scene, he seems meant to take the place of the observing woman in the other scenes: 4.7 is from Kent's perspective. Like Gertrude (about Ophelia) and Emilia (about Desdemona), Kent knows more than anyone else in the play about Cordelia *and* Lear. The faithful service of Kent and Cordelia redeems the guilt that they may feel concerning their initial behavior.

Unlike the other little performances, Cordelia's performance involves the man she loves, the rescued father-king: the recently mad Lear awakens, like a child, to his kind daughter. Like the other scenes in the other plays, this one is ritualistic and surrealistic. Instead of songs, as in *Hamlet* and *Othello*, this scene has music. Lear's new clothes, the chair, the music, their kneeling and his benediction, their exchanges of forgiveness are all choric and recapitulative. Unlike Gertrude and Emilia, Kent feels no conflict of roles, nor, though she is sister to Goneril and Regan and wife to France, does Cordelia.

The dramatic focus in these scenes is on the woman (Ophelia, Desdemona, Lady Macbeth, Cordelia) who loves the protagonist (Hamlet, Othello, Macbeth, Lear). All four of these women will die because of the actions of the men they love. Ophelia is a too-obedient daughter; Desdemona is a well-intentioned wife; Cordelia is a well-intentioned daughter; Lady Macbeth is a well-intentioned but guilty wife: she did for her husband what she thought her husband deserved and desired but was too full of the milk of human kindness to do for himself. Lady Macbeth commits suicide; Ophelia's death is questionable; Desdemona and Cordelia are victims and sacrifices.

The Gentlewoman in *Macbeth* may be said to know more than anyone else in the play about her mistress. Unquestionably, the scene under discussion (in *Hamlet, Othello, King Lear*) is presented from the perspective of the person who knows more than anyone else in the particular play about both the beloved (Ophelia, Desdemona, Cordelia) and the hero (Hamlet, Othello, Lear): Gertrude, Emilia, Kent. At the end of each play each of these three will be the victim as heart: Gertrude willfully drinks from the poisoned cup;[3] determined to redeem her mistress, Emilia is killed by her husband, Iago; heartsick Kent is determined to follow his dead master. Gertrude follows Ophelia; Emilia follows Desdemona; Kent will follow Cordelia and Lear.

* * * * *

At the end of act 3 of *Hamlet*, the Prince kills Polonius. Act 4.5 presents the result of that killing on Ophelia, Laertes, Gertrude, and Claudius. By the end of act 3 of *Othello,* the Moor is convinced that his wife is a strumpet. Act 4.3 presents the result of that conviction on both Desdemona and Emilia. In 4.1 of *Macbeth* the usurper, after viewing the apparitions, concludes:

> From this moment
> The very firstlings of my heart shall be
> The firstlings of my hand.
>
> (4.1.146-48)

Act 5.1 presents the result of that declaration and its consequent action (the murder of the Macduff family) on Lady Macbeth, the Gentlewoman, and the Doctor. In 3.6 of *King Lear* the sleeping Lear is rescued and taken to Dover; in 3.7 Gloucester, an old father and a surrogate for Lear, has his eyes plucked out by Cornwall. Act 4.7 presents the result of those actions on Cordelia and Kent. In the epilogue to 4.7 Kent remarks to the Gentleman, "'Tis time to look about"(4.7.91-92). This choric comment serves to alert the audience that in this heartfelt scene, as well as in the comparable ones in the other plays, it is time to look about, and, before moving on to the death-strewn conclusion in each instance, pause to reconsider what has happened.

The body trope, the family trope, the play-acting or stage trope are much in evidence in the four scenes under consideration.[4] The little performances themselves certify the stage trope; the family trope with its expected relationships (brother, daughter, father, husband, mother, sister, son, wife) is mandated by plot. The body trope (the head, the heart, and the hand) is of large-scale importance throughout: the head thinks; the heart feels; the hand acts. Trouble begins when the parts are disjunctive: the head acts; the hand feels. The significant point is that collectively the four scenes under discussion can be thought of as applying to the heart: "'Tis time [for the heart] to look about." Gertrude and Ophelia; Emilia and Desdemona; the Gentlewoman and Lady Macbeth; Kent and Cordelia—all have reached a kind of end. The heart is on display and is at considerable risk. These private persons will soon be at the disposal of heartless, political forces.

In 4.5 of *Hamlet* the center of concern is the heart (Gertrude and Ophelia); this center of concern shifts at once to the dangerous news of Hamlet's return (4.6) and the effect in 4.7 of that news on Claudius and Laertes. "Know you the hand?"(4.7.51) Laertes asks after Claudius has read aloud the letter from Hamlet. "'Tis Hamlet's character. 'Naked'!"(4.7.52) the King replies. As the son and prince and agent of revenge, Hamlet comes home alone: his return as hand insures that the movement to widespread destruction will proceed. Hamlet has in his possession the document that ordered his death in England; Hamlet's naked return provides Claudius with the ideal opportunity to turn Laertes into a hand against Hamlet. Whereas the Prince is the instrument of one mighty opposite (the Ghost of the other world), Laertes is the instrument of another (the King of this world). Thus the swordplay between Hamlet and Laertes in the last scene of the play is a contest between doubles or equals or brothers ("I have shot my arrow o'er the house/And hurt my brother"[5.2.243-44]) or foils ("I'll be your foil, Laertes"[5.2.255]) or sons or hands.

Everyone in 4.6 and 4.7 can be considered to be a hand: the sailor and the messenger, Horatio, Laertes, Claudius, and even Gertrude (whose announcement of Ophelia's death shuts the door on Hamlet's future as husband and makes Laertes more determined than ever to murder Hamlet). All these hands function to serve Hamlet's ironic, thematic role of minister and scourge. In the last scene, up to and including the swordplay, Hamlet functions as a hand: ". . . the readiness is all"(5.2.222); Hamlet submits like a hand or a child to the bout with Laertes.

The primary trope of *Othello* is the body. Othello is the head; Desdemona is the heart; Iago is the hand. As soon as Desdemona and Emilia leave the stage, Iago and Roderigo begin 5.1: on stage the heart gives way to the hand. Up to 5.1 Iago as a head has managed to convince others (Roderigo, Cassio, Emilia, Othello) to function as his hand. By 5.1 he has convinced Roderigo to be his sword or hand in the murder of Cassio: "'Tis but a man gone"(5.1.10). But in the scene itself Iago is forced at last to take up the role of hand and to attack Cassio. After being struck in the leg from behind by Iago, Cassio cries out, and Othello comes briefly on stage and, hearing the cry, remarks:

> Minion, your dear lies dead.
> And your unblest fate hies. Strumpet, I come.
> [Forth] of my heart those charms, thine eyes, are blotted;
> Thy bed, lust-stain'd, shall with lust's blood be spotted.
>   (5.1.33-36)

Othello knows nothing about Roderigo. The Iago-Othello simple plan has been for Iago to kill Cassio and then for Othello to murder Desdemona.

Emilia, who enters at the end of 5.1, is sent off by Iago to the citadel as his hand. But in the last scene, once Emilia learns that her mistress has been murdered, she turns from being Iago's hand to being Desdemona's. She will then do whatever she can to denounce Othello, to be true to Desdemona, and, by so doing, to destroy Iago. In the last scene, instead of a contest between equals, as in *Hamlet*, Othello strikes his duplicitous hand, Iago, with his sword, and then, at the end of his dramatic speech of self-justification, Othello extends this action by stabbing his Iago-like heart with an unexpected weapon.

To Claudius and Laertes in 4.7 of *Hamlet* the Prince is naked, alone, an unpunished murderer; to Iago in 5.1 of *Othello* the Moor is a dupe and a sword. To Angus, one of the Scottish rebels on stage in 5.2 of *Macbeth*, the tyrant is a "dwarfish thief"(5.2.22). Macbeth's decision to murder Lady Macduff and her children makes it possible for Malcolm to turn Macduff into a sword or hand against the tyrant. Hamlet submits to the plans of Claudius; Othello submits to the plans of Iago; Macbeth "submits" to the plans of Malcolm. Hamlet or Othello or Macbeth, in attacking or deserting the heart, turns himself into a hand. Like Laertes and Iago, Macduff (the victim of Macbeth's wanton murder of Macduff's family) is obsessed with killing the nominal head: he will use his sword against Macbeth or "sheathe [it] again undeeded"(5.7.20). Like Hamlet (who madly agrees to engage in swordplay with the son of the man he killed) or Othello (who insanely promises to murder his waiting wife), Macbeth foolishly leaves the secure castle for the dangerous field. Like the swordplay between Hamlet and Laertes, the swordfight between Macbeth and Macduff is between equals, doubles, swords, hands. For Macduff is Malcolm's hand as surely as Laertes is Claudius's.

Largely because Lear is an old man, he is not involved on stage in a deadly confrontation with someone directly comparable, as Hamlet or Macbeth in the last scene of each of these other plays is. In *King Lear* the obligatory, deadly confrontation is between Edgar and Edmund: brothers, doubles, equals, swords, hands. After the heartfelt reunion between Lear and Cordelia in 4.7,

Edmund and Regan appear on stage. Edmund (unlike Hamlet, Othello, Macbeth, Lear) does not love the heart, a woman: Goneril or Regan is only a means to an end. Edgar comes on stage, gives Albany a letter, and tells him that, if the British forces win, he will produce a champion (a sword or a hand). Laertes serves Claudius; Macduff serves Malcolm; Edgar will serve Albany. In a soliloquy at the end of the scene, Edmund announces that he can succeed only by and through the death of others. Like that of Hamlet and Laertes and that of Othello and Iago ("This is the night/That either makes me, or fordoes me quite"[*Oth* 5.1.128-29]) and that of Macbeth and Macduff, the state of Edmund (". . . my state/Stands on me to defend, not to debate"[5.1.68-69]) and of Edgar (who must forsake his despondent father in order to become the challenger) is desperate. In *King Lear* the contest is a designated and explicit trial by combat.

* * * * *

The general movement of the poetic thought is clearest and neatest in *Othello*: it proceeds from the heart (Desdemona and Emilia in 4.3) to the hand (Iago and Roderigo in 5.1) to the head (Othello in 5.2). Hamlet is on stage throughout the last, long scene, as Othello is in his play. In the Folio the last act of *Macbeth* has seven relatively short scenes. Lear is on stage only at the beginning and at the end of the last, long scene of *King Lear*. Still, the general features at the end of all four plays are the same: a kind of performance; a series of deaths; symbolic props; a kind of epilogue.

In *Hamlet* the duel is the performance. The three deaths (of Gertrude, Claudius, Laertes) that precede Hamlet's occur in quick succession on stage. Gertrude, Claudius, and Laertes compose a family: a mother-wife, a husband, a "son." All four deaths are a direct result of the murderous plotting of Claudius and Laertes in 4.7: the hand cut off from the heart is destructive. Gertrude is the heart; Claudius and Laertes are hands. All are guilty; all are destroyed by means of their reduced roles. Hamlet as head completes the body trope. In the brief interim between their deaths and his he becomes the head: he stops Horatio's suicide and insists that Horatio tell his story; he gives Fortinbras his dying voice. The key props are ominous: the dead bodies, the discarded foils, the cup, the drum, the noise of shooting cannons. At the end the three named characters are Osric, who is silent, and Horatio and Fortinbras. From terms supplied by 3.1, these three can be designated as the courtier (Osric), the scholar (Horatio), the soldier (Fortinbras). They also fit the body trope: Osric is the hand; Horatio is the heart; Fortinbras is the head.

By the time the Moor reaches Desdemona's bedroom in 5.2 of *Othello*, he no longer wants to commit murder: he has had a change of heart; he now wants to save her soul by sacrificing her body. As the truth about the past is disclosed, the three deaths that take place on stage follow the order of deaths in *Hamlet*: Desdemona, the heart; Emilia, the hand; Othello, the head. Knowing that he has killed his innocent wife, Othello ends by giving a long speech of self-defense. This performance, which resembles Hamlet's desire for public justification, is the occasion for his desired suicide: he bemuses his onstage audience so that he can take his own life; he uses his verbal skill as head so that he can strike his vulnerable heart with his guilty hand. He cannot bear to continue to live apart from Desdemona; he follows the heart and the hand onto the bed, stained by Emilia's blood. The bloodstained sheets re-create the most important prop of the play, the red-and-white handkerchief. And then a curtain is drawn on the bed, hiding its tragic burden. Five named men (Iago, Cassio, Montano, Lodovico, Gratiano—to name them in the order that they are introduced into the play) are left alive on stage. Lodovico, the emissary of the Venetian Duke, has the final word.

According to the Folio the three deaths in the last act of *Macbeth* take place in the last three scenes: a cry of women precedes the announcement that the Queen is dead; Macbeth kills Young Siward; Macduff kills Macbeth.[5] As in *Hamlet* and *Othello* the hero reasserts himself as head right before his death: Hamlet justifies himself to Horatio; Othello justifies himself to five men. The same essential point is strangely but dramatically made in *Macbeth* with the entrance of Macduff carrying the head of Macbeth; it remains on stage for all to see.[6] This spectacular prop reinforces the body trope: the play ends with Macbeth's ghastly head. First of all, it is a memento mori: when the thanes hail the king, they are unwittingly hailing death. Second, since Malcolm has not been crowned, the King of Scotland is still Macbeth or his armed head:[7] without meaning to, the thanes are hailing Macbeth. Third, as only the audience knows, the armed head re-creates the first apparition. As such, it is like the re-created handkerchief at the end of *Othello*. Finally, having witnessed the dramatic spectacle of Banquo's heirs as kings of Scotland, the audience knows that Malcolm will be succeeded by Banquo's descendants.

The difference between the heart scene (4.7) in *King Lear* and the comparable scenes in those other tragedies is that the protagonist in *Lear* is on stage with the woman he loves. Once Cordelia rejoins Lear (4.7), they are always together. One feature of the five deaths in the last scene is that the first three take place off stage, but the order of the five deaths seems to follow that of the other three plays: Goneril and Regan (the "heart") die first; Edmund (the hand) dies next; Lear and Cordelia (the head) die last. In having Edmund carried off stage just after the dead bodies of Goneril and Regan are carried back on stage, Shakespeare re-introduces the main participants of the initial love test. The faces of Goneril and Regan are covered, masked. Lear, who has returned to the stage, is now obsessed with Cordelia's face, her head: he asks for a mirror; he uses a feather to determine if she is breathing; he dies believing that her lips are moving. Three named men watch Lear watching Cordelia's face: Edgar (the hand); Kent (the heart); Albany (the head).

The named men on stage at the end of these tragedies provide several levels of awareness toward the dead protagonists. For instance, Horatio knows Hamlet best; Osric knows only the Hamlet of 5.2; Fortinbras sees Hamlet only after his death. Iago knows Othello best; then Cassio does; then Montano; then Lodovico; then Gratiano. Ross knows Macbeth best; then Macduff; then Malcolm; Siward sees only Macbeth's cut-off head. Kent knows Lear best; Edgar knows only the mad Lear of 3.4, 3.6, 4.6; Albany knows only the Lear of 1.1 and 1.4. After the death of Hamlet (except for a comment by the English ambassador) only Horatio and Fortinbras speak. After the death of Othello, only Cassio and Lodovico speak. After the appearance of Macbeth's death's-head (except for the thanes' "Hail, King of Scotland!"[5.9.25]), only Macduff and Malcolm speak. After the death of Lear, only Edgar, Kent, and Albany speak. In *Hamlet*, *Othello*, *Macbeth* the first speaker is the man on stage who has suffered most and who understands most (Horatio, Cassio, Macduff); the second (or in *Hamlet* the other named) speaker is the person newly in power: Fortinbras, Lodovico, Malcolm. The role of the first speaker in each "epilogue" in the other plays is divided in *King Lear* between Edgar (the champion, who has suffered) and Kent (the man who has also suffered much but who understands best). The procedure in the other three plays would support the contention that the last speaker should be Albany, the person in power, rather than Edgar.[8] Albany (like Fortinbras, Lodovico, Malcolm) has not been sufficiently tested: he arrives late to power; his understanding is shallow.

In general terms, what Shakespeare does in these tragedies is to move from the heart to the head by means of the hand. For a dominant feature in the second half of these plays is the introduction of new characters: Fortinbras, the Captain, the Gravediggers, the Priest, Osric in *Hamlet*; Bianca (3.4), Lodovico, and Gratiano in *Othello*; Hecate, Lady Macduff and her child, the two Doctors, the Gentlewoman, Seyton, Siward, Young Siward in *Macbeth*; the old man and Edgar (in three different guises) in *King Lear*. All of these characters are choric and recapitulative; they all may be doubles for earlier characters; they are all types or hands.

In a deeper sense the end is reached by means of Shakespeare's hand: the end is at the service of Shakespeare's deliberate art. The bringing of Goneril and Regan back on stage and the taking of Edmund off stage are easy examples of Shakespeare's surprising manipulations. We readily understand why Shakespeare would have to challenge realistic expectations in order to echo and mirror the beginning of *King Lear* at the end. Shakespeare brings about the obligatory confrontations; he makes the deaths occur in a specific order. Shakespeare seems to want us to be aware of how unlikely it is for Hamlet to agree to engage in swordplay with Laertes, of how odd Othello's change of heart at the beginning of 5.2 is, or how insane it is for Macbeth to forsake the secure castle, or how incredible it is for Edmund to agree to fight an unknown opposite and for aged Lear to kill the slave who was hanging Cordelia. The point is that Shakespeare challenges us. For instance, we must make an effort to understand that Edmund must defeat the unknown opposite before he can confront Albany: he can reach the head only through or by means of the hand.

As we respond to the action of these elaborate, interrelated plays, we realize that the fate of the heart seems inevitable and that the fate of the head and the hand seems imposed. The final scenes stretch our credulity and are intended, at last, to make us realize that the end of these tragedies is a deliberate product of Shakespeare's art. Shakespeare wants us to think about an end before judging it. In addition, he wants us to distance ourselves from the emotional effect by means of an ironic undercutting, an intellectual dimension that is present but not sufficiently recognized or regarded.[9] Finally, Shakespeare pushes the achievement beyond tragedy into something like spectacle or into the coolness or the sweep of epic statement: "'Tis time to look [more deeply] about."

NOTES

1. Cordelia may die off stage, but even if she dies on stage, her death is private in that the focus at the end is on Lear.

2. If Othello doesn't spill her blood, a pillow seems to be the logical prop.

3. It is conceivable that Gertrude suspects the wine is poisoned: her death, like Ophelia's, may be a suicide.

4. For a discussion of the pervasive nature of these tropes, See *Design and Closure*, 3-7; also see *The Life of Our Design*, xii-xiii.

5. The scene direction in the Folio is this: "*Enter Fighting*, and MACBETH *slaine.*"

6. Holinshed says that Macbeth's head is "upon a pole."

7. We assume that Macbeth is still wearing his helmet.

8. In the quarto these final lines are given to Albany.

9. See, for instance, Harry Berger, Jr., "The Early Scenes of *Macbeth*: Preface to a New Interpretation." *ELH* 47 (1980): 4-5.

15

Two-Part Design and the Impasse in *King Lear*

Granted the certainty of a large-scale two-part design in *Richard II, Hamlet, Measure for Measure, Troilus and Cressida,* and *The Winter's Tale,* it is not difficult to uncover the same design in *King Lear.* In its complete formulation Shakespeare's two-part design incorporates (the action turns upon it; the action is divided by it) a surprising and spectacular choric scene or event: the garden scene (3.4) in *Richard II*; the only song in *Measure for Measure,* at the beginning of 4.1; the choric soliloquy by Time (4.1) in *The Winter's Tale.* In *King Lear* this spectacular feature is 3.7: after Lear sleeps and is carried off stage at the end of 3.6, Gloucester's eyes are plucked out by Cornwall in 3.7.

The action of the first part of *King Lear* leads *down* to the blinding of Gloucester, the father; the action of the second part leads *up* from that event to the necessarily painful and necessarily sublime end of Lear, the old man-father-king, with his Cordelia, the daughter-queen-spirit. In furtherance of this second, upward movement of the action, the chilling 3.7 is also the occasion that provides the opportunity for Edgar to become his father's eyes and, as Gloucester's eyes, to conduct his blind father to Dover. Edgar begins his rise from an outcast madman-beggar in 4.1 to being the champion of Lear and Cordelia in 5.3, the last scene of the play. Edgar, alone on stage, has a soliloquy at the very end of

3.6; Edgar, alone on stage, has a soliloquy at the very beginning of 4.1. Edgar is directionless before the horrific 3.7; he is enabled in 4.1 to direct his blind father to safety.

As with the large-scale two-part design, a small-scale two-part design also incorporates a significant choric event, like the turning of the hourglass at the very center of 4.1 (the large-scale choric appearance of Time) in *The Winter's Tale* or the action indicated by the stage direction *Exit pursued by a bear* at the very middle of 3.3 (the first Bohemia scene) in the same play. In *King Lear* the putting out of Gloucester's eyes occurs in the middle of 3.7. But the clearest, most precise example of small-scale two-part design is the twelve-line 5.2, the next-to-last scene, in *King Lear*.

Gloucester on stage alone with the noise (*Alarum and retreat within*) of battle is the undramatized choric event in the scene: Edgar is with Gloucester immediately before the battle and immediately after it. Before the battle Gloucester is "father"(5.2.1); after the battle he is "old man"(5.2.5). The indoor event of the blinding of Gloucester in 3.7 has been translated into the outdoor event of Gloucester alone with the noise of the beginning (the *Alarum*) and the ending (the *retreat*) of the battle: the British have won; Lear and Cordelia have lost. In act 4 Edgar champions the cause of Gloucester, by killing Oswald; in act 5 Edgar champions the cause of Lear and Cordelia, by killing Edmund. Edgar brackets the dramatized 3.7, the wanton blinding of the now-loyal-to-Lear Gloucester; in smaller *structural* terms, in the brief 5.2, Edgar brackets the victimized Gloucester and the noise of an offstage battle that has been both won (by the British) and lost (by Lear and Cordelia).

In 3.7 a temporizing Gloucester, having turned away from his immediate master Cornwall to his regal master Lear, is blinded and cast out of doors. Gloucester's parable is related to the parable of loyal Kent in 2.2. After standing up to Cornwall in the middle of 2.2, Kent is put in the stocks and turned into a public spectacle. Structurally, the stocks correspond both to the actual blinding of Gloucester in 3.7 and to the offstage battle in 5.2. Like the public spectacle of blind Gloucester at the beginning of 4.1, Kent at the end of 2.2 is stultified and helpless: he must wait out the night in the stocks. But whereas Kent has the comfort of a letter from Cordelia, Gloucester has only the bitter knowledge that Edmund has betrayed him and that Edgar has been abused. Edgar follows 3.7 with a soliloquy; Edgar follows 2.2 with a soliloquy: 2.3 is *just* a soliloquy by an Edgar who is unaware, though we are not, that Kent is also on the darkling stage in the stocks.[1] As soon as Gloucester is blinded, an unexpected Edgar appears; as soon as unseen Kent is alone in the stocks, an unexpected Edgar appears. Like Gloucester in 3.7, Kent is stultified for his service to Lear and by his concomitant disservice to Cornwall. Edgar will be of service both indirectly to Kent and directly to Gloucester.

Edgar also makes an unexpected entrance in 3.4 in the storm; now the specific choric instrument is the hovel. In 2.2 the pertinent icon is man alone, Kent, in the night in the stocks; in 3.4 the pertinent icon is man alone, Edgar, in a hovel in a storm. In 5.2 the pertinent icon is man alone, Gloucester, with the noise of battle. The crucial point is that the thematic movement of the action is from the night to a storm to a battle, from the stocks to a hovel to an *Alarum and retreat*, from Kent to Edgar to Gloucester. The Fool discovers Edgar in the hovel, and Kent orders him to "Come forth"(3.4.45). In this scene Edgar, now in the guise of Tom of Bedlam, is considered by Lear to be what man essentially is, a naked and bereft outcast. But soon Lear comes to consider this abject Tom, unaccommodated man, as his philosopher, his Theban, his Athenian. To Lear in 3.6 mad Tom has become a "most learned [justicer]"(3.6.21), a "robed man of justice"(3.6.36), someone qualified to judge Goneril and Regan, who are figuratively on stage, Goneril as a "join-stool"(3.6.52).

Edgar's sudden presence in 3.4 as mad Tom serves to enable Lear not only to understand himself as rejected old man and despised father but also to come to harsh terms with both pomp and his downcast state: in 3.6 Lear appeals to the Fool and Tom and the other member of the commission, Kent, for justice. At the end of the first half of the play, the obsessed Lear is intent upon damning and destroying Goneril and Regan; at the end of the second half of the play, the obsessed Lear is intent upon praising and saving his true daughter, Cordelia. But Edgar will have to become Gloucester's champion before he can become the champion of Lear and Cordelia. The action will have to move upward before Edgar can appear in his knightly garb, but only after the French forces, led by the joined Lear and Cordelia, have lost the climactic battle.

* * * * *

Typically in a Shakespeare play act 1 presents the motivating event (in *King Lear*, 1.1 presents the motivating event of the main plot; 1.2 presents the motivating event of the subplot), introduces the main characters, and states the plot problem or, as in *King Lear*, the plot problems. Descriptively the action of acts 2 and 3 of *King Lear* takes place at or near Gloucester's castle. The scenes proceed, with a more-or-less alternating focus, naturally, one after the other. Again, the eleven-scene sequence can be considered to be an elaborated episode. The action culminates in the abysmal plucking out of the eyes of the host of the castle, Gloucester. By the end of act 3, Edgar, the future earl, is bereft and forgotten; Edmund, the new Earl of Gloucester, has left to accompany Goneril to her palace; the old, blind Earl of Gloucester has been thrust out of doors.

The emphasis of this eleven-scene sequence is primarily on the members of the subplot (Gloucester, Edgar, Edmund) as they are affected and changed by the arrival of outsiders to the castle: of Cornwall and Regan, of Kent and Oswald, of Lear and the Fool, of Goneril. Kent is released from the stocks and joins Lear and the Fool in 2.4; Edgar, as mad Tom, and Gloucester, as good host, join Lear and his company on the stormy heath in 3.4 and later in the farmhouse in 3.6. Since, as we have seen, a quintessential structural strategy in Shakespeare is that of the recapitulative point-of-view scene, the action from the perspective of the character or characters who remain on stage throughout a scene, it seems useful to consider 2.1 as an Edmund scene; 2.2 as a Kent scene; 2.3 as an Edgar scene. Further, we may consider 2.1 as the parable of Edmund, a bastard and a rascal, whose rise to prominence is meteoric, largely because he is self-serving and is untrammeled by a conscience. Act 2.2 is the parable of Kent, a disguised nameless servant, who overreaches himself in the scene and thus exacerbates, rather than relieves, the plight of his absent master, who will soon arrive at the castle. The brief 2.3 is the beginning of the parable of an innocent, endangered outcast, Edgar, who is about to hide himself in a base disguise in order to escape the hunt.

Thus in some sense 2.1, the second subplot scene, can be considered as the rise of Edmund, and 2.2, the scene of Kent's arrival at the castle, can be considered as the fall of Kent. In the course of these two scenes Edgar runs away, and Kent is disenfranchised, disregarded, and neglected; still, we are given bits of new, happy information. In 2.1 we hear whispers of war between Cornwall and Albany; we learn that Edgar was Lear's godson and that Lear named him and that Edgar was presumably one of Lear's knights; in 2.2 we discover that Gloucester is concerned for Kent's plight ("The Duke's to blame in this, 'twill be ill taken"[2.2.159]) and that Kent now has in his possession a letter from Cordelia. In 2.3 we see that Edgar has escaped the hunt and promises to survive as Tom. The main point is that the smaller up-down movement of 2.1 and 2.2 is at the service of the larger down-up movement of not just Edgar but of the two parts of the play. To put the matter boldly, by the end of 3.7 (for the spectacular 3.7 is not just choric) the fortunes of Goneril, Regan, and Edmund are ascendant; by the end of 5.3 the fortunes of Albany, Kent, and Edgar are ascendant.

If we consider 2.1 and 2.2 more narrowly, we can see that the design of one scene is comparable to that of the other. Each scene begins in darkness with a dialogue between two underlings (Edmund-Curan; Kent-Oswald); an inconclusive swordfight takes place (Edmund-Edgar; Kent-Oswald); one person is injured (Edmund; Oswald); the members of the court world enter (Edmund followed by Cornwall, Regan, Gloucester). At the end of 2.1 Cornwall "seize[s] on" Edmund for reward for his good service; at the end of 2.2 Cornwall seizes on Kent for punishment for his bad service. Two Edmunds (the real and the disguised) are on stage throughout 2.1; two Kents (the real and the disguised) are on stage throughout 2.2.

Because of the winning and losing of the battle in 5.2, the fate of Gloucester changes from "father"(5.2.1) to "old man"(5.2.5). But as early as 2.1, a change in Gloucester is dramatized. In the first half of 2.1 Gloucester four times calls the absent Edgar a villain and refers to him as a murderous coward. After the entrance of Cornwall and Regan, Gloucester's hard manner as vindictive father is replaced by the soft demeanor of a distraught father. Now Gloucester says that his poor heart is cracked, that "shame would have [Edgar's actions] hid"(2.1.93). A main point is that Cornwall and Regan do not see and hear the vindictive Gloucester of the first half of the scene; they know only the "noble friend"(2.1.86), "noble Gloucester"(2.1.120), "Our good old friend"(2.1.125). Gloucester shows one face to Edmund and another face to Cornwall and Regan, though Edmund, on stage throughout, sees both. We can then partially understand why Cornwall and Regan react so violently to being betrayed by this, to them, obsequious old man. But the structural point is that 2.1 has, vis-à-vis Gloucester, two main parts and two distinct Gloucesters.

In 2.2, the Kent scene, Gloucester says very little on stage until the stocks are brought out. Then Gloucester says, "Let me beseech your Grace not to [stock Kent]"(2.2.140). It is only after Cornwall and Regan have left that Gloucester declares:

> I am sorry for thee, friend, 'tis the Duke['s] pleasure,
> Whose disposition, all the world well knows,
> Will not be rubb'd nor stopp'd. I'll entreat for thee.
> (2.2.152-54)

The crucial point is that Gloucester, who has long been aware of the nature of Cornwall, will help Lear both because of and in spite of that awareness. Only Edmund is on stage in 2.1 to hear the vindictive father, Gloucester; only Kent is on stage to hear Lear's considerate friend, Gloucester. To Edmund Gloucester is always foolish or weak, an easy dupe or victim, like Edgar.

* * * * *

A basic strategy employed by Shakespeare can be called the impasse. In *Twelfth Night*, for instance, as soon as Olivia falls in love with Viola disguised as Cesario (1.5), Sebastian is introduced into the play (2.1). This new, unexpected person, the one that Viola is imitating, is the answer to Viola's plight: Sebastian is the proper, needed husband for Olivia. Thus, at this early time, the answer for Viola's (as well as the answer for Olivia's) plight appears on stage to us, the audience, but not to Viola or Olivia. Sebastian will be *the* answer, delayed until the proper time. At the end of act 3 Viola's plight as Cesario is that she is not a man, not a soldier: she is not prepared to fight a duel with Sir Andrew. And onto the stage to begin act 4 appears Sebastian as the answer to Viola's public plight, though, again, she is unaware of his presence. Olivia, now madly in love with Cesario, will take Sebastian to be Cesario, and he will, without compunction, agree to marry her; Sebastian will then physically abuse Sir Andrew and Toby when they mistake him for the cowardly Cesario. Sebastian is the answer to the plot problem of the play: the proper husband for Olivia, the proper replacement for Cesario, Sir Andrew, Malvolio, Orsino.

At the end of 2.2 of *King Lear* Kent in the stocks is at an impasse; Edgar, who then comes on stage, is the answer to Kent's plight, *in time*. Kent is stultified, and onto the stage comes the way out of that stultification or impasse. Like Sebastian in *Twelfth Night*, Edgar is the answer to Kent's plight, but he is unseen by Kent, and he is not the needed answer yet. In *Twelfth Night* Sebastian's needed presence is delayed for plot reasons; in *King Lear* Edgar's needed presence is also delayed for plot reasons. But the crucial, additional point is that Edgar, unlike Sebastian, has to change his nature; he has to be patient and endure; he has to prove himself before he can become Lear's effective (as well as his only remaining) knight. In the same manner Gloucester is at an impasse at the end of 3.7; Edgar, who in 4.1 again comes on stage alone (as in 2.3) and who is of course unseen by Gloucester, is the answer to Gloucester's plight *in time*. He will lead Gloucester to Dover, not as Edgar, but as madman-beggar. He will then rescue him, not as the son, but as a "most poor man"(4.6.221). Edgar himself will be at an impasse off stage in 5.3. When the trumpet sounds, he must forsake his father, to whom he has just revealed his true identity, in order to do what he has promised Albany in 5.1: to "produce a champion"(5.1.43). Edgar as mad Tom is a justicer for Lear in 3.6; Edgar as Albany's champion is a justicer for Lear and Cordelia in 5.3.

Kent is true to Lear and Cordelia, though to no great result, from 1.1 on; Gloucester becomes true to Lear, though to no great end, in act 3. Edgar's test at the end of 4.6 enables him to become, unlike the ineffective Kent and Gloucester, the successful champion of Lear and Cordelia. Indeed Edgar's actions in 4.6, the Dover scene, are a version of Kent's actions in 2.2 at Gloucester's castle. There Kent beats Oswald, goes out of his dialect ("Under th' allowance of your great aspect,/Whose influence, like the wreath of radiant fire . . ."[2.2.106-07]), and ends the scene with a letter from Cordelia. At the end of 4.6 Edgar goes out of his dialect ("And chud ha' bin zwagger'd out of my life, 'twould not ha' bin zo long as 'tis by a vortnight"[4.6.238-39]), beats Oswald, and ends the scene with a letter from Goneril. In an unexpected way Edgar completes what Kent started. And Edgar's actions here (rescuing his father from a prize-hunting servant, Oswald) completes in an unexpected way his service to Gloucester as madman-poor man. By his true service to Gloucester, Edgar gets in 4.6 and uses in 5.1 Goneril's letter to Edmund against both Edmund and Goneril. Oswald is the foe to Kent and Lear's cause in 2.2; Oswald is the friend to the cause of Kent, Gloucester, Edgar, Lear, and Cordelia in 4.6. After the battle Edgar must desert his bereft father in order to confront his heartless brother.

In *King Lear* the strategy of the impasse is more realistically employed as well as more thematically complex than it is in *Twelfth Night*, in part because *King Lear* is a character-driven, rather than plot-centered, drama with a more fully developed and integrated subplot. In the first half of the play Lear faces a series of related impasses. He is confronted and opposed by Cordelia and Kent in 1.1; by Goneril at Albany's palace in 1.4; by Cornwall, Regan, and Goneril at Gloucester's castle in 2.4. In each instance Lear as king-father responds directly, with mounting anger, frustration, and madness. In the second half of the play Lear *becomes* the impasse and, after his cure, is wonderfully accommodated by Cordelia. In 1.2, the first subplot scene, Gloucester and Edgar are impasses to Edmund. They are quickly dealt with by Edmund's guile and are sacrificed to his rise to power. Only at the end do Lear and Cordelia become an impasse to Edmund. Then he uses guile to insure that Lear and Cordelia are dead and no longer an impasse.

For *King Lear* is a tragedy, which ends with a series of deaths, not a comedy, which ends with a series of promising revelations and resolutions. In act 5 Edgar manages to achieve the same kind of plot-centered resolutions that are supplied by the advent of Sebastian in act 5 of *Twelfth Night*, and he, like Sebastian, is a double for other main characters. Although he does not become part of the main plot through marriage and although he rises at the expense of, rather than for, his "brother," Edgar is the champion of Lear and Cordelia. But he is an ironic champion who wins the trial by combat but is unaware of the danger to Lear and Cordelia off stage. *Twelfth Night* ends with the unaccommodated Fool singing about the wind and the rain. *King Lear* ends with unaccommodated Kent, Edgar, and Albany feebly responding to the impasse of the dead Cordelia and the wildly grieving Lear. We, the audience, have to accommodate the Fool in that comedy and have to accommodate these three despondent men in this tragedy.

* * * * *

The plot problem of both the main plot and the subplot of *King Lear* deals with the way that the initially disenfranchised are re-enfranchised. At the beginning of the play, main-plot action is bracketed by subplot action: Kent, Gloucester, and Edmund have a thirty-one-line exchange before the advent of King Lear and his court; in 1.2 Edmund, Gloucester, and Edgar follow after the love test of the main plot. In the last scene of the play (5.3) the structural procedure is reversed: main-plot action now brackets subplot action: Lear and Cordelia begin and end the scene; the centerpiece of 5.3 is the trial-by-combat between Edgar and Edmund. When Edgar, cast out in 2.1, re-enters the action in 2.3 with Kent in the stocks, he remarks, "I heard myself proclaim'd"(2.3.1). When Oswald comes upon the blind Gloucester (4.6), he cries, "A proclaim'd prize"(4.6.226). In 5.3, right before the advent of Edgar as champion, Albany says that he has "proclaimed" Edmund a treasonous villain. As mad Tom, the proclaimed Edgar replaces Kent in Lear's service; as a poor man, Edgar rescues the proclaimed prize, Gloucester, and kills Oswald;

as a knight Edgar kills the proclaimed villain, Edmund. The re-enfranchised Edgar moves to center stage at the center of 5.3.

At the beginning of 4.6, the Dover scene, Gloucester's despondent state constitutes an impasse for Edgar; he gets out of the impasse by tricking his father into taking a miraculous fall. Then this reborn, re-enfranchised Gloucester, the product of Tom's actions, is at once confronted by three separate men. Severely shaken by the first of these (the abusive, mad Lear), Gloucester is brought to "see . . . feelingly."(4.6.149). After the departure of Lear, a gentleman arrives with the news that Cordelia has returned to Britain. Gloucester is encouraged:

> You ever-gentle gods, take my breath from me,
> Let not my worser spirit tempt me again
> To die before you please!
>
> (4.6.217-19)

He is further encouraged to hear that the person in his presence (Edgar) is a "most poor man . . . pregnant to good pity"(4.6.221-23):

> Hearty thanks;
> The bounty and the benison of heaven
> To boot, and boot!
>
> (4.6.224-26)

But when Oswald appears with the intention of killing Gloucester, the old man regards Oswald's bloody declaration as welcome news: "Now let thy friendly hand/Put strength enough to't"(4.6.230-31). And when told that Oswald has been killed, Gloucester comments:

> The King is mad; how stiff is my vild sense
> That I stand up, and have ingenious feeling
> Of my huge sorrows! Better I were distract.
>
> (4.6.279-81)

Edgar has the letter from Oswald, but he hasn't managed to save his father from despair. The advent of mad Lear has had a destructive effect on this other old man. His "huge sorrows"(4.6.281) are an impasse that Gloucester cannot, and indeed does not wish to, accommodate. All of Edgar's efforts as madman-beggar-poor man on behalf of his father have been in vain. By the end of the first half of the play Lear as father and king is frustrated and vengeful; in 4.6 Edgar as child and outcast is frustrated and then rewarded with a letter he can use.

Although it is a commonplace of *Lear* criticism that the Gloucester case is at the service of enabling us to understand the Lear case, it has not been noticed by *Lear* criticism that the distraught Gloucester at the end of 4.6 helps us to understand the distraught Lear at the end of 5.3: Gloucester's death as reported in 5.3 (". . . his flaw'd heart . . ./Burst smilingly"[5.3.197-200]) is one gloss on Lear's end; the end of 4.6 is another.

Gloucester cannot accommodate his grief at the end of 4.6; Lear cannot accommodate his grief at the end of 5.3. As we have seen, the dramatic action of 3.7, the blinding scene, is translated and condensed into the action of 5.2, the battle scene. The pertinent *structural* point is that the dramatic action of 4.6 is translated and condensed into the middle of 5.2 and then the end of 5.3; the pertinent *thematic* point is that the Lear of 5.3 has replaced the Gloucester of 4.6 and of 5.2. The symbolic action of the play has moved from faithful man in the stocks (Kent) to unaccommodated man in a hovel (Edgar) to old man-father in the noise of battle in 4.6 and in 5.2 (Gloucester)[2] to old-man-father-king in a wretched world (Lear).

In 4.6 three men (Lear, a gentleman, Oswald) come upon a father and a child (Gloucester and Edgar); at the end of 5.3 a father and a child (Lear and Cordelia) come upon three men (Albany, Edgar, Kent). In 4.6 the men enter one after the other and then "leave" separately; by the end of 5.3 the men have gathered. At the end of 4.6 the saved Gloucester is destitute because of mad Lear; at the end of 5.3 the saved Lear is destitute because of "dead" Cordelia. At the end of 4.6 Edgar begins to turn away from Gloucester; at the end of 5.3 Lear turns away from everyone but Cordelia.

In 4.6, although his father is again in ill thoughts, Edgar must ignore his despondent father and use the letter given to him by Oswald. But by the end of 5.3 Edgar's public mission has ended:

his father is dead; he has managed to destroy his brother. Suddenly entering in the middle of 4.6, Lear has a shattering impact; suddenly entering at the end of 5.3, Lear has a broader, more profound impact. We hear of the joyful and sorrowful reunion of Gloucester and Edgar and of the moving reunion of Gloucester and Edgar with Kent; we hear of the ignominious deaths of Goneril and Regan. To this bemused world come Lear and the still Cordelia, unaware of all that Kent and Edgar and Albany have endured, of all that these three men have seen and heard and felt.

Coming as he does (with Cordelia in his arms), Lear constitutes a gigantic impasse for these three men: Kent, Edgar, Albany. Obsessed with his true daughter, Lear cares not at all for anyone or anything else. With shattering brutality, he wants no moral accommodation, no social acceptance. And these three men, who have served Lear so well for so long, are at an impasse: they have nothing else to care about. Each is without a family, without a friend, without a master. Just as King Lear can do nothing to save Cordelia, so these men can do nothing to save King Lear. They are indeed distraught. The best that Kent can do is to remark that only someone who hates Lear would want him to continue to live. Thus the play ends with this spellbinding tableau-like impasse that we apprehend feelingly. And we are left to deal with this side-piercing sight as best we can; only in our hearts and our understanding can we re-enfranchise these two sacrifices and these three victims.

NOTES

1. In the Folio the scene, 2.3, is not marked: it is part of the long second scene.

2. In 4.6 the battle is between Edgar and Oswald; in 5.2 it is between Britain and France.

16

Perception and Perspective in *King Lear*

The cogency of a Shakespeare play is such that its end is implicit in its beginning. Every part of a Shakespeare play—character, incident, language, story—is at the service of unfolding the initial situation to an articulated conclusion. Shakespeare's usual practice is to establish at once the motivating event and then to quickly display the essential nature of the main participants and then to dramatize the action as it unfolds into either the reconciliation of comedy or the agony of tragedy.[1] Just a moment's reflection about any of Shakespeare's major plays ought to validate the above assertion.

Although the story of *Hamlet* or *Othello* is quite simple, the plot (the addition, as E. M. Forster puts it, of causality to incident) is wonderfully human and extraordinarily precise. The adumbrated plot is documented and explored by means of Shakespeare's presentational mode. One striking feature of Shakespeare's usual structural procedure is that the major characters who are meant to be finally equated are kept apart on stage: Prince Harry is kept apart from Hotspur; Viola is kept apart from Sebastian; Hamlet from Laertes. The consequent movement of the initial action of each of these Shakespeare plays is toward a dramatic confrontation between these separated characters.[2] In these plays the broader Shakespeare principle is that, until the end, the action proceeds along separate plot lines: Prince Harry's line is kept apart from

Hotspur's; Viola's from Sebastian's; Hamlet's from Laertes's. In *King Lear*, after Edgar and Edmund are briefly together in the first two subplot scenes (1.1 and 1.2), their lines are kept apart, until the end.

Shakespeare's structural unit is the scene. If we exclude from consideration those scenes that are primarily choric in nature (for example, 4.3 of *Antony and Cleopatra*, where unnamed soldiers respond to music beneath the stage and in the air; the first scene of *The Tempest*), we can always consider the significance of point of view. Indeed, point of view is crucial to Shakespeare's documentation of character and exploration of theme.[3] But the further meaningful point is that it is essential to regard a Shakespeare play as a network of viewpoints. For the complexity of a Shakespeare play is largely a product and a result of Shakespeare's deployment of points of view.[4] Thus the gathering together of characters and of lines of action at the end of a Shakespeare play is a gathering together on stage of different viewpoints. By then, a Shakespeare tragedy becomes a network of viewpoints about the hero or, in the case of *Romeo and Juliet* or *Antony and Cleopatra*, about the hero and the heroine.[5] The last two scenes of *Hamlet* (act 5) present a number of different Hamlets; the last two scenes of *Othello* (act 5) present a number of different Othellos.

One of the main reasons that *King Lear* is so complex is that it sustains so many vital points of view.[6] Lear, Goneril, Regan, Kent, Gloucester, Edgar, and Edmund appear in each of the five acts. Kent, like Gloucester, is on stage in twelve of the twenty-six scenes; Lear, like Edgar, is in ten scenes; Edmund is in nine; Goneril, like Regan, is in eight. Lear speaks more lines than anyone else in the play (770). Edgar has 406 lines; Kent, 379; Gloucester, 344; Edmund, 323.[7] Of the seven characters named above, only Edgar is not in the first scene of the play; only Gloucester is not in the last scene.

Lear and Gloucester are on stage together in five scenes: 1.1; 2.4 (Lear's second and last confrontation with Goneril and Regan); 3.4 (a tempest scene); 3.6 (the farmhouse scene); 4.6 (the scene in which Lear returns to the action as mad king). Lear and Edgar are on stage together in four scenes: 3.4 (a tempest scene); 3.6 (the farmhouse scene); 4.6 (the scene in which Lear returns); 5.3 (the final scene). Thus in all but the last scene (5.3) whenever Lear and Edgar are together, Gloucester is also present. But Lear never recognizes or responds to the presence of Edgar as his godson; Gloucester never responds on stage to Edgar as his son. In 3.4 and 4.6 Edgar is disguised as mad Tom of Bedlam; in 4.6 Edgar is dressed as either a peasant or a yeoman. In 5.3 Edgar is wearing the armor of a knight or a champion, but to Lear at the end Edgar is one of the men of stones, a murderer, a traitor, an animal.[8] Lear and Edmund are on stage together only at the beginning of the final scene, after Lear and Cordelia have been captured. Lear's only expressed awareness (but faulty perception) of Edmund occurs in 4.6: "Let copulation thrive; for Gloucester's bastard son/Was kinder to his father than my daughters/Got 'tween the lawful sheets"(4.6.114-16). From 4.7 on, Lear's concern is almost exclusively for Cordelia: he has eyes for only his beloved daughter.

The motivating event of the main plot—the love test—is established in the first scene of the play; the motivating event of the subplot—the dissimulation of a thankless child—is established in the second scene. Unlike the long, busy first scene, the second scene, with its clear design, is a model point-of-view scene: Edmund delivers a soliloguy; he has an interview with his father; Edmund delivers a soliloquy; he has an interview with his brother; Edmund delivers a soliloquy. Edmund reveals himself to be a self-centered, self-serving, illegitimate; Gloucester is seen as a superstitious, credulous father; Edgar as an innocent child. The motivating event of the subplot and the nature of the members of the Gloucester family are given to us by means of Edmund's choric soliloquies, through Edmund's eyes. In addition, the scene reinforces the main plot; it is a subplot version of Lear and his children; it makes an incisive comment about the nature of the initial world of the play.

The next subplot scene, 2.1, is an easy extension of, or a development from, 1.2: all three members of the Gloucester family are again on stage. Again Edmund is the only person to remain on stage throughout the scene; he has a short soliloquy after Curan leaves and another short soliloquy after Edgar, following his brother's advice, runs away. Like 1.2, this scene presents the action from Edmund's point of view. He wounds himself in order to delude Gloucester. Under the influence of Edmund, Gloucester denounces Edgar. And then the two remaining members of the subplot (Edmund and Gloucester) are joined by two members of the main plot, Cornwall and Regan. Edmund's ostensible service to his father convinces Cornwall to adopt Edmund.

The very next scene, which both complements and extends 2.1, is presented from the viewpoint of Kent: he is the only person to remain on stage throughout the scene; after an interview with Gloucester, Kent ends the scene with a soliloquy. Kent's service in the cause of his absent master (beating Oswald and justifying to Cornwall his own behavior) is brazen and rude: unlike Edmund, he doesn't dissimulate for his own ends. In looking over Cornwall's head, Kent acts in the interests of what to him is a privileged Lear. The main point is that, right after Edmund enters Cornwall's service (2.1), Kent is put in the stocks by Cornwall (2.2). Since night has come, Kent must wait for the sun to rise in order to read a letter from Cordelia: "Fortune, good night; smile once more, turn thy wheel"(2.2.173). And at once Edgar announces in a soliloquy that he is going to assume the disguise of a beggar. Kent ends 2.2 in the stocks, stultified, and onto the stage comes Edgar: "I heard myself proclaim'd"(2.3.1). The role of good but ineffective servant to and for Lear will pass from Kent to Edgar.[9]

Lear leaves the stage at the end of act 1 (1.5) and does not return until 2.4. While Lear is absent, Shakespeare presents three different viewpoints (Edmund's in 2.1, Kent's in 2.2, Edgar's in 2.3) that function in terms of three related lines of action that will come together in the final scene. Edmund's service to Cornwall will result in his becoming "contracted" to both Goneril and Regan; Kent will thereafter be concerned exclusively with the welfare of Lear and Cordelia; by enacting on stage the role of Tom of Bedlam, Edgar will begin a movement that will culminate in a trial by combat against his half-brother. Again, after 2.1, Edmund and Edgar are kept apart until their confrontation in the final scene: they are both in 5.1 but are not on stage together.

In 1.4 (where he is introduced into the play), in 1.5, and in 2.4, the Fool wants Lear to become what he was; but in the storm in act 3 the Fool loses all expectation of that hope. Like Kent at the end of 2.2, the Fool at the end of act 3 is at an impasse: Lear's

world can never again be what it was. The specific point is that
3.2 is from the viewpoint of the Fool: he is the only person to
remain on stage throughout the scene. "Good nuncle, in, ask thy
daughter's blessing"(3.2.11-12) is now his sad appeal to Lear. In
this scene the Fool's rhyme (introduced by the words "He that has
a house to put's head in has a good head-piece"[3.2.25-26]) is the
Fool's "summary of the human situation."[10] During the scene the
Fool begins to lose his identity as a human being to a larger,
choric function. He sings a stanza from the Fool's epilogue-song-
soliloquy in *Twelfth Night*: man alone in a world of wind and rain.
In *this* Fool's soliloquy, which ends 3.2, he remarks that when
Albion becomes a Utopia, "Then shall the realm of Albion/Come
to great confusion"(3.2.85-86). What he says doesn't even express
what *he* thinks or feels: "This prophecy Merlin shall make, for I
live before his time"(3.2.95-96).[11]

Like Kent's role 2.2, the Fool's changed role in 3.2 contributes
to Lear's growing upset. Like Kent, the Fool and his choric
function will give way in 3.4 to Edgar and his choric and dramatic
function.[12] Edgar in 3.4, secure in his role as mad Tom, will
evince no expressed regard for Lear; however, during the mock
trial of Goneril and Regan in 3.6, he will come to express in an
aside his heartfelt feeling for the now-frantic Lear: "My tears
begin   to   take   his   part   so   much,/They   mar   my
counterfeiting"(3.6.60-61). An empathetic, choric Edgar begins to
peek through his guise as Tom.

For most of act 3 the emphasis alternates between the main plot
and the subplot. Act 3.2 presents Lear, the Fool, and Kent; act 3.3
presents Edmund and Gloucester; 3.4 presents the Lear group; 3.5
presents Edmund and Cornwall; 3.6 presents the Lear group; 3.7
presents Cornwall, Regan, Goneril, Edmund, Oswald, and
Gloucester. In this six-scene sequence the most significant subplot
character is Gloucester. In 3.3 he tells Edmund that he intends to
help Lear; in 3.4 he joins Lear in the storm in order to bring him
"where both fire and food is ready"(3.4.153); in 3.5 Edmund
betrays Gloucester to Cornwall; in 3.6 Gloucester helps Lear
escape to Dover; in 3.7 Cornwall takes revenge on the traitor,
Gloucester, by plucking out his eyes—the turning point in the
subplot and the central event in *King Lear*. Gloucester's delayed,
good service to Lear goes unrewarded: like Kent's immediate

service to Lear (in 1.1 and 2.2), Gloucester's eventual willingness to serve Lear results in his being brutally punished and stultified, reduced from active participant to victim. Act 3.3, the second of the six-scene sequence, is presented from Edmund's viewpoint: like 1.2, it ends with a self-serving soliloquy. In 3.7 the blind Gloucester does learn of his bastard's perfidy.

Both Gloucester and Edmund (what they stand for and represent) are on either side of the advent of Edgar as Tom of Bedlam, who re-enters the subplot by means of the main plot. Act 3.4 is a variation of Shakespeare's usual point-of-view practice in that the action is presented from the viewpoint of both Lear and Kent: these two are on stage throughout the scene. The only time that the Fool is off stage in the scene occurs when he enters the hovel and brings forth Tom. Lear's "Poor naked wretches"(3.4.28) speech is a kind of soliloquy, said by Lear, overheard by Kent. The significant thematic point is that, although earlier he was solicitous of his Fool, Lear, for the first time in the play, is able to look beyond himself to those worse off than he:

> Take physic, pomp,
> Expose thyself to feel what wretches feel,
> That thou mayst shake the superflux to them,
> And show the heavens more just.
>
> (3.4.33-36)

Symbolically, the speech prompts the appearance of Tom, "A servingman! proud in heart and mind"(3.4.85), "unaccommodated man"(3.4.106-07). This Tom is worse off than the abject Fool.

In the scene, after the emergence of the naked wretch from the hovel, Lear has eyes for only this madman and ears for only this beggar's history. Once Lear discovers Tom, the Fool is relegated to the company of the disguised Kent. Kent and the Fool must abide Lear in his new obsession. Lear remains unaware that Kent, the servingman at his side, is also an unaccommodated man; Lear ought to realize that the pathetic Fool is an unaccommodated man; it is beyond Lear's concern that Gloucester's good service to him (but traitorous behavior to Cornwall) may turn Gloucester into an unaccommodated man. Lear recognizes the vainglory of pomp, but he is incapable of extending his perception beyond what *we know* is a counterfeit example of unaccommodated man, Edgar as Tom.

By the end of the play none of these men will mean much to Lear: the Fool and Tom will have disappeared; Gloucester will be dead; Kent will be perfunctorily welcomed. From 4.7 on, Lear, again obsessed with his beloved daughter, will be blind to everyone and everything else.

In 3.4 and 3.6 mad Tom directs the attention of a disturbed Lear; in his soliloquy at the end of 3.6 Edgar's understandable self-concern is corrected by Lear's plight:

> How light and portable my pain seems now,
> When that which makes me bend makes the King bow:
> He childed as I fathered!
>
> (3.6.108-10)

Act 3.6 ends with a soliloquy by Edgar; the terrifying retributive action of 3.7 takes place; 4.1 begins with a soliloquy by Edgar. Gloucester and Edmund are on either side of the first appearance in the play of Tom of Bedlam in 3.4. Now Edgar, as Tom, is on either side of Edmund and Gloucester in 3.7. At the end of 3.6 Edgar, like Kent at the end of 2.2, is at an impasse: when the sleeping Lear is rescued, Edgar is left behind. And then, at the beginning of 4.1, upon seeing his blinded father, Edgar is most moved by his father's plight, his father as hopeless victim.

The world is worse than Edgar thought, but he doesn't follow blindly like Kent or collapse like the Fool or sleep like Lear. Edgar, as forgotten, unaccommodated man, begins the slow process of being accommodated as a champion of the realm. For the blind father provides the aimless Edgar the chance to be his father's eyes and the opportunity to save his father from despair. Once Tom puts on the "covering" provided for his nakedness, he will, in 4.6, still be a madman to the distraught, blind Gloucester, but he will be something quite different to the fallen Gloucester, to the mad king, to the Gentleman, to Oswald. Oswald's faulty perception of Edgar as a peasant, a slave, and a villain provides Edgar with the letters, the way toward his worldly redemption.

* * * * *

Lear is absent from the stage from 3.6 to 4.6. Edgar and Gloucester are on stage in 4.1 and again in 4.6. In the four intervening episodic scenes (4.2; 4.3; 4.4; 4.5) eleven different characters speak (Goneril, Edmund, Oswald, Albany, a messenger, Kent, a gentleman, Cordelia, a Doctor, another messenger, Regan). Only Oswald (whose thematic role in act 4 is like Edmund's in act 3) appears and speaks in more than one scene, 4.2 and 4.5. Lear and Gloucester and Edgar have escaped their enemies. While Lear and Gloucester and Edgar are absent from the stage, each of Lear's three daughters as well as Kent is presented in a separate scene: Goneril, Kent, Cordelia, Regan. Goneril is enamored of Edmund and would like to see Albany, her husband, dead; Kent is preoccupied with Lear and Cordelia; Cordelia will do anything to help her father; Regan, who is now enamored of Edmund, tries to subvert Oswald, for she wants Gloucester dead and Edmund freed from Goneril.

Like Goneril, Regan cares about only herself and her love for Edmund. Like Kent, Cordelia is devoted to her father and will sacrifice "all [her] outward worth"(4.4.10) to help him. Goneril and Regan look down to Edmund ("Down from the waist they are Centaurs,/Though women all above;/But to the girdle do the gods inherit,/Beneath is all the fiends': there's hell, there's darkness"[4.6.124-27]); Kent and Cordelia look up to Lear. Each of the first four scenes of act 4 contains a quasi-soliloquy: it looks outward and upward. The four speeches are given by those in opposition to Goneril and Regan: Gloucester, Albany, Kent, Cordelia. These four speeches ascend in spiritual value from Gloucester's despair to Cordelia's affirmation; they look forward to the heavenly reunion of Lear and Cordelia in 4.7.

In 4.1 Gloucester delivers his famous remark: "As flies to wanton boys are we to th' gods,/They kill us for their sport"(4.1.36-37). In 4.2, in reaction to the news of the way the servant responded to Cornwall's plucking out of Gloucester's eyes, Albany comments, "This shows you are above,/You [justicers], that these our nether crimes/So speedily can venge!"4.2.78-80) In 4.3, after hearing how Cordelia took the news of her sisters' treatment of their father in the storm, Kent says, "It is the stars,/The stars above us, govern our conditions,/Else one self mate and make could not beget/Such different issues"(4.3.32-35).

And in 4.4, hearing that the distressed Lear has escaped from the town and that the British forces are advancing, Cordelia, echoing *Luke, 11:29*, cries, "O dear father,/It is thy business that I go about"(4.4.23-24). It should be observed that neither Albany nor Cordelia is in acts 2 or 3; each is responding to a report. The responses are made on the basis of second-hand information.

Act 4.6, the scene in which Lear returns to the play, is from the viewpoint of both Edgar and Gloucester, who have witnessed the distraught Lear of 3.4 and 4.6. In addition to three asides, Edgar comments at the end to and about the dead Oswald; he then reads Goneril's letter written to Edmund. All of these lines resemble a soliloquy: Gloucester is so preoccupied with himself that he doesn't listen to Edgar, even if he were close enough on stage to hear him. In 4.6 the disguised Edgar, like Kent in 2.2, is serving a distraught old man, *to no immediate purpose*. In 2.2 Kent briefly affects the language of a courtier; in 4.6 Edgar briefly adopts the dialect of a rustic. In 2.2 Kent beats Oswald; in 4.6 Edgar cudgels Oswald to death. At the end of 2.2 Kent produces a letter from Cordelia; at the end of 4.6 Edgar receives at least two letters from Oswald, one from Regan (in 4.5) and one from Goneril. Edgar *uses* the letter from Goneril to become a champion.

In design 4.6 is most like 3.4 but, as we would expect, from a different viewpoint. Act 3.4 is from the viewpoint of both Kent and Lear; 4.6 is from the viewpoint of both Edgar and Gloucester. In the middle of 3.4 Edgar, as mad Tom, and Gloucester join Lear and Kent and the Fool in the storm; in the middle of 4.6 Lear as mad king joins Edgar and Gloucester in calm weather. The thought of the play determines that the beggar be accommodated by the king in 3.4 and that the king be accommodated by the beggar in 4.6.[13] In 3.4 Tom enables Lear to focus on unaccommodated man; in 4.6 Lear forces Edgar and Gloucester to focus on unaccommodated king. In 3.4 Lear wants to become unaccommodated man; in 4.6 he insists that he is "the King himself"(4.6.84). To Edgar and Gloucester in 4.6, Lear is an icon and an exemplum. Lear's indictment of *his* civilized society is bitter, corrosive. In 3.4 Gloucester is, to the Fool, "a walking fire"(3.4.114) and, to Tom, "foul [fiend] Flibbertigibbet"(3.4.115); in 4.6 Gloucester, to Lear, is "Goneril with a white beard"(4.6.96), then blind Cupid, then Gloucester. After Lear's onslaught, Edgar's efforts to delude his blind father into being miraculously reborn prove to have been in vain. Lear deepens Gloucester's despair; Gloucester cannot endure Lear's tempest: "The King is mad"(4.6.279). Like Kent in 2.2, blind Gloucester ends 4.6 being worse off than he was at the beginning of the scene.

As Gloucester's eyes, Edgar tells his father what has been seen: Edgar fabricates a perception for his father. In Edgar's vivid description of an imagined view, common things change their appearance: fishermen appear as mice. The advent of Lear's piercing perception in 4.6 mars Edgar's humane achievement. During his long interview with Gloucester, Lear tells the old man to see with his ears; to see *through* things ("Robes and furr'd gowns hide all [vices]"[4.6.165]). He tells him to translate what is seen: a creature running from a cur becomes "the great image of authority: a dog's obeyed in office"(4.6.158-59). He tells Gloucester to get "glass eyes"(4.6.170) and, "like a scurvy politician, seem/To see the things thou dost not"(4.6.171-72). Lear tells him to use his eyes to weep, not to see. Unwittingly, destroying what Edgar's perceptions have accomplished, Lear imposes a drastic series of perceptions upon Gloucester, for no substantive reason.

Both Edgar and Lear see what isn't there: Edgar is making up a scene; Lear is imagining an invisible, harsh reality. The effect of Lear's blistering words enables Gloucester to "see [the world] feelingly"(4.6.149). But that sudden sight is too much for the damaged old man to bear: Gloucester concludes that it is better to be "distract"(4.6.281). A nameless Edgar uses his manufactured point of view to rescue his unaware father from despair; King Lear's imposed point of view distracts Gloucester and turns the blind old man into a hopeless old man. Edgar wants his father to look up; Lear makes the old man look down. Cornwall violates Gloucester in 3.7; Lear violates Gloucester in 4.6.

Before Gloucester falls down, he looks down; after he falls down, he looks up. From a broad perspective, the action of *King Lear* can be described as a looking down and then a looking up. Albany, Kent, Cordelia, and Gloucester, all of whom have fallen, look up in act 4; Goneril, Regan, and Oswald have never looked up; they always look down. Until the advent of Lear on stage in

4.6, Edgar's behavior in the scene is determined by the perception he wants his father to have; he wants his father to look down and then, miraculously saved from death, to look up. When Lear imposes a deeper, downward perspective, Edgar's well-meant intentions are blasted: Lear's perception of worldly reality destroys Gloucester's will to live. In the next scene Cordelia will do for her father what Edgar tries and fails to do for his father in 4.6. Cordelia succeeds because Lear awakens as a child-changed father; Cordelia will ultimately fail because the world has not been changed by a child.

Lear looks down in 4.6; he looks up in 4.7. From the perspective of the second half of the play, 4.6 is a "looking-down"; 4.7 is a "looking-up." The second scene is the opposite of the first; in 4.6 Lear is mad king; in 4.7 he is a "very foolish fond old man"(4.7.59); dressed in fresh garments, he is a kind father. With the great rage killed in him, he awakens to the spirit Cordelia, to music, to the good offices of the Doctor and the presence of Kent and the Gentleman. The action is from the viewpoint of a still-disguised Kent, who remains on stage after Cordelia has led Lear off, who has a little dialogue with the Gentleman ("'Tis time to look about"[4.7.91-92)), and who ends the scene with this soliloquy-like remark:

> My point and period will be throughly wrought,
> Or well or ill, as this day's battle's fought.
>   (4.7.95-96)

The heartfelt, lovely reunion of Lear and Cordelia must still be submitted to the end, to the battle that is about to begin. But the scene is the end of act 4; it is a private action; it grants us a privileged perspective.

For 4.7 as a "looking-up" scene is also in opposition to 3.7, a "looking-down" scene, the blinding of an old man-father. There Gloucester is put in a chair and blinded; then the "eyeless villain"(3.7.96) is turned out. In 4.7 Lear is also in a chair, but he awakens to kindness and seeming security. Like Gloucester, he is released from the chair. In 3.7 Regan leads the wounded Cornwall off stage; in 4.7 Cordelia leads the feeble Lear off stage. Act 3.7 ends with only two servants on stage; 4.7 draws to a close with only Kent and the Gentleman on stage. None of the characters in 3.7 is in 4.7. The world has changed; the wheel has been turned; what was down is now up. Toward the end of act 3 Lear is obsessed with Edgar as unaccommodated man; at the end of act 4 Lear is obsessed with Cordelia, the spiritual daughter.

We look down to a beggar in 3.4 and look up to a mad king in 4.6 and to a recovered old man and father in 4.7. In a sense 4.7 looks backward to 4.6 and then, further back, to 3.7 and then to 3.6 (where Lear falls asleep) and then to 3.4 and ultimately to 1.1, Lear's love-test and his treatment of Cordelia. "You have some cause, [your sisters] have not"(4.7.74), Lear says in 4.7, to which Cordelia replies, "No cause, no cause"(4.7.75). And then Lear: "You must bear with me./Pray you now forget, and forgive; I am old and foolish"(4.7.83-84). Lear manages to recover himself in the last scene, before his final fall. But then Cordelia never sees the corrosive, fallen, ugly Lear of 4.6.

* * * * *

The center of the eleven-line 5.2 is the stage direction *Alarum and retreat within. Enter* EDGAR. When the alarum and then the retreat are sounded, Gloucester is on stage alone: the British have won; Lear and Cordelia have lost. The noisy center is bracketed by Edgar and Gloucester. Before the battle is both lost and won, Gloucester is to Edgar a "father"; after the battle, he is to Edgar an "old man." Since the British have won, Edgar must do what he promised Albany in 5.1 he would: produce a champion. For the brutal, other truth is that, once the British have won, Edgar will have to forsake his eyeless father, who has been victimized by Cornwall (3.7) and Lear (4.6) in order to challenge the risen Edmund: he must relegate his desperate father to his status at the end of 3.7, that of a forsaken old man.

Lear and Cordelia are on either side of 5.2: at the beginning of the scene Lear and Cordelia walk across the stage before the battle; at the beginning of 5.3 Lear and Cordelia come onto the stage, after the battle, as prisoners. Edmund brackets Lear and Cordelia. Gloucester and the noise of battle are at the center of 5.2; Edgar and Gloucester bracket that center; Lear and Cordelia bracket Edgar and Gloucester; Edmund brackets Lear and Cordelia. What will happen to Edmund, to Lear and Cordelia, to Edgar, to Gloucester is determined by what happens *off stage* at the center of 5.2, the winning and losing of the battle.

While Edmund is briefly off stage in 5.1, Edgar appears and gives Albany Goneril's letter, which was written to Edmund. After Albany comes back on stage (5.3), he tells Edmund that he holds him "but a subject of this war/Not as a brother"(5.3.60-61). Off stage Albany has been busy controlling or bracketing Edmund. Structurally, therefore, bracketing may be considered as frames or as a series of encompassing circles, each one primarily concerned with the circle immediately inside it: Albany's circle; then Edmund's; then Lear and Cordelia's; then Edgar's.[14] In terms of the present discourse, each circle is a viewpoint that has been documented by the play. The still center is Gloucester and the winning and losing of the battle: his viewpoint is now the static one of victim. The dramatic point is that, because of Albany's larger actions, Edmund *will have to* "defend" himself rather than to debate. After Edgar leaves the stage in 5.1, Edmund's first words upon his re-entrance in the scene are these: "The enemy's in view"(5.1.51). From our perspective, Edgar, Edmund's enemy, has just been in view.

A familiar tension in Shakespeare roughly corresponds to a frame or bracketing; it has to do with the tension between the outside and the inside: the outside is in opposition to the inside. In sonnets 74 and 146 the terms are the body and the soul: "The worth of that is that which it contains"(74.13); "Poor soul, the centre of my sinful earth"(146.1). A closely related tension is even more familiar. In act 2 of *The Merchant of Venice* the Prince of Morocco discovers that the golden casket contains "carrion Death"(2.7.63). In *King Lear* Edmund agrees to fight the unknown opposite because, so he says, "[his] outside looks so fair and warlike"(5.3.143). Oswald, Regan, Goneril, and Edmund are destroyed because they are bemused by outside appearance. Unaware of his base nature, Goneril and Regan are enamored of Edmund's goodly outside. Until the end Edmund, Goneril, and Regan are obsessed with the body, with gold, with getting what they desire.[15] Until they "marry in an instant"(5.3.230) in a series of rash deaths, they are never out in the storm; they do not "see

. . . feelingly"(4.6.149). They do not look up; they do not look within. They never perceive Cordelia or Lear as being good or valuable: to them Cordelia is not the heart or love or truth or the spirit.

The outside-inside tension reinforces the trope of looking downward and then upward. Bemused by the outside, Edmund looks downward; bemused by the inside, Cordelia looks upward. Self-centered Edmund intends to destroy; love-centered Cordelia intends to save and protect. As soon as Edmund (what he stands for or represents; his cynical perception) is borne off stage, Cordelia (what she stands for or represents; her hopeful belief) is borne on stage in the arms of Lear. Apparently Lear sinks down, and if he is lent a looking-glass, as he requests, he holds it up to her face. It seems certain, however, that he holds a feather up to her mouth to see if she (what she represents or stands for) still has breath. For just a short while then, with Kent kneeling, all three are together again, as they were in 1.1 and in 4.7, the reunion scene. Lear now acknowledges Kent. In addition, the other two daughters have been brought back on stage and their faces covered: their faces cannot be seen; they are masked. The dramatic point is that the principal actors of 1.1 have gathered. The little family is together again; the failed love-test of the first scene has come to this incredible conclusion. All of the preceding scenes provide gathered perspectives on this final one.

Lear's last words concern his beloved daughter: "Do you see this? Look on her!/Look her lips,/Look there, look there!"(5.3.311-312) And then he faints or dies, falling forward to join his beloved daughter in death. But before he falls, a kind of spatial, instant bracketing takes place. Cordelia is the sacrifice and victim as center; Lear is obsessed with this center, her life, his spirit. Albany, Edgar, and Kent now stand around Lear and Cordelia. They are obsessed by the spectacle of this pair. The important point, however, is that each onlooker sees a different Lear and Cordelia: each observer has a viewpoint of this father and daughter, one that the action of the play has rendered. Albany knows only the Lear of act 1; Edgar has never seen Cordelia and knows only the frantic Lear of acts 3 and 4; Kent did not see the mad Lear of 4.6. Kent knows Lear and Cordelia best, but his perception of Lear is still partial, incomplete.

In reporting his reunion with his father, Edgar remarks to Edmund and Albany:

> But [Gloucester's] flaw'd heart
> (Alack, too weak the conflict to support!)
> 'Twixt two extremes of passion, joy and grief,
> Burst smilingly.
>
> (5.3.197-200)

Bradley's familiar argument that Lear's death, resembling Gloucester's, has also a "fleeting, ecstatic joy" is rejected by J. Stampfer:

> But the similarity only serves to accentuate the basic difference between the two deaths. Gloucester died between extremes of joy and grief, at the knowledge that his son was miraculously preserved, Lear between extremes of illusion and truth, ecstacy and the blackest despair, at the knowledge that his daughter was needlessly butchered. Gloucester's heart "burst smilingly" at his reunion with Edgar; Lear's, we are given to conclude, burst in the purest agony at his eternal separation from Cordelia.[16]

Gloucester's end does provide us with a perspective on Lear's. More pertinently, the Gloucester-Edgar situation functions as a gloss on the Lear-Cordelia situation. In 4.6, before the great rage in him was killed, Lear saw deeper than Gloucester ever did; in 4.7, in his sublime reunion with Cordelia, he saw higher than Gloucester ever could. Lear and Cordelia are King and Queen, not just a father and a child. In her service to her father, Cordelia, unlike Edgar, is determined, direct, and unswerving. Edgar deserts his father and kills his brother. Lear killed the slave who was hanging Cordelia: he tried to rescue his beloved, blameless daughter and failed. The main point is that the Gloucester-Edgar situation enables us to better understand and appreciate the poignancy of the Lear-Cordelia end. For the sad truth is that the Gloucester-Edgar situation at the end is more complex than the Lear-Cordelia one, as the beginning of 5.3 predicted:

> So we'll live,
> And pray, and sing, and tell old tales, and laugh
> At gilded butterflies, and hear poor rogues
> Talk of court news; and we'll talk with them too—
> Who loses and who wins; who's in, who's out—
> And take upon's the mystery of things
> As if we were God's spies; and we'll wear out,
> In a wall'd prison, packs and sects of great ones,
> That ebb and flow by th' moon.
>
> (5.3.11-19)

Holding his beloved companion, Lear asks the three men on stage to look down. Seeing that Lear is looking down, Edgar responds, "Look up, my lord"(5.3.313). From the perspective of 4.6, Edgar, as he had with Gloucester, wants Lear, having looked down, to look up. From the perspective of both 4.6 and 4.7, we must look down and then look up. The dynamics of the full play require that procedure. Responding to Edgar, Kent wants *his* Lear, not to look up, but to go up: "Vex not his ghost. O, let him pass"(5.3.314). From his perspective, which is a product of 4.7, Kent feels that it would be a relief for Lear to die; with Cordelia dead, there is no earthly reason for Lear to continue to live. The mute testimony on stage of the dead bodies of Lear's other daughters reminds us of Kent's earlier upward-looking comment about "the stars above"(4.3.33) and "Such different issues"(4.3.34) as Cordelia and her two sisters. Although Lear doesn't want Cordelia's ghost to pass, Kent does want Lear's ghost to pass now, *at this moment*. From Kent's perspective, Lear and Cordelia should be together (like Romeo and Juliet, Othello and Desdemona, Antony and Cleopatra).

Cordelia is a victim and a sacrifice; as a spirit and soul, Cordelia rises victorious; as transcendent love, she has been released from this earthly prison. Both Cordelia and Lear have come from the prison house to die in this public way. Recognized at last ("My master calls me, I must not say no"[5.3.323]), Kent will follow after Lear and Cordelia: the full significance of their deaths is contingent upon the belief in a spirit and in a spiritual life. For one of the public points that the end of *King Lear* makes is related to the private point made by King Richard (after shifting in a soliloquy from king to beggar to king to beggar) in his final words, after being struck down by Exton in *Richard II*:

> Mount, mount, my soul! thy seat is up on high,
> Whilst my gross flesh sinks downward, here to die.
>   (5.5.111-12)

Like Richard II, Lear and Cordelia and Kent have to die in order for their souls to rise. These related sacrifices (Cordelia, then Lear, then Kent), canonized by their earned, mutual love, demand both our sorrow at their death and our joy at their redemption from this world.[17]

It is, however, a singular error to overlook the ironic, negative aspects of a world bereft of Lear and Cordelia. We look down: "Is this the promis'd end?/Or image of that horror?"(5.3.264-65) To Kent it is a "tough world"(5.3.315); to Albany the state is "gor'd"(5.3.321); to Edgar it is a "sad time"(5.3.324). The grim 3.7 ends with a brief epilogue by two servants; the resplendent 4.7 ends with an epilogue by Kent and the Gentleman; 5.3 ends with an epilogue by a distraught Kent, Albany, and Edgar. Kent's "point and period"(4.7.95), like the battle, will be both "well" and "ill." The British win; Lear and Cordelia and Kent lose. In the first scene of the play Kent tries to make Lear "See better"(1.1.158) and is thrust out of doors for his trouble; in 2.2 he tries to serve the changed Lear's cause and ends up worsening that cause; in 4.7 he refuses to be acknowledged until the proper time, and now, in 5.3, when he has rejoined Lear and Cordelia and has been acknowledged, it is too late for acclaim or celebration. Sorrow overwhelms his long-anticipated joy.

In 5.3 Albany, who has been supplanted by Edmund in the arms of Goneril, publicly denounces his murderous wife. When he hears of her suicide, he remarks, "This judgment of the heavens, that makes us tremble,/Touches us not with pity"(5.3.232-33). Upon hearing that Edmund is dead, he responds, "That's but a trifle here"(5.3.296). When Lear enters, Albany offers to resign his power so long as Lear lives; after the death of Lear, Albany offers to give the office of king to Kent and Edgar. What Albany has done and what he has been forced to do have hardened him as a man and depleted him as a king: he is wifeless, childless; his state is "gor'd"(5.3.321). He has seen too much too soon and has been too much a part of the "general woe"(5.3.319).

Edmund agrees to combat the unknown opposite because he knows that, having been stripped of power by Albany, the only way he can now defend himself is, first, to defeat the champion and then to defeat the champion's master, Albany. After being fatally wounded, Edmund exchanges charity with Edgar and encourages Edgar to tell his story. The real reason for this unexpected behavior is not that Edmund has been converted, but that Edmund still wants (as he did at the beginning of the scene) Lear and Cordelia dead. Edmund still manipulates Edgar: he hasn't changed his nature. In seeming to be penitent and helpful, Edmund is still desperately trying to defend himself. At the end, paying lip service to looking upward and looking within, he just collapses into "goodness."[18]

And indeed, while Edgar is exchanging forgiveness and charity with Edmund, Cordelia is being hanged off stage. Hostage to his role as champion or man of justice, Edgar, the ostensible good son, can speak unfeelingly about his dead father: "The gods are just, and of our pleasant vices/Make instruments to plague us"(5.3.171-72). By chance and circumstance Edgar has been forced to desert his desperate father and to kill his half-brother: this good man becomes the instrument of death and heartbreak. If the last speech is indeed his, he seems perhaps aware that he is partly responsible for the deaths of Cordelia and Lear:

> The weight of this sad time we must obey,
> Speak what we feel, not what we ought to say:
> The oldest hath borne most; we that are young
> Shall never see so much, nor live so long.[19]
>
> (5.3.324-27)

If Cordelia is already dead when Lear enters with her in his arms, Lear is the only person to die on stage in the last scene: Lear's death is bracketed, on one side, by a series of deaths and, on the other side, by a series of responses to his onstage death. Within 112 lines, five deaths are reported or occur on stage. If Cordelia is already dead, then this is the order of the deaths: Gloucester, Regan, Goneril, Cordelia, Edmund, Lear.[20] Men bracket Lear's three daughters. More pertinently, the oldest men, who have borne most, bracket the young: Gloucester dies of heartbreak; a deluded Lear succumbs; the others die justifiable deaths.

If, however, Cordelia dies on stage in Lear's arms, Gloucester, Cordelia and Lear bracket three violent off-stage deaths: Regan is murdered by Goneril; Goneril commits suicide with a knife; Edmund dies a bereft villain. *King Lear* begins with three men on stage as a kind of prologue: Kent, Gloucester, Edmund. In the last 129 lines of the play nine perspectives come to a close. In the course of the play the three men who introduce the action join at last three separate, distinct groups. Edmund has joined Goneril and Regan: they "marry in an instant"(5.3.230). Gloucester has joined Cordelia and Lear: they are killed by care. Kent has joined the other survivors, Albany and Edgar, in a series of sad remarks: their discourse is totally unlike the brittle, unfeeling talk of the three men who performed the prologue. We may well consider the Edmund-Goneril-Regan group as symbolizing the hand; the Gloucester-Lear-Cordelia group as symbolizing the heart; the Edgar-Albany-Kent group as symbolizing the head.

The end of *King Lear* is both a dramatic contraction and a thematic expansion. The focus narrows down to this singular event, a dying old man-father-king with his dead child-queen-spirit: looking *down* at Cordelia's *uplifted* face, Lear rejoices; they are "God's spies"(5.3.17). From Lear's limited, singular perspective, Cordelia is alive. But the context for that remarkable occasion is an elaborate network of perceptions, each one cogently and dramatically presented, pungently put forth, and, valorized by and in an exceptional, composed text. Although it may be impossible to do full justice to the contextuality of Shakespeare's masterful end, it is certainly wrong to diminish the force of the end by sentimentalizing it as being optimistic or pessimistic. The end is what it must be: layered and multi-faceted. Only by trying to distinguish the various perceptions and perspectives can we begin to understand and thus appreciate the true nature of Shakespeare's transcendent vision and unmitigated genius in this, the best of all possible plays.

NOTES

1. We more or less exclude the histories because of their special, large-scale nature.

2. Macbeth and Macduff are not on stage together from 2.3 till the end of act 5; although the procedure is slightly different, Antony and Caesar are not on stage together after 3.2.

3. See Kenneth Muir's comment in the Introduction to the Oxford *Troilus and Cressida* (Oxford: Oxford UP, 1984), 20. In the typical point-of-view scene, one character remains on stage while others come and go; that character delivers at least one soliloquy.

4. S. L. Bethell uses the term *multiconsciousness* to describe an aspect of our concern. See in particular Chapter 6 ("Further Ramifications of Multiconsciousness") in *Shakespeare and the Popular Dramatic Tradition* (Durham NC: Duke UP, 1944), 132-69. Bertram Evans documents "Shakespeare's devotion to a dramatic method that gives the audience an advantage in awareness, and thus opens exploitable gaps both between audience and participants and between participants and participants" in *Shakespeare's Comedies* (London: Oxford UP, 1967), viii.

5. Although Antony dies at the end of act 4, attitudes toward Antony are expressed in both scenes of act 5 in *Antony and Cleopatra*.

6. See Stephen Booth, "On the Greatness of King Lear" (*"King Lear,"* *"Macbeth," Indefinition and Tragedy* [New Haven: Yale UP]), 1983, 5-57). The "inclusiveness" of *King Lear* and its "multiple dimensions" are in large part a product of the points of view developed by Shakespeare in the play. A consideration of perceptions and perspectives repudiates what Booth considers to be the "inconclusive" nature of *King Lear*.

7. The line count is from the Globe edition. We have assumed that The Riverside text has validity. We have avoided textual considerations (such as the absence of 3.6 from the Folio) in order to try to keep the argument clear and cogent.

8. These are the words used by Lear about the men on stage near the end of the play.

9. See Jonas A. Barish and Marshall Waingrow, "'Service' in *King Lear*," *Shakespeare Quarterly* 9 (1958), 347-355. Their assessment of Kent ("the quintessence of the good servant and the touchstone for service throughout the play" [349]) needs qualification.

10. These are John Danby's words (*Shakespeare's Doctrine of Nature: A Study of King Lear* [London: Faber and Faber, 1951], 110).

11. For a brief discussion of the social significance of the Fool's soliloquy, see Danby, 107.

12. On the general subject of the many fools and madmen in *King Lear*, see John Reibetanz, *The Lear World: A Study of King Lear in Its Dramatic Context* (Toronto: U of Toronto P, 1977), 81-107.

13. The king-beggar tension is familiar. See, in particular, its use in *Richard II*, 5.3 and 5.5.

14. For a discussion of the use of bracketing or circles or frames, see "Encompassing Actions" in Thomas B. Stroup, *Microcosmos: The Shape of the Elizabethan Play* (Lexington, KY: U of Kentucky P), 1965, 37-87.

15. Edmund's words in 5.3 make the point: ". . . some good I mean to do/Despite of mine own nature"(5.3.244-45).

16. J. Stampfer, "The Catharsis of *King Lear.*" *Shakespeare Survey* 13 (1960): 4.

17. For an excellent expression of the plangent *King Lear*, see Alfred Harbage, Introduction to *The Pelican King Lear* (Baltimore: Penguin Books, 1965), 14-27.

18. The case for a last-minute conversion by Edmund may have some merit.

19. In the quarto the final speech is given to Albany.

20. Goneril may kill herself before Regan dies.

17

Affirmation in *Troilus and Cressida*

Troilus and Cressida deserves its reputation as a difficult play. It is difficult; it is not ambiguous. The clear emphasis is on unpleasantness, on the failure of faith, honor, love, and patience. Much of the difficulty in approaching the play arises because the clues to goodness are not so obvious as they are in perhaps every other Shakespeare play, particularly in the superb early plays where, for example, the emphasis on redemption in *1 Henry IV* or on ceremony in *As You Like It* makes clear major affirmative intent. We are asked to bring the affirmation to a vicious *Troilus and Cressida*, for the play is sophisticated, truly sophisticated, in that in it Shakespeare immediately is counting more on us—is counting on us to see more—than he usually does.

In *1 Henry IV* the King, Hotspur, and Falstaff make clear what Prince Harry is not. Although Touchstone and Jaques are in the forest in *As You Like It*, that world is still green. Prince Harry is "successful"; Orlando and Rosalind are "true." But in *Troilus* there seems to be no superior being, no Hamlet or Othello or Lear or Antony, to whom things happen but do not violate, no hero who is destroyed but not defeated. In the play an affirmative figure is not readily apparent. Experience does violate Troilus, who is in fact another Romeo, but a Romeo not redeemed by a Juliet.

The first sentence of the Prologue, "In Troy there lies the scene"(Pro.1), indicates that the setting is to be Troy, but since the play also has the Greek camp and the field between Troy and the camp as settings, the sentence would seem to be not completely true and would seem then to serve another purpose. The sentence may mean that *the scene lies in Troy* or that *the seen lies there* or, further, that *in Troy their lies are seen* or that *in Troy their lies are the scene.* At least Shakespeare at once alerts us not to believe what we see in Troy. And just about everyone in Troy seems to be concerned with appearances, with keeping up appearances: the society is based on a series of lies. And since it is, we can understand the main reason why Troilus fails Cressida and why he is failed by her.

The Trojan world is infected by Paris's crime. In the royal family the ugly truth beneath the enormous lie they are all living is apparent from the start. Hector, we are at once told, has just "chid"(1.2.6) Andromache. Later Troilus can insult Helenus, can call Cassandra mad, and can finally blame Hector for being too pitying. Paris can blame his defender, Troilus, for the delay in delivering Cressida up to Diomedes. One of the first pieces of information we get is that Helen and Hecuba have gone to the battlements together: the two queens—one the mother of the royal family, the other an adulteress—preserve the public lie by being seen together. For, though the ugly truth lurks in Troy, the royal family manages to keep up appearances and the war. Significantly, it is not until the last act, on the battlefield, that Margarelon, Priam's bastard son, appears, as if to make clear that the sickness goes deeper than Paris's crime.

At the Trojan council meeting, Hector can declare to Paris and Troilus that Helen should be given back:

> . . . yet ne'er the less,
> My spritely brethren, I propend to you
> In resolution to keep Helen still,
> For 'tis a cause that hath no mean dependance
> Upon our joint and several dignities.
> (2.2.189-93)

The ill-founded Trojan cause is dedicated to preserving the divorce between Menelaus and Helen. And this fracture in that family has far-reaching effects not only in Troy but also in the Greek camp: "Troy in our weakness stands, not in her strength"(1.3.137).

Ajax's mother, Priam's sister, was exchanged for Helen; Ajax, a second Achilles, is half-Trojan. The "self-willed" Achilles gets a letter from Hecuba and a token from his fair love, Polyxena, Priam's daughter, reminding him of his vow not to fight.

We may say that setting in *Troilus and Cressida* determines action: Troy is a decadent city; the Greeks are encamped; the battlefield is anarchic. Troy is a place of lies, of vanity; the Greek camp is the scene of a struggle for power; the battlefield provides simple choices, amoral and final, where action is determined by feeling and chance. It would seem then that the way the characters act is somewhat decided by the "society" they are a part of or find themselves in. When Cressida is taken to the Greek camp, she, "married" and now, like Helen, "divorced," has to accommodate herself to the new world. It is on the battlefield that Achilles breaks his vow to Polyxena in order to revenge the death of Patroclus; that Ajax, who has also lost a friend, is trying to find Troilus in order to kill him; that Troilus is hoping to find Achilles in order to relieve his frustrated love. On the battlefield we see the frustration of those who, reduced to mad dogs, seek to eat each other up. Nothing means anything.

The Prologue emphasizes the pride of the Greek leaders; in the play Trojan vanity is an expression of Greek pride:

> . . . and their vow is made
> To ransack Troy, within whose strong immures
> The ravish'd Helen, Menelaus' queen,
> With wanton Paris sleeps—and that's the quarrel.
> (Pro.7-10)

Whereas Hector wants to lift himself to honor, Ulysses wants to bring Achilles down to earth: Hector wants the name; Ulysses wants the thing. Until the end Achilles and then Ajax (for Ulysses manages to make sure that Ajax becomes another Achilles) don't care what others think of them; they are concerned only with what they think of themselves. The vain Trojans are attacked by the proud Greeks.

By the end of the play Hector on the battlefield can give up his concern for honor in order to kill a Greek and to acquire that Greek's armor. He finds that the armor covers a putrefied core, which is perhaps meant to signify a putrefied *cor* or heart. Achilles has Hector murdered in order to achieve the honor of having the Trojan hero dead. Each is concerned with death: Hector sacrifices his honor for a putrefied core; Achilles sacrifices his honor for the dead body of Hector. When the soldiers shout, "Achilles! Achilles! Hector's slain! Achilles!"(5.9.3) we can easily see what Shakespeare apparently wants us to understand by the way the line can be read: just as surely as Achilles has slain Hector, Hector has slain Achilles. A dead body causes these two heroes to give up honor.

Without doubt the play explicitly contains small, clear affirmations of a sort. Though weak and unenlightened, Cressida is capable of a kind of love: relying on Pandarus, her surrogate father, and Troilus, her frail "husband," she finds that she cannot depend on either, and she is forced in the Greek camp to put on, like an armor, the manner of Helen. It is instructive, for example, to notice that, although Cressida has been delivered to the Greeks at the insistence of her father, the two are never on stage together. Troilus's feelings for Cressida, though erotic, sensual, and selfish, are real: he is an infatuated boy, not an evil man. Achilles does love Patroclus. Thersites's invective, rooted though it is in his envy and malice, is a kind of cry for morality and order. Margarelon, outside the Trojan family, can still fight bravely and honorably for it. When Margarelon confronts Thersites on the battlefield, it is Thersites who rejects and renounces himself as a bastard and a coward, thus effectively silencing his own shrill voice.

One reason for the unhappiness and the misery in the play can be traced to a breakdown in the family in both societies. Family ties are loose or broken. The only real family or society in the play is in Troy, and we are made to see the nature of that society. We must bring to the play the notion of what a real family is, a "society" based on love and duty, where every member has his or her place. A recognition of the full significance of the family is the first major insight toward an understanding of the play. The second major insight concerns the largely absent gods and the Apple of Discord. For the Apple of Discord is the striking missing fact in the Prologue: our awareness of its importance serves to make clear the essential poetic idea of the play.

When Paris gave the Apple of Discord to Venus, he turned Minerva and Juno against the Trojans: Venus is served and worshipped by the Trojans; Minerva and Juno are served and worshipped by the Greeks. Importing the commonplace idea of the Apple of Discord into the play, we realize that the Trojans have love; the Greeks have wisdom and power. Troy must fall because love is alone; we are made to see what love becomes when it is not informed by wisdom and power: "Troy in our weakness stands, not in her strength"(1.3.137). Conversely, the Greeks must fail because their wisdom and their power are not instructed by love. The Trojans are stultified by their lack of wisdom and power; the Greeks are stultified by their lack of love and, subsequently, honor. The Trojans are destroyed by their unwise concerns; the Greeks by their unlovely concerns. Hector and Ulysses try to control public policy, to the mutual disgrace of them as individuals and as standards of society: Hector has no wisdom or power; Ulysses has no love.

To state the lovers' case quite clearly, the affair between Troilus and Cressida fails because the two young people are hustled into bed before they can know each other; their affair is based on appearance, on sensation, on lust, on love cut off from that which could in a happier world secure it. Thersites is the fool of wisdom and power in the Greek camp; Pandarus is the fool of love in Troy. Both are left at the end with nothing because their premises are based on an uninstructed conception of what the possibilities of human life are.

This is the way Pandarus responds to Cressida in their verbal fencing match: "You are such a woman, a man knows not at what ward you lie"(1.2.259).[1] This apparently simple line proffers a poetic statement of the play's dramatic movement. But first it is necessary for us to see a pun on ward (word), a quite elaborate pun that is common in Shakespeare, as the beginning of *All's Well That Ends Well* or the end of *The Merry Wives of Windsor* plainly indicates. *Lie* at the end of the cited line ekes out the first pun and establishes another, for we seem asked to think of the first sentence of the Prologue.

The sentence is loose: we can stop reading it at a series of places. Pandarus's second rejoinder is "You are such another!"(1.2.271) as if to prove that we can stop with "You are such a woman." Or we can read "You are such a woman a man knows," for it is Pandarus's purpose in his interview with Cressida to get Troilus to "know" her, and it is Troilus's "knowledge" that destroys them and their love. Or we can read "You are such a woman a man knows not." For Troilus admits in the "noting" scene that he does not know Cressida: "This is, and is not, Cressid!"(5.2.146) We can appreciate Shakespeare's usual pun on *not*, *naught*, evil. Or we can read the whole line: at what ward (word) did she lie? at what ward (word) did she begin lying?

The line would seem then to image the concatenation of events: we are being poetically shown how one event depends on another. The cited line contains the individual statements that make up the final line, which is one version of the plot movement: in a sense the line *is* the condensed plot. Each additional word or phrase changes the meaning. To get the total meaning of the line we have to read the whole line, but the whole line contains the other, disparate meanings, and *they* really go to make up the true, total meaning of the line and of the plot. The line dramatically engages the total work, so that we can understand how ward (word) depends upon ward (word).

Immediately after the Pandarus line, the talk turns to Cressida's watches; we seem to be given then a *ward-word-watch* complex that looks toward the crucial scene at the end of the play (5.2), where Cressida and Diomedes have their verbal skirmish in the night before Menelaus's tent, which significantly contains Calchas, while Troilus and Ulysses watch the "lovers" from a distance and while Thersites watches both sets of figures from a farther distance. Each person is in some sense ignorant. We see it all. The scene renders what is implicit in Cressida's situation in 1.2. We see her, after the fall, trying to preserve what she can: her betrayed and betraying lover and the wily Greek comment; the diseased Thersites, without either wisdom or power, "coins [his] slander like a mint"(1.3.193). They are all now trapped in an expanded prison, which has several wards. The scene converges the various lines of poetic development; the public and the private failures are expressly identified. The range is from the father, who is hidden in Menelaus's tent, to Thersites, who is soon to admit that he is both a coward and a bastard.

Perhaps we are meant to understand that it is Troilus's word that could save Cressida even here, in 5.2. He made a vow to her and he has an obligation to keep it, rather than to do nothing but indulge in the verbal sleight of hand that produces two Cressidas, his and Diomedes's. But *when* should he have decided to be true? At what word did he lie? At the end of the next scene Troilus tears up Cressida's letter to him: "Words, words, mere words, no matter from the heart"(5.3.108). It doesn't make any difference now that she is speaking from the heart, for things have gone too far, and Troilus has been so brutalized by "knowledge" that he can utterly disregard both her heart and his. Troilus now settles for the deeds of death: love, the person as well as the emotion, has been sacrificed to the sordid cause.

In 1.2, right after Pandarus has left her, Cressida says:

> Words, vows, gifts, tears, and love's full sacrifice,
> He offers in another's enterprise.
>
> (1.2.282-83)

The *He* in the quotation may also refer to any of the Greeks who have come to rescue Helen. The quotation sounds as if all five items of the list are being equated, as if one of the five is no more important than the others, except that one sequentially follows the other. And this is probably all that Cressida means; it is not all that Shakespeare means. The quotation gives us another poetic statement of the play's dramatic movement; specifically, the five items roughly signify the five acts of the play. For once words subvert vows, vows can subvert gifts, and then tears and sacrifice follow. The next three scenes after 1.2 deal with the words and the vows of the public plot: first, the Greek council meeting; second, the verbal and physical skirmish between Thersites and Ajax; third, the Trojan meeting of state. In 1.3, Ulysses uses words to undermine Greek effort; in 2.1, Thersites is beaten because he won't reveal what the proclamation says; in 2.2, Hector uses words to pay lip service to truth, before submitting to the vows of Paris and Troilus. Hector doesn't mention the real truth behind his challenge to the Greeks: he wants to redeem "the disdain and shame"(1.2.34) of having been struck down by Ajax. The public plot both extends and establishes the private plot. Cressida gives herself to Troilus in act 3; she is a "gift" to the Greeks in act 4. Cressida cries in act 4, and Priam and the women of Troy cry in act 5. Then love's full sacrifice is paid.

Immediately after the lines cited above, Cressida gives her philosophy: she must defend herself; as soon as she has given in to love, her value will drop. She has no overriding moral beliefs: her attitude is defensive and negative, for she has no wisdom. She depends on others, for she has no power: those others and her beliefs betray her. It is altogether possible that Shakespeare wants us to remember that in the beginning was the Word and that it is this that she has no way of knowing. She is unaware of any transcendence. In this sense as well as historically the play is pre-Christian.

Charity, the idea of Christian love, is the final answer to the dilemma posed by the action of the play. It is the final affirmation to the horrible negation rendered, but it is an answer largely outside the play. The play does contain two other clear affirmations, which we also have to partially import and which really don't cancel the idea of Christian love, but, rather, reinforce it. The first of these affirmations is more or less implicit; it concerns Ulysses, for, while reading *Troilus*, we seem meant to remember the *Odyssey*. After the action of the play Ulysses will have to undergo his series of trials. He finally gets his true wife and rescues his bereft family. The destruction of Troy releases him for his education: his growth begins after his trickery ruins Troy; then he is secularly redeemed.

It is, however, Aeneas and his affirmation that the play expressly asks us to consider, Aeneas, the founder of Rome (the seat of Christianity), the father of the Western World. It seems very significant that after the Prologue Pandarus, Troilus, and Aeneas are the first characters to speak and that at the end of the play these three are the last characters to speak. It is Aeneas in the play who comes as an outsider to the Greek council meeting, disrupting it; it is Aeneas who metaphorically kills Pandarus;[2] it is Aeneas, as an agent in delivering Cressida to the Greeks, who helps to destroy Troilus and Cressida; it is Aeneas, the willing servant of Hector, who follows that hero to his ignominious end. For, above all, Aeneas submits himself to others; he serves willingly and faithfully something outside himself. With the possible exception of Ulysses, the quotation "Words, vows, gifts, tears, and love's full sacrifice,/He offers in another's enterprise"(1.2.282-83) applies to Aeneas in a way completely different from the way it applies to anyone else. The destruction of Troy—and Troy must be destroyed before he can act—releases him to fulfill his destiny: to serve something else and someone else. At the end of the play Pandarus explicitly bequeaths us his diseases, and Aeneas implicitly bequeaths us his service or, rather, the results of his service.

After being absent from the play from 1.3 to 4.1, Aeneas has the following as his first speech upon his return:

> Is the Prince there in person?
> Had I so good occasion to lie long
> As [you], Prince Paris, nothing but heavenly business
> Should rob my bed-mate of my company.
>
> (4.1.3-6)

The obvious points to be made are that Aeneas has not lied as long as Paris has—Aeneas has been true—and that Aeneas will forsake Dido precisely when heavenly business will call him from her: only that will rob Dido of the company of Aeneas. And "heavenly business"(4.1.5) also reflects Cressida's plight, for if her "marriage" had been true, only heavenly business or death would have robbed her of Troilus.

A few lines later Aeneas speaks to Diomedes, who will soon be comparable to Paris as Troilus will be comparable to Menelaus:

> In humane gentleness,
> Welcome to Troy! now, by Anchises' life,
> Welcome indeed! By Venus' hand I swear,
> No man alive can love in such a sort
> The thing he means to kill, more excellently.
>
> (4.1.21-25)

For the first time in the play Aeneas mentions his father, whom he will rescue from the ruins of Troy, and his mother, Venus, the goddess of love, thus imaging a complete, other family. For once Pandarus has become Cupid, the blind son of Venus, Aeneas can become the true son of love, the apostle of Agape, the new love that can exist after Eros is discredited: the "destruction" of Cupid-Pandarus is accomplished by the rightful son of Venus. And Aeneas will marry Lavinia.

As Cressida is being escorted from Troy, Hector's trumpet sounds, and Aeneas says:

> [. . . . Yea, with a bridegroom's fresh alacrity
> Let us address to tend on Hector's heels.
> The glory of our Troy doth this day lie
> On his fair worth and single chivalry.]
>
> (4.4.145-48)

The first line constitutes a rebuke to Troilus, the bridegroom, at the same time that it posits Aeneas's advance and his future. And the third line with its *lie* tells us the value of the glory of Troy that depends on Hector and his chivalry. As if to reinforce the new role that Aeneas is in the process of assuming, the very next lines, by Agamemnon in the next scene, although addressed to Ajax, are to be seen as a comment on the future of Aeneas:

> Here art thou in appointment fresh and fair,
> Anticipating time. With starting courage . . . .
>
> (4.5.1-2)

When the trumpet sounds in the Greek camp, it is not the anticipated Hector who comes. It is Cressida. (We see how the lines just cited apply to her and her future, thus drawing a parallel and a contrast between Aeneas and Cressida.) Hector follows. When the trumpet sounds again, it is Aeneas who first speaks. And all of this is as it should be, for Cressida and Hector are now to be identified together: one is the victim of love; the other is the victim of honor. What love and honor really can be is left for Aeneas to prove, since Troy has now been effectively destroyed.

Troilus and Cressida is difficult but not ambiguous. Simply stated, we immediately have to read it more alertly and more diligently than we have to read most of the other plays, not that the others are simple, for they are not: they are just not so initially difficult as *Troilus* is. In the end *Troilus* is essentially like the other Shakespeare plays; that is, it is true and finally affirmative. The Shakespeare ethic clearly instructs us that true love and ethical duty are the only viable answers to the inhumanity of man to man. We see what we are; we see why we are what we are; we see what we can be.

NOTES

1. This is the line as it appears in the 1609 Quarto, which according to T. W. Baldwin in the *Variorum* seems to be the more substantive text. In the Folio the line is "You are such another woman, one knows not at what ward you lie." In part the Quarto line has been chosen in order to more emphatically make the point, though essentially the same argument can be conducted from either line.

2. As Pandarus is playing the naughty mocking uncle, after Cressida has given herself to Troilus, Cressida says, "Would he were knock'd i' th' head!"(4.2.34), and then a knock comes at the door. It is Aeneas.

18

Thematic Point of View in
Troilus and Cressida

That the Greek camp and Trojan society are to be viewed from the
perspective of the Apple of Discord is made clear in the first two
council scenes (1.3, the Greek scene; 2.2, the Trojan scene).[1] Each
scene proffers a discussion of a public plight: Why haven't the
Greeks been successful in their objective of bringing down Troy?
Should Helen be returned to her rightful husband? In 1.3 Ulysses
properly concludes that "Troy in our weakness stands, not in her
strength"(1.3.137). To the Greek camp, accompanied by a
trumpeteer, comes the Trojan Aeneas in order to deliver Hector's
vain, love-couched challenge:

> [Hector] hath a lady, wiser, fairer, truer,
> Than ever Greek did couple in his arms,
> And will to-morrow with his trumpet call,
> Midway between your tents and walls of Troy,
> To rouse a Grecian that is true in love.
> (1.3.275-79)

This challenge brought by love (Aeneas, like Cupid, is the son of
Venus) and in the name of Hector's love for his wife (Hector's
real purpose is to redeem the shame received when Ajax "cop'd
[him] in the battle and strook him down"[1.2.33-34]) is subverted

at the end of the scene by Nestor (power) and Ulysses (wisdom), who, by rigging the lottery, will substitute the half-Trojan Ajax (who has just defeated Hector) for the vain Achilles (whom Hector hopes to vanquish) as Hector's opponent.

The Trojan council meeting (2.2) is disrupted by Helenus (the brother-priest, the Trojan representative of moral power) and then by the entrance of Cassandra (the sister-seer, the Trojan representative of prophetic wisdom). The self-centered, love-besotted Troilus contradicts Helenus's power and, joined by Paris, dismisses Cassandra's wisdom. After asserting his moral superiority over Paris and Troilus, Hector, who has already issued the challenge (by Aeneas in the name of love) to the Greeks, subverts and dismisses his rational, moral conclusion that Helen, Menelaus's lady, must be returned to her rightful husband. But the further, ironic point is that Nestor's power and Ulysses's wisdom at the end of 1.3 have made Hector's real, self-concerned cause (confronting Achilles) to be in vain.

In his introduction to the Oxford *Troilus and Cressida*, Kenneth Muir observes:

> *Troilus and Cressida*, indeed, is unique even among Shakespeare's works in its changes of viewpoint from scene to scene. In the first scene, for example, every reader and every member of an audience looks at the situation through the eyes of Troilus, in the second through the eyes of Cressida, in the third through the eyes of Ulysses, in the fourth through the eyes of Thersites, and in the fifth through the eyes of Hector.[2]

There is nothing unique about "changes of viewpoint" in Shakespeare's works: it is always in evidence, always in force, though, as Muir indicates, not always so extensively as it is in *Troilus and Cressida*. Although Muir's insight is incisive, he does not develop it, and thus we may be excused for concluding that he does not fully understand it, its purpose, its utility.

The first scene may be said to be from Troilus's viewpoint and the second from Cressida's. But the third scene is from the viewpoint of Nestor (power) and Ulysses (wisdom); the fourth scene (2.1) is from the viewpoint of Ajax; the fifth from the viewpoint of the "joint and several dignities"(2.2.193) of Priam,

Hector, Paris, Troilus, and Helenus. For the constant feature of the strategy employed by Shakespeare in these five scenes is that of a character (Troilus; Cressida; Ajax) or two characters (Nestor and Ulysses) or five characters (the Trojan Princes and their father, the King) who remain on stage throughout the particular scene; that is, the character or characters who remain on stage throughout a scene may be said to present the viewpoint of and in that scene. In the Trojan council scene (2.2), though Hector overrules his brothers, the viewpoints of Paris and Troilus are just as necessary as Hector's to an understanding of the scene and of the play: for different reasons all three do not want Helen returned; Hector capitulates to these love-sick brothers because he wants to serve his own "dignity." Patently, the viewpoints of Priam (neglectful wisdom) and Helenus (ineffective power) are important.

Like the histories and the tragedies and two of the romances (*Cymbeline* and *Pericles*), *Troilus and Cressida* employs a name or names for its title. And it is not strange for Shakespeare in his character-oriented plays to establish in an early scene the essential nature of a young person who will be of major concern later on in the action. Act 1.1 of *Troilus and Cressida* presents the plight of a love-sick young prince: "Why should I war without the walls of Troy,/That find such cruel battle here within?"(1.1.2-3) Act 1.2 presents the plight of a love-stricken young girl, forsaken by her treacherous father (now in the Greek camp) and being pushed by her sodden uncle into a love relationship, as her scene-ending soliloquy makes clear:

> Words, vows, gifts, tears, and love's full sacrifice,
> He offers in another's enterprise,
> But more in Troilus thousandfold I see
> Than in the glass of Pandar's praise may be;
> Yet hold I off. Women are angels, wooing:
> Things won are done, joy's soul lies in the doing.
>   (1.2.282-87)

Therefore it is inexact and perhaps even misleading to consider 1.1 and 1.2 of *Troilus and Cressida* as just viewpoint scenes. It is more meaningful and more useful to consider such scenes as involving and expressing character, plot, and theme. The first scene of *Troilus and Cressida* focuses on Troilus's initial plight and establishes his essential character; it proffers a trope (the process of baking and eating a cake) and the concomitant quality (patience or the lack thereof) that serves to clarify his actions in the rest of the play. Pandarus's last words in the scene, as he leaves Troilus, state the sad truth about Troilus's frustrated beginning and unhappy ending: "I will leave all as I found it, and there an end"(1.1.87-88). An *alarum* (a beginning of the day's battle) off stage emphasizes the importance of the remark. As a digestion or recapitulation of the full Troilus action, 1.1 is perforce proleptic.

And the second scene presents Cressida, the object of Troilus's desire and the begetter of his plight, in what is the essential Cressida scene. Her trope is a procession of Trojan warriors crossing the stage, one replacing the other, at the end (signaled by a *retreat*) of a day's battle. In 4.5, having been delivered to the Greeks, Cressida will be accosted by a procession of Greek warriors. In 1.2 Shakespeare wants us to perceive her insecure future as being like that of a hostess greeting customers at the door, each being quickly replaced by the next.[3] Vulnerable Cressida thus concludes her only soliloquy in the play:

> Therefore this maxim out of love I teach:
> Achievement is command; ungain'd, beseech;
> Then though my heart's content firm love doth bear,
> Nothing of that shall from mine eyes appear.
> (1.2.292-95)

Her love will subvert her wisdom. After surrendering herself to Troilus, she is then delivered by him to Diomedes. Her maxim will prove bitterly prophetic: she will be powerless, helpless among the Greeks, bartering her charms for an imperiled existence.

Mentioned in 1.2 and 1.3, Ajax is not introduced till 2.1. Of the four characters (Ajax, Thersites, Achilles, Patroclus) in that scene, Ajax is the only one to remain on stage throughout the scene, and thus the viewpoint is his. Ajax's essential character has already been satirically set forth in Troy in 1.2 by Cressida's man, Alexander:

[Ajax] is melancholy without cause, and
merry against the hair; he hath the joints of every
thing, but every thing so out of joint that he is a gouty
Briareus, many hands and no use, or purblind Argus,
all eyes and no sight.

(1.2.26-30)

Act 2.1 *dramatizes* the essential Greek character (power without wisdom or love) of Ajax: he "beats" Thersites, just as he "beat" Hector in battle and will want to "beat" Troilus on the battlefield. In addition, 2.1 may be considered as a thematic gloss on the Greek plight: unwise power (Ajax) foolishly thrashes powerless wisdom (Thersites) because it won't divulge what it knows (the proclamation). Or the private 2.1 may be considered as a gloss on the public 1.3: power and wisdom, divorced from love, must be at vicious odds.

One of the structural-thematic features of *Troilus and Cressida* is that of closely related scenes, of a kind of double-scene. Act 1.1 and 1.2 are directly comparable, just as 1.3 and 2.2 (the two public scenes) are. In a different way 1.3 and 2.1, the first two Greek scenes, make up a double scene: 1.3 presents one group of Greeks; 2.1 presents a completely different group of Greeks. If we employ the terms made available by the Apple of Discord, 1.3 may be considered as the viewpoint of Greek wisdom (Nestor and Ulysses) and 2.1 as the viewpoint of Greek power (Ajax). In addition to serving other complex purposes of character and plot, the first five scenes of *Troilus and Cressida* proffer structural and thematic permutations of the Judgment-of-Paris trope or the Apple-of-Discord paradigm.

Whereas 2.1, the Ajax scene, dramatizes the folly of power that has neither wisdom nor love, 3.1 dramatizes the folly of love that has neither power nor wisdom. Act 2.1 and 3.1 make up a still different double scene: power alone is brutal; love alone is sodden. Act 3.1 has three readily distinguishable parts: Pandarus with a nameless servant; Pandarus with Paris and Helen; Paris with Helen. As the only scene in the play in which Helen appears and as the only scene in the play to contain a song, it is the centerpiece of degenerate love. Degenerate power in 2.1 gives way to degenerate love in 3.1. Pandarus, the fool of the private plot and the purveyor of erotic love, is the singer of *Troilus and Cressida's* song of love:

> "Love, love, nothing but love, still love,
> > still more!
> > For O, love's bow
> > Shoots buck and doe.
> > The [shaft confounds]
> > Not that it wounds,
> > But tickles still the sore.
> > These lovers cry, O ho, they die!
> > > Yet that which seems the wound to kill
> > Doth turn O ho! to ha, ha, he!
> > > So dying loves lives still.
> > O ho! a while, but ha, ha, ha!
> > O ho! groans out for ha, ha, ha!—hey ho!"
> > > > (3.1.114-26)

Troilus has a revealing soliloquy in 1.1; Cressida has a revealing soliloquy in 1.2; Pandarus has a revealing song in 3.1, right before Troilus and Cressida meet for the first time (3.2). Pandarus is urged by irresponsible lovers (Paris and Helen) to sing about irresponsible love. In plot terms Pandarus has come to ask Paris ". . . that if the King call for [Troilus] at supper, [Paris] will make his excuse"(3.1.76-77). Pandarus's song, sung at Helen's behest, celebrates Cupid-love: "This love," so Helen avers, "[that] will undo us all"(3.1.110-11). Paris documents the generation of this erotic love:

> [Pandarus] eats nothing but doves, love, and that
> breeds hot blood, and hot blood begets hot thoughts,
> and hot thoughts beget hot deeds, and hot deeds is love.
> > (3.1.128-30)

Granted the sodden context, Paris's concluding comment to Helen is especially significant: "Sweet, above thought I love [thee]!"(3.1.159) The full scene functions as a prologue to 3.2, the assignation between Troilus and Cressida, and thus certifies, before it is ever consummated, the future of that insecure relationship. Unlike Venus or the half-mortal Helen, Cressida is not a wife, not a queen, let alone a goddess or "the mortal Venus"(3.1.32); she is on her way to becoming a beleaguered and devalued girl, as her soliloquy predicted.

Paris's nameless servant appears on stage only in this scene, 3.1. Although the servant is silent after Paris and Helen appear and although Pandarus is silent at the end, there is no evidence in the quarto or Folio texts that either the servant or Pandarus leaves the stage. If they do remain on stage, the scene is from the viewpoint of both the servant and Pandarus. The servant, who is too cunning for the courtly Pandarus, enables us to understand that Pandarus lacks true power and neglects real wisdom. In the first part of the scene we hear that the servant follows Paris only when Paris goes before him; that the servant does not depend upon Paris but upon the Lord. To Pandarus's confusion and consternation but for our enlightenment, the servant employs such morally prepossessive terms as *faith, grace, honor, lordship, love.*

Largely by means of these words, the servant helps us to establish a superior viewpoint toward Pandarus and the pre-Christian world as well as toward the "Sodden business"(3.1.41) of Paris and Helen. The servant's viewpoint informs ours. After Paris documents the generation of love, Pandarus asks, "Is love a generation of vipers?"(3.1.132-33) The presence of the prepossessive servant encourages us to think of the generation of Christian love and to apply the appropriate New Testament references.[4] Moreover, one of the features of this choric scene is that of iterated words: *fair* is used eleven times; *queen*, fifteen times; *sweet*, fifteen times; *lord*, twenty-two times, *love*, twenty-two times.[5] These iterated words serve to emphasize, not just the meaning of these complex words, but the play-wide tropes of the bee and the bee-hive (Helen as queen-bee) and of the Elizabethan fair, where animals were bought and sold.[6]

* * * * *

Closely related scenes are a function of closely related characters: Troilus and Cressida; Paris and Helen; Ajax and Achilles; Troilus and Paris; Troilus and Hector; Cressida and Helen; Cressida and Antenor; Pandarus and Aeneas. The play itself is a network of these closely ordered relationships. We have no trouble seeing

Ajax as replacing Achilles or seeing Antenor as replacing Cressida
or seeing Diomedes as replacing Troilus or even seeing Troilus as
replacing Hector: such relationships are mainly a consequence of
plot. But Cressida as replacing Helen and Aeneas as replacing
Pandarus are something more than plot. As a consequence of
Cressida's giving herself in 3.2 to Troilus, 4.1 is related to 3.1 for
plot reasons; but on a richer, structural-thematic level, 4.1 is, in
terms of characters, an extension and a revision of 3.1. In both
scenes Paris is an agent in the Troilus-Cressida plot. But instead
of Pandarus as in 3.1, Aeneas, the servant of Hector and an
exponent of a better love, appears in 4.1; instead of Helen as in
3.1, Deiphobus, Antenor, and Aeneas attend Paris on stage. In the
play's last scene, Paris is again pointedly accompanied by Aeneas,
Antenor, and Deiphobus.

Like 3.1, 4.1 is a prologue to Troilus-Cressida action: their
unsanctioned love having been consummated off stage in 3.3, the
lovers are rudely divorced in 4.4. Helen is celebrated as being
sweet in 3.1 and denounced by Diomedes as being bitter in 4.1.
Helen is not on stage after 3.1; after being delivered to Diomedes,
Cressida is on stage in 4.5 and 5.2, though in each instance as a
manipulated object. When an unregenerate Troilus chooses to
remain a Trojan prince rather than to become a husband, Pandarus
and Cressida fall in value, as they must: erotic love, which cannot
transform Troilus as a greater, sanctioned love might, is sacrificed
to power and wisdom. In addition, Cressida doesn't want the
assignation known, and Pandarus is more concerned with Troilus's
unhappiness than he is with Cressida's fate. As a kind of
mitigating explanation of his increased brutishness, Troilus never
hears and sees Cressida's immoderate grief at being forced to leave
him for the Greek camp.

Although Paris, Deiphobus, Antenor, and Diomedes are on stage
throughout 4.1, Antenor is silent, and Deiphobus speaks only one
line. The asides exchanged between Paris and Aeneas are perforce
private. Instead of a soliloquy (1.1; 1.2) or a song (3.1), asides are
used to secure viewpoint: Aeneas leaves; Paris remains. Act 4.1
is then from the viewpoint of Paris, whose love has been exposed
as being degenerate in 3.1. Before he leaves the stage, Aeneas
exchanges insults with Diomedes; by means of their asides (in
which Aeneas agrees to tell Troilus about the exchange of Antenor

for Cressida), Paris and Aeneas are equated; Paris in a question to
Diomedes equates himself with Menelaus: "Who, in your thoughts,
deserves fair Helen best,/Myself, or Menelaus?"(4.1.54-55) The
scene ends with an unpleasant exchange between Paris, the seducer
of Helen, and Diomedes, the seducer of Cressida. The scene
strengthens the equation between a Helen, who is bitter to the
Greeks, and a fallen Cressida, who will be bitter to Troilus, and
alerts us to the coming equation between Troilus and the cuckold
Menelaus. Thematically, Troilus, like Cressida, unaware of a
higher love, will go to the Greek camp and be contaminated by
"wisdom" and victimized by "power."

As the action expands, character equations multiply and change.
In 4.5 the trumpet "blowest for Hector"(4.5.11), but Cressida, not
Hector, appears. In the first half of the scene Cressida is kissed by
a number of Greek leaders; in the second half of the scene Hector
embraces a series of Greek leaders. Cressida is accompanied by
Diomedes; Hector is accompanied by Aeneas and Troilus, both of
whom may be equated with Diomedes. Act 4.5 is an obligatory
scene of major importance: Cressida and Hector arrive at the
Greek camp; Hector inconclusively fights Ajax and confronts
Achilles. Love (as represented by Cressida, Hector, Aeneas, and
Troilus) arrives at the Greek camp, the stronghold of power and
wisdom. But nothing of moral consequence happens: no
meaningful accommodation of unreconstructed love by immoderate
power and wisdom does occur or can occur. The storied end,
which crowns all, is stressed as early as 3.2, the assignation scene.
At the end of that scene, the bargain between Troilus and Cressida
is made; Pandarus bears witness to the kiss that seals it. Before the
love of Troilus and Cressida is even consummated, their collective
fates are secured: "Amen"; "Amen"; "Amen"(3.2.205-07). As the
play proceeds, we are reminded that Troy must fall for the story
of these lovers to be completed: they cannot escape their fate.

As we have been taught to expect by the play, 4.5 depends on
the strategy of what may be called the viewpoint scene: because
Ulysses is the only character to remain on stage throughout it, the
perspective is his. The lottery, rigged by Nestor and Ulysses in the
Greek council scene (1.3), is concluded in 4.5. Instead of a
soliloquy or a song or asides, Ulysses delivers wise
pronouncements upon the three principals of the love plot: on

Diomedes ("He rises on the toe. That spirit of his/In aspiration lifts him from the earth"[4.5.15-16]); on Cressida (". . . set [creatures like Cressida] down/For sluttish spoils of opportunity,/And daughters of the game"[4.5.61-63]); on Troilus ("a true knight"[4.5.96]; "Manly as Hector"[4.5.104]; "A second hope [for Troy]"[4.5.109]). Ulysses expresses what the Greek world in its power and wisdom may now believe about this famous threesome. But we, who have seen Diomedes, Cressida, and Troilus in ways that Ulysses has not, know how wrong Ulysses is in his dark assessment of Cressida and in his bright assessments of Diomedes and Troilus.

At this time there is no signal character on stage to guide us, no cunning servant as in 3.1, no Thersites, who will damn Diomedes at the end of 5.1. Act 4.5 ends with Troilus and Ulysses on stage together; these two are now to be equated. Troilus asks Ulysses to lead him to the brutal Diomedes and the embattled Cressida. In 5.2 Troilus "creates" two Cressidas in order to resolve his dilemma; in retrospect, we are encouraged to create in 4.5 two Troiluses in order to resolve ours. This "other" Troilus has become infected with spite. Thersites, a signal character of joyless, heartless wisdom, watches the four participants of 5.2 and vilely comments on all but Ulysses. In 5.1 and 5.2 Thersites encourages us to see Diomedes, Cressida, and Troilus in a heartless light.

Hector's strange actions in the council scene, 2.2, which were designed to enable him to confront a reluctant Achilles, are in vain because the rigged lottery has made it impossible for him to meet Achilles in the way he desires. Since the "maiden battle"(4.5.87) between Hector and Ajax in 4.5 resolves the lottery issue, Hector and Achilles ought to be now free to fight. They don't. Instead Shakespeare again uses the plot device of subversion found in the council scenes, 1.3 and 2.2. In 5.1 Achilles is ready to fight Hector, but a letter from Queen Hecuba and a token from Polyxena convince him not to fight. In 5.3 Hector, in a version of 2.2, insists on having his way against those who would stop him (his wife, his sister, his brother, his father): he is again determined to fight Achilles. But we know that Achilles has decided to remain in his tent, though Hector, who is with Achilles in Achilles's tent at the end of 5.1, does not. Hector's actions in 5.3, like his actions in 2.2, the council scene, are in vain. Now, however, Hecuba and

Polyxena (neither of whom appears in the play), rather than Nestor and Ulysses, control the fate of both Achilles and Hector. We may perhaps conclude that Trojan love will have a salubrious effect on Greek power. But this is not so. When Patroclus is slain on the battlefield, Achilles breaks his major vow to Hecuba and Polyxena, enters the field, and, to our horror, has Hector brutally murdered.

None of the three pre-battlefield scenes of act 5 has a specified viewpoint: Thersites, except for a prologue in 5.1 and 5.2, is on stage throughout both scenes. A composite viewpoint is directed toward a single person in 5.2 and in 5.3. Act 5.2, the last Troilus-Cressida scene, presents Troilus's Cressida, Diomedes's Cressida, Ulysses's Cressida, Thersites's Cressida: each view is valid but partial; all are negative, none hopeful. In 5.3, the last council scene, the viewpoints of Andromache, Cassandra, Troilus, and Priam toward Hector are presented: each view is valid but partial; all are negative and hopeless, though not viciously so. Rather than presenting first Cressida and then Hector in the same scene, as 4.5 does, act 5 uses separate scenes: 5.2 presents Cressida; 5.3 presents Hector. Act 5.2 gives us a composite "Greek" view of Cressida (love); 5.3 presents a composite "Trojan" view of Hector (vanity).

The main action of the pre-battlefield section of act 5 concerns three warriors who will be of first importance on the battlefield: Achilles, Troilus, Hector. In 5.1 Achilles's love for Polyxena is tested; in 5.2 Troilus's love for Cressida is tested; in 5.3 Hector's love for Andromache is tested. The order of these love tests is from the one that seems least secure (Achilles's) to the one that should be most secure (Hector's). In 5.3 Hector rejects his wife: "Andromache, I am offended with you,/Upon the love you bear me, get you in"(5.3.77-78). Later in 5.3, Troilus rejects Cressida's declaration of love and tears up her letter. In 5.5, after Patroclus is killed, Achilles rejects his major vow to Polyxena and angrily seeks to destroy Hector. The order of these love rejections is the reverse of that of the love tests: Hector rejects his Trojan wife; Troilus rejects his Trojan lover; Achilles rejects his Trojan maiden.

In 5.1, while Achilles is reading the letter from Hecuba, Patroclus and Thersites are exchanging curses and vile insults: "adversity"(5.1.12);   "masculine   whore"(5.1.17);   "box   of envy"(5.1.25) "ruinous butt"(5.1.28); "cur"(5.1.29); "gall"(5.1.35); "Finch-egg"(5.1.36). Thersites invokes the rotten diseases of the south. The foul language, which the audience hears but which Achilles apparently does not, seems meant to be equated with the fair appeal being made to Achilles in a letter: it is an onstage replacement for the love appeal; it is a voiced qualification of that appeal. Greek "wisdom" qualifies Trojan "love." This same strategy of onstage unpleasant comment while an appealing letter is being read is employed at the end of 5.3: while Troilus reads a love letter from Cressida, Pandarus complains about a cough, a rheum in his eye, an ache in his bones. Again, a reminder of physical decay qualifies and subverts a love appeal.

One dramatic effect of the comparable situations is to emphasize a series of character equations: Troilus with Achilles; Pandarus with Patroclus and Thersites; Cressida with Hecuba and Polyxena. Achilles responds to Hecuba's appeal by turning his back on the war; Troilus responds to Cressida's appeal by tearing up her letter and turning his back on love: "Words, words, mere words, no matter from the heart"(5.3.108). He has embraced the war: his determination now (to pursue war) is the opposite of his determination in 1.1 (to pursue love). Right before the battle Troilus chooses war over love; on the battlefield Achilles chooses war over love. Like Achilles, Ajax enters the fray because his friend has been killed: Ajax is then intent upon killing Troilus; Achilles is then intent upon killing Hector.

There are no women on the battlefield, no heart: after 5.3 no matter from the heart has any effect. Both love and honor are negated and neglected. The obligatory public action in the play is the long-delayed encounter between Achilles and Hector on the battlefield, the testing place of love and honor by brutality and savagery. The occasion itself is not at all what might be expected. Indeed there are two encounters, and even they are broken by other action. Achilles and Hector fight; they pause to rest; Achilles departs. Troilus appears; he leaves in order to rescue Aeneas from Ajax. A Greek soldier appears; enamored by the soldier's armor, Hector pursues the Greek: "I'll hunt thee for thy hide"(5.6.31). Achilles reappears on the empty stage and orders his Myrmidons to murder Hector. Paris and Menelaus cross the stage fighting. Thersites comments on them, and then he is confronted by the bastard Margarelon. Hector returns to the now-empty stage. Having expended himself to attain a Greek's armor, the unarmed Hector is butchered by the Myrmidons. A *retreat* sounds; the battle has ended; the day is over; ugly night will come on; Troy will fall.

In spite of being Priam's crutch and the hope of Troy, the married but neglectful Hector is concerned, particularly (when he is with his family) in 2.2 and 5.3, only for his own "dear" honor: he is preoccupied with self-love, self-aggrandizement, lost honor, vanity. On the battlefield Achilles and Troilus sacrifice love and honor to revenge and violence. Hector foolishly sacrifices himself for Greek armor and then, having achieved it, discovers that it contains a "putrefied core"(5.8.1), a rotten heart. Hector's mistake is to be obsessed with appropriating a sumptuous outside that is only then discovered to contain rottenness and death. Like the Prince of Morocco with the golden casket in *The Merchant of Venice*, Hector learns a symbolic lesson and is destroyed by the lesson and for it. In *Troilus and Cressida* this linking of something valuable with something worthless or deadly is an elaboration and an extension of the recent strategy of letters (Hecuba's to Achilles in 5.1; Cressida's to Troilus in 5.3). In these two instances Achilles and Troilus (apparently unaware, though we are not, of the expression on stage of putrefaction) respond in opposite ways to a love appeal, to ostensible value.

Characterization and symbolism are at the service of trenchant thematic concerns. Even before the appearance of the wordless Greek soldier, Hector behaves in an unexpected way. In the first meeting, at the Greek camp in 4.5, Hector is disdainful of and rancorous toward his long-sought antagonist, Achilles. In their first encounter on the battlefield Hector is courteous and oddly dispassionate: "Pause if thou wilt"(5.6.14). Granted his play-long desire to meet Achilles in battle, it is incredible for Hector to now say, "I would have been much more a fresher man,/Had I expected thee"(5.6.20-21). He is led in 4.5 to expect Achilles on the battlefield: "Dost thou entreat me, Hector?/To-morrow do I meet thee, fell as death;/To-night all friends"(4.5.268-70). And then for Hector, having fought with Achilles, to waste his freshness on the battlefield by chasing after a soldier for some ornate armor seems to be the sheerest folly. What does Hector's irrational behavior mean? What thematic purpose is being served?

But, really, in a larger, Shakespearean context, Hector's behavior at the end is no stranger than that of Hamlet's (agreeing to a fencing match with Laertes) or Macbeth's (leaving the secure castle). Upon inspection, it will be discovered that the dramatic context for the confrontation between Hector and Achilles is no stranger than that between the Prince and Hotspur, between Hamlet and Laertes, between Macbeth and Macduff, between Edgar and Edmund. All of these episodes are part of the same procedure of thematic closure used by Shakespeare in these plays that end with the death of at least one of the equated participants. As in these other masterpieces, the reason for the extended Hector-Achilles "duel" on the battlefield is to bring together related lines of meaning in a cryptic, symbolic way. A "duel" or onstage dramatic equation is just the centerpiece of the concluding dramatic action.

In *Troilus and Cressida*, while Hector is off stage pursuing, catching, killing, and then discovering Greek putrefaction, other "pairs" replace Hector and the Greek soldier: Achilles and the Myrmidons; Paris and Menelaus; Thersites and Margarelon. Achilles, who has just disclaimed Hector's courtesy, now behaves (and orders his men to behave) in a cold-blooded, dishonorable way. Thersites applauds the end of illegitimate, unsanctioned love ("The cuckold [Menelaus] and the cuckold-maker [Paris] are at it"[5.7.9]; and then "I love bastards [Margarelon and himself]"[5.7.16]). Thus the full dramatic episode gathers together for our consideration and enlightenment Greek power (Achilles) discrediting itself; Greek wisdom (Thersites) discrediting itself; Trojan honor (Hector) discrediting itself. Meanwhile off stage Troilus is rescuing Aeneas (Trojan love) from Ajax (Greek power). This offstage action by Troilus brackets or frames, *not* the first encounter on the battlefield between Hector and Achilles, but the disreputable other action, "presented" both off stage and on. Chastened but uninformed Trojan love in the persons of Troilus and Aeneas brackets and then survives the hopeless carnage:

Like or find fault, do as your pleasures are,
Now good or bad, 'tis but [Shakespeare's] war.
(Pro.30-31)

* * * * *

Pandarus appears in eight scenes: in 1.1, the Troilus scene; in 1.2, the Cressida scene; in 3.1, the Paris-Helen scene; in 3.2, the assignation scene; in 4.2, the morning-after scene; in 4.4, the divorce scene; in 5.3, the rejection-of-Cressida scene; in 5.10, the rejection-of-Pandarus scene:

> *Tro.* Hence, broker, lackey! [*Strikes him.*] Ignominy, shame
> Pursue thy life, and live aye with thy name!
> (5.10.33-34)

Cressida is on her way to disease and shameful death; Troilus has turned from lover to revenger ("Hope of revenge shall hide our inward woe"[5.10.31]). For Pandarus to wonder why his endeavor was so loved and his performance so loathed is to mistake the truth. Pandarus just did what Troilus and Cressida wanted done; he provided the stimulus and the occasion. Troilus and Cressida failed because they lacked wisdom and power.

The play ends from the point of view of Pandarus alone (not as in 3.1, with the servant), in an epilogue. The fool of the Trojan world, of the private plot, of the love theme, Pandarus in 3.1 sings the only song of *Troilus and Cressida* ("Love, love, nothing but love. . . ."[3.1.115]); in 4,4 he embraces Troilus and Cressida at their divorce and proffers the only "rhyme" in the play ("O heart, heavy heart. . . ."[4.4.16]); in the epilogue he sings the only "verse" in the play:

> Full merrily the humble-bee doth sing,
> Till he hath lost his honey and his sting;
> And being once subdu'd in armed tail,
> Sweet honey and sweet notes together fail.
> (5.10.41-44)

In the epilogue Pandarus addresses, not the collective audience, as the armed Prologue had, but those in the audience who, like him, are "Good traders in the flesh"(5.10.46) or "Brethren and sisters of the hold-[door] trade"(5.10.51). If they can't weep for his aching bones and at his fall, they should at least be able to weep for their own aching bones. When he dies, he will bequeath to his particular audience his diseases. Even now, he has no power and gives no evidence of wisdom.

This foolish man, who was so preoccupied with serving the lustful needs of his young master, the Prince, has nothing of value to say to a fully informed audience now. Unlike the armed Prologue, Pandarus is just a disenfranchised lackey. He feels no kinship with those in the audience who are not traders in the flesh. He is talking to his modern confederates. In 3.1 he was too courtly, and the servant was too cunning. Now he is just a pathetic figure, a rejected broker. And we, who have observed the sad plight of Cressida in the Greek camp and who have watched the vainglory of Hector and the battlefield brutality of Achilles and Troilus, can judge Pandarus and his fall with accuracy and some spiritual authority. Pandarus emphasizes putrefaction; we must supply the concomitant love. In the epilogue to *Troilus and Cressida* we must bring an awareness of corrected and instructed love and a belief in the value of a true, not wanton, sacrifice.

NOTES

1. See the preceding chapter.

2. See Kenneth Muir's introduction to The Oxford *Troilus and Cressida* (Oxford: Oxford UP, 1984), 20.

3. See Ulysses's comment to Achilles in 3.3 while Troilus and Cressida are consummating their relationship off stage.

4. Cf. *Matthew* 3:7; 12:34; 23:33; and *Luke* 3:7.

5. Kenneth Muir notes the following: "In the ensuing dialogue the word 'fair' is used eleven times, 'sweet' fifteen times, thereby helping to create the sentimental and enervating atmosphere of the court (The Oxford *Troilus and Cressida*, 109).

6. See, for example, the *fair* reference in Troilus's soliloquy (1.1) and in Paris's comment to Diomedes in 4.1. The significance of the words in the scene urge us to consider the significance of letters in the song. For example, the song ends with a *hey* (A) and a *Ho* (O), the alpha and the omega.

Conclusion

Plight-Directed Action

As a boy Shakespeare must have been fully aware of the intended scope of *The Canterbury Tales*; at his arrival in London Shakespeare surely was cognizant of *The Faerie Queene*, a remarkably ambitious work-in-progress. But it is an unnecessary error to conclude that Shakespeare initially intended his work to have the shape of a gigantic enterprise: he began as a practicing playwright; he wasn't a deliberate artist, like Virgil or Milton or Joyce, with some masterwork in mind. But even in the earliest plays we can glimpse Shakespeare's enormous talent and artistic genius. Shakespeare mastered his craft so effortlessly that the stage must have been stunned by a profound early masterpiece like *Richard II*. With the completion of the second tetralogy, Shakespeare exhausted the possibilities of English history. He had to go deeper than that: *Henry VIII* is an afterthought. As a closet artist Shakespeare could complete a sonnet sequence, but the dramatic, presentational mode is a different, ongoing enterprise. In a very short time he managed to indite a comedic tetralogy and a tragic trilogy. He was able to digest the Trojan War in *Troilus and Cressida*; he fashioned a visionary spectacle in *The Tempest*. As a dynamic artistic development, the Shakespeare canon remains the wonder of the literary world.

A Shakespeare play is relentlessly human, resonantly alive; it clarifies our humanness, expresses our hopes and fears.

Characteristically, a Shakespeare play begins with a meaningful event, something as small as the arrival of a prince and his band of men (*Much Ado*), something as large as the murder of a king (*Hamlet*). A play itself is an exploration of the effect of that initial cultural shock: as they work their way through the society, the attendant difficulties and problems are clarified, certified, and then accommodated. A dramatic end is reached and declared. For example, the coming of a usurping monarch to power (*1 Henry IV*) affects the court world, the tavern world, the rebel world. We witness the way Prince Harry, Falstaff, Worcester, Hotspur, and Douglas react to the developing and developed situation. Once Hal as Prince Harry becomes the Prince of Wales in deed, the office of the usurping Henry IV is assured.

A Shakespeare play is an artistic gathering of all of its constituent parts, some more significant and trenchant than others, all essential to an understanding of the meaning of the action: a Shakespeare play is coherent and complete. *Hamlet* helps us understand an essential point. We are intended to distinguish Claudius's Hamlet from Gertrude's Hamlet or from Ophelia's or from Horatio's as we extend ourselves in order to realize the Hamlet creation and the creation of *Hamlet*. A Shakespeare play becomes a collection of points of view, a network of attitudes and positions, a mosaic of parables and story lines. In Shakespeare everything is rooted in the text; everything is given a local habitation and a name. Still, every mature Shakespeare play is artistically kinetic: as the action evolves, it involves us.

As we try to understand the nature of Shakespeare's achievement, it is necessary to consider the art that informs his material and that enables us to perceive Shakespeare's intention and meaning. Here, at the conclusion of this study of Shakespeare's deliberate art, let us consider a structural pattern in a number of Shakespeare's plays. We will begin by inspecting those scenes that render the plight of what we may call the heroine and how that plight is resolved. At the church in *Much Ado* (4.1), Beatrice witnesses Claudio's brutal treatment of Hero. Unlike the temporizing Friar Francis, she is determined to get revenge at once, but her plight is that she is only a powerless woman. She desperately needs a man to right an unconscionable wrong. She tricks Benedick, who professes to love her, into agreeing to challenge, if not kill, Claudio, his erstwhile best friend. After a subplot scene involving Dogberry and Verges (4.2), Benedick in 5.1 fulfills his promise to Beatrice and challenges Claudio to a duel.

In the forest in *As You Like It* (4.1), after Orlando departs to attend the Duke at dinner, Rosalind, disguised as Ganymede, confesses to Celia that she is deeply, hopelessly in love: "I cannot be out of the sight of Orlando"(4.1.216). After a brief subplot scene involving Jaques, some foresters, and a song (4.2), Oliver arrives (4.3) with the news that Orlando has rescued his hated brother from a hungry lioness. On learning that Orlando has been wounded, Rosalind faints: she is not what her costume declares. As we have seen, once Benedick has proven himself, he is qualified to marry Beatrice; once Orlando has overcome his earlier self, he is qualified to marry the revealed Rosalind and to become in time the new duke.

In Olivia's garden in *Twelfth Night* (3.4), Viola in the guise of Cesario is forced into a duel with Sir Andrew. Like Beatrice and Rosalind, Viola is only a woman: she is unqualified and unable to fight a duel. Like Beatrice and Rosalind, Viola is at an impasse and needs a man to rescue her from her plight. After Viola leaves the stage, there is a brief subplot episode (as in the other two comedies) involving Toby, Fabian, and Sir Andrew. The next scene begins with Sebastian, the real Cesario. coming on stage. Like Benedick and Orlando, Sebastian is the answer to the heroine's plight: he strikes Sir Andrew and confronts Toby and Fabian. He immediately proves himself qualified and ready to marry Olivia, and, by so doing, he resolves Viola's plight of being in the guise of Cesario and in love with Orsino. Like Beatrice and Rosalind in their plight scenes, Viola in 3.4 is aware of what the needed answer is:

> He nam'd Sebastian. I my brother know
> Yet living in my glass; even such and so
> In favor was my brother, and he went
> Still in my fashion, color, ornament,
> For him I imitate. O, if it prove,
> Tempests are kind and salt waves fresh in love.
> (3.4.379-84)

Viola, as well as Beatrice and Rosalind, needs a virtuous, eligible bachelor to rescue her from her plight, but it is interesting that neither Beatrice nor Viola is in her resolution scene and that Rosalind, but not Orlando, is in her resolution scene: the point is that the couples do not meet in the resolution scene. In *All's Well* the forsaken Helen needs Bertram, her rash, susceptible husband, to consummate their marriage and to impregnate her. Thus her plight is substantially different from that of the other three heroines: the man she needs is already her husband. But, like the Duke in *Measure for Measure*, Helen comes to need the good services of two women in order to forestall a powerful man's evil design. Still, Helen's plight and its resolution follow the same general pattern observed in the three earlier comedies. Instead of just two or three scenes (as in *Much Ado* and *As You Like It*), *All's Well* employs six scenes that for the most part alternate between women in one and men in the other.

In Florence the newly arrived Helen discovers (3.5) that her husband intends to commit adultery with a maid, Diana. In the next scene (3.6) Bertram is told that Parolles is not the brave soldier he professes to be. In 3.7 Helen takes the Widow (Diana's mother) into her confidence. In the next scene (4.1) Parolles is captured by some French lords, his supposed friends. In 4.2 Diana agrees to an assignation with Bertram. In 4.3 Bertram hears the confession of the blindfolded Parolles: Parolles is a coward, a fool, and a traitor. Bertram does not change (like Benedick and Orlando); he is not revealed as being virtuous (like Sebastian); he simply observes the true nature of Parolles, and he then rejects his erstwhile friend and companion. In terms of the general pattern, we should see the scene in which Parolles is captured (4.1) as corresponding to the subplot episode (Dogberry and Verges; Jaques and the song; Toby, Sir Andrew, and Fabian) that occurs in the comedies after the plight scene.

After Benedick confronts Claudio in the resolution scene in *Much Ado* (5.1), Claudio learns that Hero was belied and innocent: the same scene makes certain not only that Benedick will marry Beatrice but also that Claudio will marry Hero. Before Oliver arrives with a bloody napkin in the resolution scene in *As You Like It* (4.3), Silvius enters with a letter: the same scene makes three marriages certain: Orlando and Rosalind; Oliver and Celia; Silvius and Phebe. After Sebastian confronts Sir Andrew, Toby, and Fabian in the resolution scene in *Twelfth Night* (4.1), Olivia arrives and tells Sebastian to be ruled by her: the same scene makes sure not only that Sebastian will marry Olivia but also that Viola will be free to marry Orsino.

The subplot scene that comes between the plight scene and the resolution scene presents a threat to future security: the inept Dogberry and Verges; the cynical Jaques; the self-centered Toby, Sir Andrew, and Fabian; the corrupt Parolles. Margaret is not in the resolution scene in *Much Ado*; Touchstone and Audrey are not in 4.3 of *As You Like It*; Maria is not in 4.1 of *Twelfth Night*. At the end, each of these comedies accommodates an unsteady and insecure marriage or relationship: Borachio and Margaret (*Much Ado*); Touchstone and Audrey (*As You Like It*); Toby and Maria (*Twelfth Night*). Occurring at roughly the same time (the middle of the play) as in the earlier comedies, the resolution scene of Helen's plight in *All's Well* does not have the hopeful, steadying influence of a second, secure marriage: the end does not involve another prospective bride and groom.

At the end of her soliloquy in 4.2, Diana pointedly remarks, "Since Frenchmen are so braid,/Marry that will, I live and die a maid"(4.2.73-74). Although the concord at the end of the earlier comedies is threatened by the presence of a dangerous relationship, the concord at the end of *All's Well* is more than threatened: it is insecure or tenuous. At the end the King of France seems determined to repeat his earlier mistake: he tells Diana to choose a husband, and he will pay the dowry. And since Parolles has been rescued by Lafew and will become part of that household, there is at least the possibility that Maudlin, Lafew's daughter, will succumb to Parolles's wiles. Thus *All's Well* goes beyond the comedic tetralogy (*Much Ado, As You Like It, Twelfth Night, Measure for Measure*) in emphasizing the very real prospect of an unfortunate, hopeless end.

There is, however, a difference in *Measure for Measure*. Isabel's plight is never that of love-thwarted maiden: that is Mariana's role. And so the fourth-act procedure (plight-subplot-resolution) is necessarily modified. In the middle of 4.3 the Duke as Friar has an interview with Isabel; then he has an interview with Lucio. Three short scenes follow: Angelo and Escalus; the

Duke in his own person and the new Friar Peter; Isabel and Mariana, who are joined by the Duke's agent, Frair Peter. In effect a series of doubles parades across the stage, bringing act 4 to a close. The interview between the Duke as friar and Isabel replaces the plight-of-the-heart scene in the other comedies in the tetralogy. Hearing Isabel approaching, the Duke remarks:

> She's come to know
> If yet her brother's pardon be come hither.
> But I will keep her ignorant of her good,
> To make her heavenly comforts of despair,
> When it is least expected.
>
> (4.3.107-11)

This episode is followed by four subplot, "hand" scenes: the Duke as friar and Lucio; Angelo and Escalus; The Duke and Friar Peter; Isabel, Mariana, and Friar Peter. The order of these countervailing scenes tracks the development of the plot and leads up to the resolution scene, 5.1, the public appearance of the Duke.

This fourth-act pattern (the plight of the endangered heart, the countervailing subplot, the appearance of the presumptive head) so clearly in evidence in the comedies is also much in evidence in the tragedies. In *Coriolanus* after Coriolanus turns his back on Rome (4.1), Volumnia, his mother, and Virgilia, his wife, confront Brutus and Sicinius, the tribunes, and berate them for incensing the rabble to banish Coriolanus (4.2). Volumnia is at a furious impasse (Sicinius says that she is mad) because her son has been stripped of the consulship he was given and much deserved. The next scene (4.3) introduces two spies: a Roman, Nicanor, and a Volscian, Adrian. The traitor Nicanor tells Adrian that Coriolanus has been banished, that the nobles, upset with the rabble, are threatening to remove the tribunes from power, and that Tullus Aufidius, Coriolanus's mortal enemy, ought to be victorious against Rome. The next scene (4.4) presents Coriolanus *in mean apparel, disguis'd and muffled*. He is much changed, no longer the boastful, forward-looking hero of 4.1. In his changed state his resolution will be to beat Rome into submission: he will become a traitor to Rome.

In the plight or endangered-heart scene (4.2) Volumnia violently says to the tribunes: "The lady's husband here—this (do you

see?)/Whom you have banish'd—does exceed you all"(4.2.41-42).
One modification of the structural pattern is that the heroine is not
simply a maiden as in the comedies (up to the assignation Helen
is a wife in name only); here she has the important role of mother
(Volumnia) and is seconded by the other role of wife (Virgilia).
The second modification is that the plight is readily or swiftly
resolved. A comedy will end with marriages or (as in *All's Well*)
with the confirmation of a marriage. In this tragedy the heroine's
plight is resolved but at the high cost of the hero's violent death.
At the end Coriolanus will respond to the appeal of Volumnia,
Virgilia, Valeria, and young Martius. Coriolanus will become
again the son-husband-friend-father and, as an ironic hero, will
save Rome once more. In order to right an acknowledged,
grievous wrong, he will sacrifice himself in an act of deliberate
bravado: he will prod Aufidius into killing him.

As in *As You Like It* and *Coriolanus*, the plight scene in *Othello*
(4.3) presents two women, the wives Desdemona and Emilia. The
heroine's plight in *Othello* is more desperate and considerably
more dangerous than the heroine's plight in the comedies or in
Coriolanus. Othello, the man (not young and not unmarried)
needed to resolve the heroine's plight, is, like Coriolanus, a
renowned soldier and a beloved husband. Othello, who is briefly
in the plight scene, speaks to Desdemona: "Get you to bed on th'
instant. I will be return'd forthwith. Dismiss your attendant there.
Look 't be done"(4.3.7-9). At the close of her plight scene, as she
wishes her attendant adieu, Desdemona (like Beatrice, Rosalind,
Viola, Helen, Volumnia) glimpses a resolution:

> Good night, good night [God] me such uses send,
> Not to pick bad from bad, but by bad mend.
>   (4.3.104-05)

In the comedies the countervailing subplot scene presents a
threat to the emerging concord: Dogberry and Verges; Jaques;
Toby, Sir Andrew, and Fabian; Parolles. In these two tragedies the
comparable scene is a countervailing counterplot to a prosperous
resolution. Nicanor and Adrian are political conspirators. The
counterplot scene in *Othello* begins with Iago conspiring with
Roderigo to murder Cassio. In the scene Iago reaches an impasse:

he can no longer depend on the services of other men (Roderigo, Cassio, Othello) to carry out his subversive deeds: he must act for himself, with the help of his wife. Othello briefly appears in the counterplot scene. Upon hearing Cassio's cry for help, Othello remarks:

> Minion, your dear lies dead,
> And your unblest fate hies. Strumpet, I come.
> [Forth] of my heart those charms, thine eyes, are blotted;
> Thy bed, lust-stain'd, shall with lust's blood be spotted.
>   (5.1.33-36)

But the Othello who begins the resolution scene (5.2) is a different man, much changed: he arrives at the bed chamber like a bridegroom-priest, calm, almost restrained, serious, determined. He no longer wants to chop his wife into messes. He intends to resolve what he considers to be her plight by taking her life in order to save her soul. Upon discovering the truth about Desdemona, he recovers himself as best he can and, by taking his own life, joins his wife and the devoted Emilia on the bloody wedding bed.

The plight scene itself (4.3) mentions and presents a range of unhappy women. Desdemona's mother had a maid called Barbary. In 4.3 Desdemona sings Barbary's song about a maid who loved a man who proved to be mad and did forsake her. The song of Willow expresses Barbary's fortune (as well as Desdemona's): she dies singing the song. In 5.2, the resolution scene, Emilia will die with the song on her lips. The plight scene (4.3) ends with Emilia's disquisition on unhappy wives. In 5.2 Emilia will fail as a wife (though not as a heroine) because of her husband's grievous fault. In *Hamlet*, as in *Othello*, the procedure of endangered heart-hand-head or plight-counterplot-resolution occurs later than it does in the comedies, close to the parade of deaths at the end. The plight scene in *Hamlet* presents two unhappy women: a wife and mother, Gertrude; a maid, Ophelia. In *Othello* Desdemona is pathetic and innocent; in *Hamlet* Gertrude is anxious and guilty. In her bedroom (3.4) Hamlet made his mother see "such black and [grained] spots/As will not leave their tinct"(3.4.90-91). Now, in 4.5, Gertrude for the only time in the play speaks to herself:

To my sick soul, as sin's true nature is,
Each toy seems prologue to some great amiss,
So full of artless jealousy is guilt,
It spills itself in fearing to be spilt.

(4.5.17-20)

As in *Othello*, the plight scene in *Hamlet* contains a song about a forsaken maid. Ophelia and the maid in her song find themselves in the same position that Desdemona and Barbary and the maid in Barbary's song were in: betrayed and forsaken by a loved one. As queen-wife-mother, Gertrude in the scene feels compelled to try to protect her king-husband from a mad Laertes, Hamlet's double and a prospective king.

If we overlook the short 4.6, in which Hamlet's return to Denmark is reported, the counterplot scene (4.7) presents (as in *Coriolanus* and *Othello*) a conspiracy: Claudius and Laertes plot to murder Hamlet. The scene ends with our awareness of Hamlet's increasingly desperate plight: now Hamlet can have no future as a husband. In the reappearance scene Hamlet (like all of the other heroes in these plays) is much changed. He is not the same man who left the stage in 4.4 with the remark, "O, from this time forth,/My thoughts be bloody, or be nothing worth!"(4.4.65-66) Now Hamlet is quietly observant, almost relaxed, philosophical, until he discovers that the "maimed rites"(5.1.219) are for the now-beloved Ophelia. Gertrude in 5.2 will resolve her plight by drinking from the poisoned cup intended by her husband for her son: ". . . the drink, the drink—O my dear Hamlet—/The drink, the drink! I am pois'ned"(5.2.309-10).

Although the procedure of heart-hand-head or plight-counterplot-resolution remains constant, the different situations and the changed emphases mandate that Shakespeare modify the procedure in *Macbeth* and *King Lear*. The hero of *Macbeth* is, like Claudius, a murderer, a usurper, and at last the husband of a guilt-stricken wife: unlike Hamlet, the usurper (the Claudius figure) is the hero. Act 4.2 presents the plight scene from the perspective of the subplot: Lady Macduff and her children have been betrayed and forsaken by Macduff. The plight of an innocent mother and child is ironically resolved at the end of the scene when Macbeth's men murder them. This plight scene is followed by a counterplot scene (4.3) featuring a conspiracy: Malcolm and Macduff conspire to move against the tyrant, Macbeth. The murder of Macduff's family, reported at the end of the scene, is used by Malcolm to harden Macduff's resolve to kill Macbeth. Thus the end of the counterplot scene in *Macbeth* (the effect of the murder of loved ones) is clearly akin to the end of the counterplot scene (4.7) in *Hamlet* (Ophelia's death is reported, and Laertes is much affected).

The next scene (5.1) in *Macbeth* presents the plight of the heroine: a doctor and a gentleman observe the sleepwalking Lady Macbeth guiltily reliving the horrible events of the past. She too has been forsaken by her husband, who has gone into the field. The next scene, 5.2, presents, not a counterplot scene, but a subplot one: the Scottish noblemen have turned against Macbeth and have become rebels and traitors. Even if Macbeth were to defeat the English invaders, the subplot scene makes certain that his future reign would be strife-filled and short-lived.

The Macbeth of 5.3 is not much changed from the man who left the stage in 4.1. He is still confident and headstrong: "The mind I sway by, and the heart I bear,/Shall never sag with doubt, nor shake with fear"(5.3.9-10). And then, at once, Macbeth's security is shaken by the appearance of a "cream-fac'd loon"(5.3.11). The change has begun. Macbeth's insecurity deepens in 5.5 upon hearing the cry of women, the signal that his wife, the queen, is dead, her plight resolved: "To-morrow, and to-morrow, and to-morrow . . ."(5.5.19). Foolishly abandoning the security of the castle, he ventures forth to his waiting death. Like Coriolanus, Othello, and Hamlet, he commits a kind of suicide.

As we would expect, the basic procedure is significantly altered in *King Lear*. The emphasis is on the king-father rather than on the son-prince or husband-usurper. Act 4.2 presents the plight of Goneril: a daughter-wife, she is married to Albany but committed to Edmund. The next scene (4.3) presents a subplot situation: loyal Kent responds to the news of Cordelia's upset at the treatment of her father by her sisters; Kent also learns that Lear is distressed. The following scene (4.4) presents the plight of Cordelia, a daughter-wife: her husband, the King of France, has returned home; she has been left in command of the French army. Cordelia's position acts as a counter to Goneril's. She loves her husband, but her immediate concern is for another man, the welfare of her father: "No blown ambition doth our arms

incite,/But love, dear love, and our ag'd father's right"(4.4.27-28).
The next scene (4.5) presents the plight of Regan: a daughter-
widow, she is in love with cruel Edmund, but she knows that
Goneril possesses him.

The next scene opens with a subplot episode (4.6): Edgar has
brought Gloucester to Dover in order to save him from despair. To
this subplot scene comes the changed man, who will in time
resolve the plight of each of his daughters: the mad King Lear. He
is no longer the pathetic figure who put his evil daughters on trial
in 3.6. And he is not the man described by Kent in the subplot
scene, 4.3: "A sovereign shame so elbows him . . ."(4.3.42). Now
he is the King himself, a powerful, disturbing presence,
iconoclastic and terrifying. Act 4.6 ends with another subplot
episode, involving Edgar, Gloucester, and Oswald.

Act 4.7 presents the resolution of Cordelia's plight. Lear has
again dramatically changed: ". . . the great rage,/You see, is kill'd
in him"(4.7.77-78). Lear and Cordelia have come together in love
and harmony, as devoted father and beloved daughter. This
beautiful resolution scene gives way to a counterplot scene: Lear
and Cordelia are the leaders of the invading French army. In 5.1
Albany understands the necessity of gathering forces in order to
defeat the French enemy. In the middle of the scene Edgar gives
Albany Goneril's incriminating letter written to Edmund. At the
end of the scene Edmund delivers a soliloquy:

> As for the mercy
> Which [Albany] intends to Lear and to Cordelia,
> The battle done, and they within our power,
> Shall never sec his pardon; for my state
> Stands on me to defend, not to debate.
>
> (5.1.65-69)

Regan's plight is resolved by Goneril's poison; Goneril resolves
her own plight by suicide. The beloved Cordelia, rescued too late
by her dutiful father, dies calmly; the vexed King dies with his
true daughter in his arms. His death too is a kind of suicide.

Being neither a comedy nor a tragedy, the ambitious *Troilus and
Cressida* necessarily modifies its fourth-act plight. The first half of
the last scene of act 4, 4.5, presents the public plight of the
heroine. Trumpets replace the expected music. After being kissed

by a series of Greek leaders, Cressida leaves with Diomedes. Nestor and Ulysses, the conspirators of the first Greek scene, 1.3, reinforce the Greek perception of a fallen Cressida: "A woman of quick sense"(4.5.54); "a daughter of the game"(4.5.63). "The Troyans' trumpet"(4.5.64), the exclamation made by all the Greeks, is heard by the audience as *The Troyan Strumpet*. Though not a maiden, Cressida is love-thwarted. Troilus, a possible answer to Cressida's plight, arrives on stage after Cressida has left it.

The second half of 4.5 presents the plight of Trojan honor in the person of Hector. After a fight with Ajax (the product of the lottery) is aborted, Hector greets a series of Greek leaders, ending with Achilles. The scene closes with an interchange between Ulysses (who was responsible for rigging the lottery in 1.3 and denying Hector his opportunity of meeting Achilles in single combat) and Troilus (whose savage behavior in 5.3 will make it impossible for Hector to remain peacefully at home). Ulysses will guide Troilus to Menalaus's tent, where they will eavesdrop on the love-struck Diomedes and Cressida.

As we might expect, the first half of the next scene, 5.1, presents a subplot (Achilles, Patroclus, Thersites). Achilles's decision to keep his peaceful vow to Hecuba and Polyxena will deny the opportunity that Hector thought he had (in 4.5) to combat Achilles in the upcoming battle. Observing the imperiled Cressida in 5.2, Troilus concludes, "This is, and is not, Cressid!"(5.2.146) In the comedies the plight of the heroine is resolved by marriage; in the tragedies it is resolved by death; in *Troilus and Cressida* it is "resolved" by rejection. Hector rejects Andromache in 5.3; Troilus rejects Cressida in 5.3; Achilles rejects Hecuba and Polyxena in 5.5. The Troilus of 5.2 and 5.3, the Hector of 5.3, the Achilles of 5.5 are changed from what they were: Troilus once loved Cressida; Hector once loved Andromache; Achilles once loved Polyxena.

* * * * *

After the presentation of the plight of the heroine and its constituent scenes, Shakespeare recapitulates this heart-hand-head procedure in act 5 in order to bring about the play-ending marriage in comedy or death in tragedy. Propelled by the plight of the endangered heroine or the heart, fifth-act procedure, at least in the comedies, dramatizes the now-public plight of the hero as the ironic purveyor of moral authority.

As we would expect, this tripartite fifth-act procedure is clear in the famous early comedies: in the last scene of *Much Ado*, with Benedick; in the last scene of *As You Like It*, with Duke Senior; in the last scene of *Twelfth Night*, with Duke Orsino. Except for the very beginning of the last scene of *Twelfth Night*, each hero, the purveyor of moral authority, is on stage throughout the final scene; in each scene he is confronted by characters from both the main plot and the subplot. Ironically, his last words are at once followed by a dance in *Much Ado*; Rosalind's epilogue in *As You Like It*; Feste's epilogue-song in *Twelfth Night*.

This tripartite fifth-act procedure is readily perceived in *Measure for Measure*. In the last scene the Duke returns to Vienna in his own person: he had not left the city; he is not the Duke he once was. His plight is that he cannot safely assume his ducal authority until the ugly truth about his surrogate, Angelo, is publicly disclosed. Leaving the stage as Duke, he returns to the stage as Friar and is confronted by a member of the subplot (Lucio) and by a member of the counterplot (Angelo). Revealed by Lucio to be the Duke in disguise, the Duke addresses the gathered participants. Now that the truth about the society has been revealed, he assumes his office-role of duke-friar-husband of this now-corrected and now-instructed society.

The procedure is closely followed in *All's Well*. In the final scene, 5.3, the King arrives at Rossillion: like Duke Senior and Duke Orsino, the King has been absent from the stage since act 2. He is still upset that Bertram deserted Helen. After forgiving Bertram and accepting Bertram's marriage to Maudlin, the King notices that Bertram's ring once belonged to Helen. How did that happen? The King is then confronted by two members of Helen's counterplot (the Widow and Diana) and then by a member of the subplot (Parolles). Finally, the King's renewed public plight is resolved by the appearance of the supposedly dead Helen and the reuniting of the young husband and his wife:

All yet seems well, and if it end so meet,
The bitter past, more welcome is the sweet.
(5.3.333-34)

The King then steps forward and in an epilogue appeals to us for a resolution that only we can provide:

Ours be your patience then, and yours our parts:
Your gentle hands lend us and take our hearts.
(Epi.5-6)

In *The Tempest* Miranda does not recognize her plight: she is not the usual love-thwarted maiden. Still, the full fifth-act procedure, including an epilogue by the purveyor of moral authority, is certain. At the beginning of the last act, Prospero's changed plight is that of being the newly reinstated Duke of Milan. Instructed in mercy by Ariel and suddenly aware of Gonzalo's present plight as the past savior of Miranda and her father, Prospero embraces his king (Alonzo), confronts the two members of the counterplot (Antonio and Sebastian) and forgives them; he then reveals Ferdinand and Miranda playing chess; he then accepts a member of the subplot (Caliban) as his own. Prospero's public plight as Duke will be resolved by the marriage of Ferdinand and Miranda and by his retiring to Milan to await his death. In the epilogue he turns to us for a resolution:

But release me from my bands
With the help of your good hands.
Gentle breath of yours my sails
Must fill, or else my project fails,
Which was to please.
(Epi.10-13)

Though clearly in evidence, the fifth-act procedure in each of the great tragedies (*Hamlet*, *Othello*, *Macbeth*, *King Lear*) is modified by the role-office tension (son-Prince in *Hamlet*; husband-general in *Othello*; husband-usurper in *Macbeth*; father-king in *King Lear*) and the concomitant public-private aspects of the poetic action. Understandably, each tragedy ends with a speech, not by the hero, but by an ironic figure of moral authority.

Of course, *Hamlet*, *Macbeth*, and *King Lear* must be considered in consort.

In 5.1, although he has killed Polonius and has ordered the death of Rosencrantz and Guildenstern, his former friends, the Prince is calm, reflective. He is not upset that he has not fulfilled his promise of revenging his father's death: his initial plight has not changed. Hamlet confronts a "member" of the subplot (Yorick's skull), and his heart is aroused by the arrival on stage of the dead Ophelia. Grappling in the grave with Laertes does not relieve his heartfelt grief. His private plight as rejected lover and as hopeful husband, however, is resolved by the death of the heart. In 5.2, the last scene of the play, Ophelia's name is not even mentioned.

At the beginning of 5.2, Hamlet's public plight is still in abeyance: he rejects a feeling about his heart. He is confronted by a member of the subplot (Osric); he is then confronted by his counterplot adversary (Laertes). In the swordplay Hamlet is the sword or hand of the ghost; Laertes is the sword or hand of Claudius. By killing the King, Hamlet fulfills his promise of revenge. The dying Hamlet reasserts himself as Prince, designates Fortinbras as his successor, and directs Horatio to tell the story. Hamlet's resolution is in terms of son and prince. As expected, the final speech is given by an ironic purveyor of moral authority, a victorious son and prince, a soldier, a hand, Fortinbras.

Though crucial, the role-office tension is not so dynamic in *Othello* as it is in *Hamlet*, *Macbeth*, and *King Lear*. Act 5.2 of *Othello* begins with the emphasis on role, not office, with an emphasis on the heart. In 5.1 of *Hamlet* the Prince is distraught lover; in *Othello* the General is distraught husband. Othello intends to sacrifice his wife's body to save her soul. After the death of Desdemona, Othello is confronted by a member of the subplot (Emilia) and then by a member of the counterplot (Iago). Although the hero does not engage in swordplay, as Hamlet does, Othello, like Hamlet, does wound his adversary, Iago, with a sword. At the end Hamlet, the hero, reassumes his office as prince; at the end of *Othello* the hero reassumes his office as general ("Soft you; a word or two before you go" [5.2.338]), justifies himself, and resolves his plight by committing suicide. Like the epilogues in *All's Well* and *The Tempest*, Lodovico's final speech reinforces the head-heart-hand trope:

> Myself will straight aboard, and to the state
> This heavy act with heavy heart relate.
>   (5.2.370-71)

In 5.5. of *Macbeth* the hero's plight is that (although in the secure castle) he is under siege by his enemies. Unlike Hamlet and Othello, Macbeth does not see his dead beloved. He just hears the cry of women that signifies the death of the Queen. His reaction to the news is, not the heartfelt grief shown at once by Hamlet and, after Desdemona has been vindicated, by Othello, but rather resigned despair: "She should have died hereafter"(5.5.17). Almost at once, like Hamlet and Othello, Macbeth becomes a hand: he forsakes the secure castle for the public battlefield. There he is confronted by (as Hamlet and Othello are) a member of the subplot (Young Siward) and then a member of the counterplot (Macduff). In the swordfight, Macbeth does not wound his adversary (as Hamlet and Othello do), and he is defeated. The expected final-act movement from the heart to the hand to the head is grimly emphasized by the appearance on stage of Macbeth's bloody head. Malcolm's epilogue-like final speech ends with unmitigated irony:

> So thanks to all at once and to each one,
> Whom we invite to see us crown'd at Scone.
>   (5.9.40-41)

The last scene of *King Lear* begins, as we would expect, with an emphasis on the father-daughter roles, on the heartfelt concern that Lear and Cordelia have for each other. Now that they have been captured, they know that they can expect little mercy. In terms of the main plot, the movement to the hand takes place off stage: Lear kills the slave who was hanging Cordelia. On stage a member of the subplot (Edgar) confronts a member of the counterplot (Edmund). Edgar is the hand of Albany; Edmund is an isolated hand. Lear returns to the stage with the dead Cordelia in his arms and, unintentionally, reassumes his authority. Unlike the end of *Hamlet* or *Othello* or *Macbeth*, the plight of the hero in *King Lear* is not resolved by the spilling of his blood. Instead, the emphasis is on Lear's head as he gazes transfixed on the face of Cordelia, hoping that she is still alive. The play concludes with either Albany or Edgar assuming the epilogue-like task of the ironic purveyor of moral authority.

The fifth act of *Troilus and Cressida* presents the plight of two Greeks (Achilles and Ajax) and the plight of Two Trojans (Hector and Troilus). The procedure of plight-subplot (counterplot)-resolution proceeds along parallel plot lines, side by side. In 5.5, upon learning that Patroclus has been slain by Hector, Achilles renounces his vow to Hecuba and Polyxena and goes to the field determined to kill Hector. Upon learning that his friend has been slain by Troilus, Ajax turns away from indolence and goes to the field determined to kill Troilus. In 5.6 Troilus fights with both Ajax and Diomedes: this little conflict is a direct consequence of the plot action: Troilus wants to kill his hated successor, Diomedes; Ajax wants revenge on the murderous Troilus. The three combatants leave the stage fighting. Hector and Achilles enter and fight: this little conflict is what Hector hoped to achieve from the very beginning of the action. But these two leaders discontinue fighting, and Achilles leaves the stage. None of the four plights has been resolved.

Troilus begins the elaborate counterplot by returning to the stage and announcing that he is going to rescue Aeneas from Ajax. While Troilus is engaged in rescuing Trojan love from Greek power, Hector, instead of waiting for Achilles to return to the stage, declares his intention to kill a nameless Greek (who comes on stage and then leaves) for his armor. Hector's counterplot action is in direct contradiction to Troilus's: Hector wants to kill for a "goodly" outside; Troilus wants to save a valuable "inside." While both Troilus and Hector are off stage, the double onstage action is that of Paris fighting with Menelaus and of Margarelon confronting Thersites. In effect, three doubles parade across the stage, one after the other: each of three Trojan brothers is paired with a Grecian moral equivalent: Paris and Menelaus; Margarelon and Thersites; Hector and Achilles. We may consider these pairs as representing the heart (Paris and Menelaus), the hand (Margarelon and Thersites), and the head (Hector and Achilles).

Having discovered a "putrefied core"(5.8.1) within "goodly armor"(5.8.2), a disillusioned, weary Hector disarms himself and is brutally murdered by Achilles's Myrmidons: "Hector's life is done"(5.8.8). Achilles resolves his own plight and Hector's with a sordid murder. A bitter, disillusioned Troilus returns with a rescued Aeneas. Ajax's plight remains unresolved, as does Troilus's. Now that Hector is dead, Troilus decides to "starve . . . out the night"(5.10.1): "Hope of revenge shall hide our inward woe"(5.1031). He then rejects Pandarus, instrument of love: "Hence, broker, lackey!"(5.10.33) The play ends with an epilogue-like address by Pandarus, an ironic purveyor of moral authority.

The plight-subplot(counterplot)-resolution or heart-hand-head procedure outlined above functions as a blueprint for the second half of the typical Shakespeare play. Although the procedure is not clearly in evidence in the history plays, it is present, though modified, in, for instance, *Romeo and Juliet*, *Antony and Cleopatra*, and *The Winter's Tale*. It seems safe to then conclude that the first act of a Shakespeare play presents the plot problem and introduces the main characters; that the next two acts comprise an extended episode; and that the final two acts resolve the impasse reached at the end of the extended episode by a concentration on the accentuated plight of, first, the heroine and, then, the hero. Within the guidelines of this structural formulation, Shakespeare trenchantly and vividly renders the plight-directed action.

Index

All's Well That Ends Well,
47-57; puns in, 107; world
of, 48
Anna Karenina, xviii
Apple of Discord, 206, 215,
219. See also Trope
As you Like It, xviii, 68; ages-
of-man-speech in, 69-71,
91; as part of social
tetralogy, xxi, 93, 98;
ceremony in, 203; compared
to Hamlet, 99; hero in, 98;
plight-scenes in, 235-37;
readjustment in, 59; roles
in, 91-92, 98. See also
Social tetralogy
Austen, Jane, xiv

Bache, William B., See Design
and Closure in
Shakespeare's Major Plays
Back, Guy, 18n.14
Baking bread. See Trope
Baldwin, T. W., 213n.1
Barish, Jonas A., 200n.9
Barton, Anne, 56n.2, 71-72,
75, 76n.5
Bastard, in King John, 21-30;

in King Lear, 21; in Troilus
and Cressida, 204, 206,
208, 226-27, 228
Battenhouse, Roy, 45n.8
Battlefield. See Trope
Bedford, Brian, xv
Bee. See Trope
Berger, Harry Jr., 167n.9,
17n.4
Bethell, S. L., 200n.4
Body. See Trope
Booth, Stephen, 200n.6
Bracketing. See Strategy
Bradley, A. C., 195
Braunmuller, A. R., 30n.1
Brower, Reuben A., 18n.6, 7,
9
Bullough, Geoffrey, 37, 45n.1
Bonjour, Adrien, 30n.1

Cacicedo, Alberto, 115n.1
Calderwood, James L., 30n.1
Campbell, Oscar James, 117
The Canterbury Tales, 233
Character equation, in All's
Well That Ends Well, 48-49,
52-53; in Hamlet, 166; in
King Lear, 166; in Macbeth,